I0235160

Feodor Rojankovsky

The Children's Books and Other Illustration Art

Irving Allen and Polly Allen

with

Tatiana Rojankovsky Koly

Wood Stork Press Englewood, FL

Feodor Rojankovsky
The Children's Books and Other Illustration Art

v3.0

Cover designed by Russell Jenkins.

Wood Stork Press
P.O. Box 5315, Englewood, FL 34224

ISBN: 978-0-578-13558-8

Library of Congress Control Number: 2013921055

PRINTED IN THE UNITED STATES OF AMERICA

For our friend, the late A. L. de Saint-Rat, a true connoisseur of the book and graphic arts created by the Russian community in Paris between the wars. André inspired us with his enthusiasm for the illustration art of the émigrés in general and of Feodor Rojankovsky in particular.

CONTENTS

Acknowledgments

Our greatest debt is to Tatiana Rojankovsky Koly. She shared with us recollections of her father and guided us through his personal library, clippings, sketch books, and family photographs, and she translated letters and notes in his often difficult handwriting. Her bibliographic diligence in her own library and investigations in Paris led to the inclusion of several elusive books illustrated by her father. She contributed especially to our compilation of book covers and other graphic designs and to the list of published sources about her father. The many days and thoughts she has given to our effort, her deep knowledge of her father's work, and her expert advice and close reading of the typescript have made this book more complete and accurate. Any later errors are ours, not hers. Tanya's husband, Mohsen Koly, made the photographs to reproduce most of the illustrations that appear in the e-book version. Mohsen, and Elena Koly Jenkins, the artist's granddaughter, cheerfully indulged our invasions on more than a few visits. Russell Jenkins, Elena's husband, generously contributed the design for the cover of the book.

Interviews with people who knew Rojankovsky in the 1930s or in later years also deepened our understanding: Elizabeth H. Alexander, Olga Andreyev Carlisle, Ruth S. Gritsch, Dr. Catherine Lodyjensky, Margaret K. McElderry, Ole Risom, and Thomas P. Whitney. Conversations with specialists in children's books also gave us valuable direction: Brian W. Alderson, Barbara Bader, H. Nichols B. Clark, A. L. de Saint-Rat, James Fraser, Gregory Gillert, Pamela K. Harer, Michael Patrick Hearn, Lee Bennett Hopkins, Solomon Ioffe, John Langstaff, Billie Levy, Elisabeth Lortic, Leonard Marcus, and Justin G. Schiller.

For the Polish materials, we are grateful to Barbara Bulat, Piotr Hordyński, and Anna Sienkiewicz, Biblioteka Jagiellońska, Krakow; Mirosława Zygmunt and staff, Biblioteka Narodowa, Warsaw; Konstanty Kalinowski, Muzeum Narodowe w Poznaniu; Katarzyna Mikocka-Rachuba and staff, Instytut Sztuki, Polskiej Akademii Nauk, Warsaw; and Radislaw Wasiak, Storrs, CT.

For the help with some of the more elusive French materials, we are grateful to Béatrice Michielsen and Isabelle Nières-Chevrel, and to Béatrice Michielsen for the photograph of the mural at Montgeron (in the e-book). François Faucher, the son of Paul Faucher and now president of l'association "Les Amis du Père Castor," was generous with his recollections of his childhood encounters with Rojankovsky and has been supportive and helpful in facilitating permissions to reproduce illustrations from the Père Castor books in the e-book.

Our debts are deep to many institutional librarians and curators who went out of their way to help us. Some we imposed on heavily or on several occasions: Mary Bogan, Emporia State University; Margaret Coughlan, Library of Congress; Allison Cowgill, University of Denver; Margaret Danowski, Madonna University; Polly Elkin, Victoria and Albert Museum, London; Julia Gauchman and Jan Adamczyk, University of Illinois; Mary Janaky, Golden Books Publishing Company; Dolores B. Jones, University of Southern Mississippi; Dorothy G. Knaus, University of Oregon; Sandra Kroupa, University of Washington; Deena Kushner, American Artists Group; Anne-Claude Lelieur, Bibliothèque Forney, Paris; Françoise Lévèque, Bibliothèque de l'Heure Joyeuse; Charles Mann, Pennsylvania State University; Olena Nessen, Ukrainian Research and Documentation Center, New York; Kath Pennavaria, Kinsey Institute, Indiana University; Jonathan Riddell, London Transport Museum; Chantal Rousseau, Montreal Public Library; Jim Soester, Chadron State College; Carrie Tahtamouni, University of Minnesota; Anne Tracy, Michigan State University; Robert Vrecenak and Lynn Sweet, University of Connecticut; Eva Wolynska, Central Connecticut State University.

The staff people we met on visits to research libraries were always helpful: Northeast Children's Literature Collection, The Dodd Center, University of Connecticut Library; Special Collections, Harvard University Library; the Slavic and Baltic Division and the Central Children's Room, New York Public Library; Special Collections, Center for Russian Culture, Amherst College; Special Collections, University of New Hampshire; Bakhmeteff Archives and the Rare Book and Manuscript Library, Columbia University.

Author's Note

In the mid-1990s my husband, Irving Allen, and I were looking for a complete list of the children's books illustrated by Feodor Rojankovsky, as part of our larger interest in book illustration by Russian artists in the early 20th century. We could not find such a list, so decided to compile one. As we began to learn more about the eventful life and varied work of this accomplished artist, our interest and our ambitions grew, from a simple list to a biography and a descriptive bibliography of all of his published work.

While Rojankovsky is known primarily as an illustrator of children's books in France and the United States, his contributions were much broader. He also illustrated books and book covers, magazine stories and covers, and a wealth of commercial and advertising art for general adult audiences, in four countries, from WW1 until his death in 1970. Researching this book has been a fascinating intellectual journey into the history of Russia, Poland, and France and into the development of children's literature and illustration over four decades in France and the United States.

Early on, Irving and I came to know Tatiana Rojankovsky Koly, the artist's daughter, who was enthusiastic about our project and exceedingly generous with her time, effort, recollections, and materials from the Rojankovsky archive. Indeed, Tanya's contributions have become an integral part of the research and writing of this book.

While working primarily as an illustrator, Rojankovsky made large numbers of drawings and paintings. These are widely dispersed, sometimes destroyed, and largely impossible to account for. We have not tried to account for this original work, but have limited ourselves to the published work, however ephemeral. I feel reasonably confident that we have accounted for Rojankovsky's illustrated books, with the possible exception of some early book from Poland or a small Russian language book. But our lists of his ephemeral advertising and commercial work will always remain incomplete.

With Irving's death in 2002, I stopped working on the manuscript for a number of years. Recently I revived the project, updating and completing the research, with Tanya's active participation and support, for publication as an illustrated e-book and a hardcover book without illustrations.

Interest in Rojankovsky remains high, and seems to be growing. I hope that this work will fill a gap in the general knowledge about this remarkable Russian-American artist.

Polly Allen

I.

BIOGRAPHY

1

An Artistic Life

Feodor Rojankovsky was one of the most popular and highly regarded illustrators of children's books in the middle decades of the 20th century and has a secure role in the history of modern picture books. The Caldecott Medal for 1956, the highest American recognition for children's illustrators, is among his many honors. Rojankovsky's earlier contributions to French children's books in the years between the two world wars are equally admired in Europe.

His artistic career spanned half a century, two continents, six countries, and as many cultures and languages. The illustrator's life and travels followed the westward course taken by many artistic and literary men and women who fled the Russian Revolution of 1917 and its aftermath. A common pattern was to resettle first in a central European city such as Prague, though in Rojankovsky's case it was the newly repatriated Polish city of Poznan.

Many went on to Berlin, as Rojankovsky also did briefly in 1922, to join the large Russian émigré community that had assembled there. But the hyperinflation soon caused the German economy to collapse in 1923, and many of the Russians fled to Paris. Traveling from

Poznan, Rojankovsky arrived in Paris in late 1925 and stayed sixteen years. After the Germans occupied France in 1940, many Russians fled southward and some to the United States. In late 1941 Rojankovsky went to New York and began a new career, just a few months before the American entry into the Second World War.

An extraordinary story lies in the artist's romantic childhood in Old Russia in the years around 1900, his adventurous young manhood in the turmoil of revolution and civil war from 1914 to 1920, and then twenty years of exile in cities across the expanse of Europe. The artist's European career is one of the most diverse and cosmopolitan of all the children's illustrators who came to work in America before the Second World War. In France he became known as "Rojan," as he is still known to many of his friends and older fans.

After 1930, Rojankovsky's decisive move into children's illustration influenced the new, modern look of children's books in France. Upon coming to the United States in 1941, he brightened the look of American children's books during the war and immediate post-war years and through the 1950s and 1960s. Today, Rojankovsky is regarded as one of the wittiest of illustrators, whose pictorial humor is equally popular with adults, whether they discovered him first as children or as grownups.

The French and American children's books have been translated into many languages and read around the world. Three decades after the artist's death, children still enjoy his timeless pictures and their worlds of make-believe. Several of the most popular books remain in print in the United States, France, Japan and other countries—some first published seventy years ago.

The artist was a keen amateur naturalist and observer of animal behavior, abiding interests from his boyhood in Imperial Russia. As "Rojan," he was a favored *animalier* to generations of French children, especially through the famous Père Castor animal books. And he is just as famous in America for the joyous pictures of domestic and wild animals that inhabit two thirds of his children's books. Equally skilled in drawing children in natural attitudes and activities, he drew them full of facial and bodily expression, catching the sheer joy of childhood.

Rojankovsky depicted sturdy youngsters, socks falling down, running and tumbling with abandon.

A superb draftsman, he had the gift of catching a subject—animal or human—in precise lines. An artist friend in Paris who sketched with him at sidewalk cafés in the 1920s marveled at Rojankovsky's ability to draw proportion and perspective without conscious calculation, starting with the part of a person's body or other thing nearest and drawing as if backwards into the picture.

Countless Americans were brought up on Rojankovsky's many colorful picture books of the 1940s, 1950s, and 1960s. Now in their middle years, many are nostalgic about the books of their childhood. Some are serious collectors, or at least are reassembling their childhood favorites—the very books their parents so outrageously discarded.

Pictures from the best-known books are reproduced in many anthologies and scholarly histories of children's books. Leading research libraries in several countries are gathering in the first editions and preserving them in special collections of children's books deserving of admiration and study. The early and now scarce books are seen in the catalogs of rare book dealers—and at ever escalating prices. But commercially unsophisticated children are still reading battered copies from the open stacks of libraries.

Despite this ardent attention, the full scope of Rojankovsky's remarkable career and prodigious bibliography are not well known. In the United States, he is usually remembered as the illustrator of thirty eight titles in the popular line of Golden Books. Yet he illustrated just as many books for twenty other American publishers, and some of these won prestigious awards.

In his careers in Europe and the United States, Rojankovsky illustrated altogether 144 books and eighty short stories—mostly for children and young people. He illustrated original texts, many by famous children's authors, in Russian, Polish, French and English and in every genre of books for youngsters.

People who know his work in Paris in the 1930s value the innovative and modern picture books he made for Esther Averill's expatriate Domino Press, especially the path-breaking *Daniel Boone* of 1931. And he is just as well known, especially among the French, for the trend-setting picture books in Paul Faucher's Père Castor series for Flammarion publishers. Historians of twentieth-century illustration agree that these books helped to give a new look to children's books in France, setting a new and modern direction, and their influence spread to England and America. But fewer know the striking illustrations produced in the early 1920s for young people's books in Poland or those in the late 1920s for the Russian-language émigré presses in Paris.

In a parallel world of work, Rojankovsky created for other audiences a great variety of graphic art and design. In the legendary decade of the 1920s, he participated as a commercial artist in the French *Moderne* or art deco movement in graphic design. In the 1930s, he brought his special look to several British travel posters. Hundreds of published works created in pre-Revolutionary Russia, Poland, France, Britain, and the United States include book covers, illustrations and covers for general-interest magazines, travel posters, advertising brochures, scenic postcards, greeting cards, and even a popular Fisher-Price pull-string toy for tots—graphic art and design of every kind.

Prime examples of his contributions to modern graphic design in Europe between the wars were in their day reproduced in leading professional magazines of commercial art, such as *Gebrauchsgraphik* and *Arts et métiers graphiques*, and more recently in American anthologies of art deco graphic design. The brochures and catalog covers for Paris department stores and his British steamship, railway and Underground posters are today collected as exemplars of their kind and are held in major British and French museums. All these graphic designs, coupled with his skill in the deployment of integral letter forms, made arresting commercial messages and showed a mastery of the modern motifs of the 1920s and 1930s.

The hundreds of drawings for general-interest magazines and newspapers are, for the most part, conventional of their times and places. Yet a wicked knack for humorous derision and cultural commentary shines in the covers and drawings for Polish, French, and Russian émigré popular humor and satirical magazines. Some of the best work was for France's famous *Le Rire* in the early 1930s. Had magazine work ever offered itself as a way to make a dependable living, Rojankovsky could have topped himself as a cartoonist and caricaturist.

Aside from the applied graphics work, Rojankovsky was an active fine artist, working chiefly on paper—drawing with pen and pencil and painting in watercolor and gouache. The palette is usually light and bright. Over the years he produced many portraits of friends and female figure studies of informal candor. And he was, too, an accomplished artist of rural and city scenes. The interest in landscape began in Russia, came to fruition in Poland in the 1920s, and continued in travels to many parts of Europe, North Africa and the United States.

In Moscow just before the First World War, Rojankovsky trained in theater design and worked as a student apprentice with senior stage designers in the Moscow Art Theater. After settling in Poland in 1920, he worked several years executing designs and painting scenes for the newly-formed Poznan opera and theater, and probably made original but uncredited contributions as well. Surviving sketches of costume designs and other drawings with theatrical themes hint at their richness. In Paris he painted sets and visual effects for at least one well-known silent film in the late 1920s. All through life he kept up an interest in designing for amateur and other small theatrical productions, making his last maquettes in the mid-1960s for ballet-school productions in small Paris theaters.

In the book illustrations, this theatrical and cinematic turn of mind was ever present, if just in the wings. The principles of stage and scene design are apparent in the layouts for his early children's books. Critics have pointed out influences of theater and film on the presentation and unfolding of scenes in his *Daniel Boone.*

Viewing Rojankovsky's illustration art over the full-career of fifty years, he worked within and occasionally beyond the dominant graphic styles of the day. Modernistic influences became apparent in his Polish work shortly after 1920. He sometimes diverted with touches of German-style Expressionism, but quickly turned to the lighter French style. In France, his graphic art of the middle and late 1920s and early 1930s revealed understandings of French Cubism, Fauvism, Russian Constructivism, and the French Art Décoratif of 1925. Some of the early children's illustrations show a Fauvist, colorist sensibility and here and there reflect Constructivist impulses. But he did not consistently follow in any of these fashionable styles.

Rojankovsky's early work clearly shows the influences of admired Russian artists, such as Boris Grigoriev and, later, of the fashionable semi-cubistic styles of the émigrés working in Paris between the wars. In children's books, he admired and occasionally quoted the styles and themes of the innovative Soviet illustrators. Yet Rojankovsky's work is distinct at a glance and creates its own world. In the best work, such as the creative bursts in his children's art of the early 1930s and again in the early 1940s, he breaks away entirely.

By 1930 Rojankovsky had made a conscious decision to pursue children's-book illustration as his artistic specialty and for the rest of his life devoted himself chiefly to children's illustration and other graphic art of this style and subject. The illustrator's understanding of children was less sentimental than deeply empathetic, and this good humor and realism show in the art. The later American advertising art, story illustrations for general-interest magazines, and commercial wall calendars feature animals and children and derive from his children's art. And some of the advertising and calendar art were, conversely, made into children's books.

At its best, Rojankovsky's art for children was singular, and its spirit touched two generations of younger artists and illustrators. The Paris fashion designer, Christian Lacroix, has written of how the illustrator's picture books touched him as a child and eventually played into his own taste and design work. And other artists have written of Rojankovsky's influence on their decisions to become illustrators and of how his style and *élan* touched them.

* * *

People who knew Rojankovsky personally, some recalling him from the 1930s and the years in Paris, have all told us that he was, indeed, the man we might hope to meet as the illustrator of his children's books—open, generous to all, humorous, filled with a zest for living, and a man of great personal charm. He spoke five languages (Russian,

Polish, German, French and English) and sometimes mixed them in speech and writing to express himself to best advantage. But Russian was his first and preferred language, and Russian culture and art sustained him throughout his life.

A well-educated man in the tradition of the European gymnasium, Rojankovsky read widely all his life and kept a library filled with classics in world literature and art history. Like many cultured people of his generation, he was an enthusiastic writer of letters, trading news and everyday experiences of life with friends and editors. Many of the letters are decorated with calligraphy and humorous drawings, mostly in color.

A man of the world, Rojankovsky was a seasoned veteran of two wars who served honorably as a military officer for the Tsar of Russia in the First World War and later, reluctantly, in 1919 for the White Army. In certain ways, he lived by an old code of masculine conduct in his personal life, and was courtly with women and popular with men. As we might expect, he had a few old-school manly touches in his ways and about his person. On his left arm, he sported large tattoos of a striking serpent, a seahorse, and an elaborate monogram, no doubt from army days. He liked the out of doors—gardening in summer and skiing in winter. And true to a certain popular image of artists, he sometimes wore a beret.

Rojankovsky enjoyed a successful career in France during the Depression years of the 1930s, when the incomes of other talented émigré artists suffered. He kept a leg up because of his energy, push, and willingness to promote himself and his talents and to engage all kinds of illustration work. In some of the bawdy magazine and book illustrations for adult audiences in Paris of the 1930s, he mischievously stretched the boundaries of decorum and taste—and clearly enjoyed the work. Even in the children's art, the social candor and impish humor of his first Mother Goose book in America stirred controversy among parents and librarians, and many years later one drawing was suppressed in new editions.

In 1946 Rojankovsky married Nina Fedotova, a glamorously attractive young Russian woman of a distinguished émigré family. Nina was a skilled pianist and, in many attitudes, a patient model for the artist. The couple's only child, Tanya, was born when Rojankovsky was in his late fifties, and she was a joy in his life. One of her earliest and fondest memories is of her father reading to her from Russian folk tales and French and American children's classics. While young Tanya was not made to sit still as a direct drawing model, the vicarious adventure of her childhood was a presence in many of her father's books of the 1950s.

Traditional holidays, especially Christmas, had special meaning for the family and were times for gathering friends. Rojankovsky's own birthday coincided with Christmas eve, making the season doubly a time for celebration. The artist loved the atmospheres of Russian, French and American Christmases, and their traditional scenes and symbols were a specialty in his art. In the 1930s he expressed the special feeling and atmosphere of French Christmas in illustrations for children's stories and in some of his best commercial designs. In the United States, a popular series of timeless Christmas cards of his design brought images of joyful woods animals into many thousands of American homes.

An artist through and through, Rojankovsky was sensitive to the aesthetics of his surroundings and, when he could, liked to improve them. A plain wall might be improved with a mural, or a homely radiator with a decorated cover. He liked to arrange and furnish his home in pleasing ways—never fussily or expensively, but with a few handmade comforts and humorous touches. His studios were always cheerfully decorated with bright pictures and eye-catching objects. Wherever he settled, even in hotel rooms, he added a decoration to make it more attractive and home-like.

Over many years he combed beaches in Europe and America and made elegant driftwood sculptures of wild animals. From found wood he made rustic furniture, retrieving a boyhood pleasure in woodwork. For much of his European career, he had worked in and around the worlds of fashion and design—and had ideas about how things and people ought to look. An old friend told of how he took a rare man's interest in the style of his wife's clothing.

Highly disciplined and steady in work habits, Rojankovsky spent long hours in his studio in total absorption—so absorbed that he was known to sip at the water in the jar he used for cleaning brushes, mistaking it for his glass of tea. He was fastidious about his work, striving over and over for just the right effect, ruthlessly discarding drawings that disappointed him, sacrificing hours, even days of work. Like most artists, he had individual ways of working. He made drawing tools to meet special problems, sought and prized brushes that brought up just the right effect of animal hair on the painted surfaces, and whimsically used a bird's feather to brush away eraser crumbs.

But when work was done, Rojankovsky played just as hard, organizing festive occasions, dinner parties, and costume balls. Animated by music, he would leap to his feet and spin in solo dances, out-dancing the children. Or he would enliven events by playing the balalaika. Slight of build and easy of movement, he was a physically graceful man who looked and acted years younger. Tales abound of his climbing trees like a monkey and leaping over couches like a gazelle. The mature man's agility and boundless energy, well into old age, amazed his friends.

Old friends, who as children knew the artist, tell how he delighted in making fanciful decorations, organizing games and staging antic stunts. François Faucher, the son of Rojankovsky's Paris editor Paul Faucher, recalls the late summer of 1940. The Faucher family and some of his circle had fled Paris on the eve of the German occupation and were domiciled at the Faucher family estate in the provinces. To liven things up one day, Rojankovsky walked waist-deep into a lake wearing his best new suit, pretending to be preoccupied reading a newspaper. The adults were stunned at the absurdity; the children screamed with delight.

Other friends remember excellent meals prepared and served with flair, the special dishes he liked to cook, his fastidious tastes in good food and drink, and the offerings of herb-flavored vodka. Even in his last illness, too ill to leave his bed and on the evening before he died, he directed in detail his wife's preparation and serving of a leg of lamb for dinner guests.

* * *

Though world politics and events propelled the course of his life in Europe and even in America, the illustrator was too busy with his art and making a living to be much involved in émigré or other local politics. For Rojankovsky, the political life was for the most part personal and expressed among friends and intimates. Nor was he much interested in ideologies or political parties. Despite his professional-class Russian background and former military allegiances and unlike many other exiles, Rojankovsky was not enamored with the Old Regime. Nor was he church-going, except to observe major holidays in community affirmation. He joined a few organizations, such as the French Freemasons in 1934 and, in New York, the American Institute of Graphic Arts, chiefly for their social and professional benefits.

As a young man, Rojankovsky was direct witness to the political turmoil and events leading to the Russian Revolution of 1917 and, eventually, by 1920 found himself exiled in Poland, all but banished from his homeland. But his deep love of Russia and its possibilities were never severed. Years later he was asked which among the array of political parties in Russia he most identified with as a young man in the years leading up to the Revolution. He replied that he felt closest to the Constitutional Democratic Party, once part of the Provisional coalition, and a party promptly banned when the Bolsheviks rose to power.

In Paris he lived an essentially bohemian, but disciplined artistic life and was at one with the world of art and making picture books. From 1920 to 1941, Rojankovsky's whole life was in the French and Russian intellectual and arts communities in great European cities. His personal friends were a cosmopolitan crowd—variously of Russian, American, French, Hungarian, German and British origins, people of Orthodox, Catholic, Protestant, Jewish and secular backgrounds. Most were people of liberal to democratic-left sentiments. Most of the Paris artists and intellectuals watched with dread the rise of Hitler and understood some of its awful implications. Rojankovsky and his friends were staunchly anti-fascist from the beginning.

His mother, brothers and sisters had all suffered greatly, most perishing, in two wars with Germany or at the hands of the Bolsheviks and Stalin. Through all his years in exile, a beloved younger sister and other family lived in Russia. A 1959 reunion with his sister, after a forty-one year separation and his first visit to Russia and St. Petersburg since 1918, must have been emotionally overwhelming. Russia was where his heart was, and his attachment to the past grew with years in exile.

After he came to America, Rojankovsky liked to discuss Cold War politics with Russian friends of various opinions. Irritated by political certitude in others, he sometimes maddeningly defended the Soviet Union as the flawed reality of modern Russia, though he had little use for the repressions of Soviet communism. People who knew him best say a romantic haze clouded his view of the post-war Soviet Union, especially after the death of Stalin in 1953 when hopes rose for liberalization. But Rojankovsky's views were no more or less innocent than those of many American liberals at the time, particularly in the arts and academic communities.

Another soft place in his heart was Paris, but now a lost Paris—as it was between the wars. In 1960, then in his late sixties, he moved the family to Paris with every intent of staying. The immediate rationale was to seek superior French schooling for Tanya, now twelve. But it was also a nostalgic quest, seeking to recover a few pleasures from a world and a time long gone and forever changed.

Five years later they all came back to Bronxville, New York, and Tanya finished high school at the Lycée Français in New York City and entered New York University. Though his robust health was now weakened, Rojankovsky enjoyed a few more good and productive years at home in Bronxville. After a long illness, he died on October 12, 1970—a few months before his seventy-ninth Christmas.

2

The Early Years in Old Russia

Feodor Stepanovich Rojankovsky was born on December 24, 1891—as he reset the date by the New Calendar. His parents, Lydia Kiprianovna (Kordasevich) and Stepan Fedorovich Rojankovsky, were middle-class and cultured Russians of Orthodox church traditions. His father, a Russian native of Bessarabia whose forebears were small landowning orthodox gentry from Galicia, was headmaster and teacher of classical languages at a secondary school for boys in Mitava, a town then in Imperial Russia. About fifty kilometers southwest of Riga in independent Latvia, today Mitava is named Jelgava.

Feodor was the second youngest of five children. All his life, Feodor had a special attachment to his sister, Tatiana, younger by two years and an accomplished pianist and choir director. Though separated for decades by war, revolution and exile, they kept close in mind and heart, exchanging letters when possible and beginning in 1959 visiting about every two years.

The father's assignments to various schools had taken the family across Imperial Russia. Children were born in Kishinev (eventually part of Romania), Odessa (in Ukraine), in Estonia, and near Moscow—all to give the family an international cast. To add to the confusion, the surname *Rojankovsky* is of remote Polish origin, and the artist is sometimes mistaken as Polish, especially as he lived and worked in Poland in the early 1920s. Another branch of the family is Ukrainian, some with interests that almost presage Feodor's own ardor for theater. The paternal grandfather, Theodor Rozankovski, was a priest whose widow, Feodor's grandmother, joined the Ukrainian National Theater as a wardrobe dresser—in the company of her two daughters who were actresses in the traveling company.

In his late years, Rojankovsky joked about the "mixed" nationalities of his family and particularly the notion that he was Latvian, as his immigration papers read, simply because he was born in Latvia. He was fond of repeating the old east European saying, one born of so much historical confusion of ethnic and national identities, "Listen, if a sparrow is born in a stable, that does not mean he is a horse." Rojankovsky and his family were decidedly Russian, and he eventually married a Russian woman of distinguished family. For the most part, he grew up in the historic Estonian city of Reval and in St. Petersburg, and later spent several years in Moscow on the eve of the First World War.

The Rojankovsky siblings and their spouses were a tight-knit family. The older sister, Aleksandra, a great beauty in her photographs, married a wealthy, landed, and prominent man some twenty years her senior. Upon the death of Feodor's father in 1897, Aleksandra's husband became the responsible patriarch, helping support the Rojankovsky family and the expense of educating his wife's four younger brothers and sister.

Aleksandra and the brothers, Pavel and Sergei, all more than a decade older than Feodor, assumed a parental role with the two youngest children and encouraged Feodor's and Tatiana's cultural interests. The middle brother, Pavel, was an electrical engineer and an avocational artist who contributed drawings and paintings to magazines. A circus poster of Pavel's design with two French pugilists is preserved today in the Durov Circus Museum in Voronezh, Russia. Sergei, the oldest brother, also studied at a technical/engineering institute in Russia. But

Sergei was more attracted to art and *la vie bohème*, and went on to study art in Paris before the First World War.

Owing to a handwritten memoir in Russian that Rojankovsky wrote late in his life and left in his papers, we have a rich picture of his early years in Russia. In 1893 when Feodor was about one year old, the family moved to Reval, where his father had a new assignment as headmaster of the Revel'skaia Aleksandrovskaia Gimnaziia, a secondary school. The lovely old seaside city is on the Gulf of Finland, about 325 kilometers west of St. Petersburg. Today, Reval is named Tallinn and is the capital of Estonia.

Rojankovsky's earliest recollection of effortful drawing was when he was only three or four years old. After a visit to the Reval zoo, his parents gave him a box of German-made Caran d'Ache colored pencils to draw pictures of animals he had seen there. He recalled how he relished the sweet odor of cedar when the pencils were sharpened, and how they were used up mostly in repeated attempts to draw the zoo's elephant.

Early childhood memories of life in the family quarters of his father's school were of the daily routines, the hourly bells, the shouts of the older schoolboys in recess, and the odors of birch burning in wood stoves and of kerosene. In a long hallway, the boy peered into cabinets of scientific curios and what he saw there were all lingering impressions. One glass-fronted cabinet contained plaster casts of supposed countenances of the world's national and ethnic types. One of the casts used for drawing models was the head of an American Indian, the face painted to make him look fierce.

One memorable evening in 1896 the Lumière group, representing Auguste Lumière, an early inventor of the movies, visited the school to demonstrate the new Cinématographe. The French company was in Russia filming the coronation of Tsar Nicholas II and traveling about to promote the invention. The boy of four remembered the famous scenes on the flickering screen of a train arriving in a station and of workers streaming from a factory.

Tragedy struck the family in 1897 when the father, Stepan, suddenly died. Feodor was five years old. His widowed mother went to St.

Petersburg to be near her married daughter, Aleksandra. Lydia rented a small apartment on Galernaia Street in the heart of the city, just off the Neva Embankment and less than two kilometers from the Winter Palace. Feodor and his younger sister soon joined her, and the family remained in St. Petersburg four years. The experience of the great Imperial city lay just beyond his doorstep and he soaked up all within his grasp.

Young Feodor was deeply impressed with the sensations of St. Petersburg at the turn of the century and recalled its stylish public life, its splendid architecture, military atmosphere, and imperial pomp. The Tsar's magnificent private yacht, "The North Star," was moored just a block away on the English Quay. The yacht's spit and polish, the bells that rang, the whistle of the boatswain, and the deckside drills of the Naval crews were spectacles the boy never tired of. He yearned to be closer to life on the ship. "A yellowish dog and a cat lived on the yacht and I was jealous of them."

"It was in St. Petersburg that my interest in books grew and developed." The family valued their father's personal library and kept it intact—until it was lost in the First World War. Rojankovsky remembered many of the exact editions that impressed him and decades later was thrilled to find identical copies in used bookstalls in Paris. Young Feodor poured over the many picture books in natural history, the illustrated literary classics like Gustave Doré's *Bible* and *Paradise Lost*, and other great parlor favorites of that era. These books were a matrix of his interests in art and drawing.

On his last Christmas in St. Petersburg, he received the gift of a Russian translation of Daniel Defoe's *Robinson Crusoe*, illustrated by Grandville. He and his younger sister, Tatiana, drew "improved" illustrations of Crusoe's improvised island house, pictures they thought better matched the text.

Always fond of the classic, in 1938 he planned to illustrate Crusoe for his Polish publisher, R. Wegner, and painted a proposed cover with a garland of seven scenes from the story. But the edition was never published, probably because of the German invasion of Poland in 1939 and Wegner's death during the war. Many years later, he illustrated a juvenile edition for Golden Books in 1960, using a redrawn, less detailed version of his 1938 cover to decorate the title page, and probably brought forward other ideas as well. Taking on the assignment, he wrote his editor, Lucille Ogle, that *Crusoe* was "my first adventure in the world of illustration"—some sixty years earlier, and he expressed high enthusiasm for the project.

In 1901, his mother, Lydia, and the two youngest children left St. Petersburg and returned to Reval. Feodor completed his last year of primary education in a cavernous, bilingual German and Russian school under the watchful, "watery colored" eyes of two elderly German sisters and school mistresses, whose surname was Howen. He read German books printed in Fraktur and wrote lessons in the angular old script.

Then came secondary school or *gimnaziia* in the same institution where his father had so briefly served as headmaster. A teacher of natural history at the school stimulated the boy's life-long love of nature and its artistic expression. Taking the students on nature walks in the woods and by the sea, the teacher encouraged Feodor to draw animals and nature scenes in his notebooks.

In 1904 the family of three returned to St. Petersburg and stayed about a year with the older children. The two brothers encouraged Feodor to paint landscapes in watercolors and show them to the world. The boy of twelve was bold enough to offer ten of his pictures for sale to the Daziaro gallery at 11 Morskaia Street, a fashionable street of galleries near the Nevskii Prospekt. Mr. Daziaro bought them on the spot, paying 50 kopeks each—the young artist's first sale.

Returning to secondary school in Reval, he became involved in studies and school activities. He played musical instruments, brass and string, in all three of the school's orchestras—the symphonic group on second violin, the military band on French horn, and the balalaika ensemble. The repertory of the balalaika group included the Overture to Mikhail Glinka's opera *Ruslan & Lyudmilla*, which remained a lifelong favorite of the artist with a taste for stirring music. Making light music just for fun remained a part of his life. Musical themes and instruments recur as symbols in his illustrations and graphic designs.

And young Feodor had all the other usual boyhood interests. He and his friends collected drawings from magazines and made pin-ups of Gibson Girls—those tall, slim shirtwaisted ideals of young American womanhood at the beginning of the new century—so famously drawn by the illustrator Charles Dana Gibson.

In 1909, Rojankovsky traveled to the Crimean city of Yalta and stayed with his older brother Pavel, the engineer and now headmaster of a technical school. While continuing studies for final school exams, he made pocket money painting murals for a local roller skating rink and decorated the foyer of the Miniature Theater in Yalta. An uncle fell ill and required Pavel's return to St. Petersburg. Feodor also decided to end his stay in the southern city and went directly to Moscow. There he lived in the welcoming household of his father's old friend, who had a son about Feodor's age.

The capital city of Moscow, quite different in spirit from St. Petersburg, offered many diversions for a young man. Feodor contemplated several careers, fleetingly even one in ballet. Though untrained in dance, he once seized a moment in the presence of a famous ballerina and danced impromptu for her. She assured him good naturedly that, with training and practice, he could become a character dancer in a corps de ballet. But deeper interests and talents in pictorial art soon dominated. The son of his host family urged him to visit two art exhibits then in the city, at the Stroganov Central College of Art and Design and a student show at the Moscow School of Painting. Something about what he saw on the walls turned his head toward a career in art.

He became intent on going to art school in Moscow. In 1911 he plunged into a preparatory crash course of only three months, took the entrance exams for art school—and failed. Not discouraged, he studied at Fedor Rerberg's studio in a longer preparatory course. He passed on the second try in 1912 and more than redeemed the earlier pratfall. This time the young artist was ranked first in his class of only twenty five students selected from among 300 applicants, and he entered the renowned Moscow School of Painting, Sculpture and Architecture. Among the teachers there, he studied with Konstantin Korovin, the chief artist for the Imperial Theatres in Moscow, and with Apollinarii Vasnetsov, the head of the landscape studio at the School.

In his second year, Rojankovsky entered a school competition in which paintings were judged to find students with an aptitude for stage design. He won the contest and the chance to work at one of the Imperial Theaters. Stanislavskii was then at the Moscow Art Theater, and this was the young artist's first choice. Early in the summer of 1914 he worked as assistant to the stage director and helped on a production of *Peer Gynt*, with sets and costumes by Nicholas Roerich. Gordon Craig came from London and staged *Hamlet*, all giving the young artist a chance to meet and see at close hand the work and methods of accomplished theatrical designers.

The First World War

But art education was cut short in August 1914 by the outbreak of the War. Rojankovsky was inducted within a few days and, with his middle-class background and gymnasium education, was commissioned as an infantry reserve officer in the Russian Imperial Army, eventually with the rank of Staff Captain. Put in command of one of the first motorized units in the Russian military, he served throughout the campaign of 1914-1917.

In the first winter of the war, he took a bullet in the left arm and was evacuated to St. Petersburg. The unexpected leisure gave him time to paint and draw with his good arm. Upon recovery and return to active duty in 1915, he traveled with his regiment through Poland, Prussia, Austria, and Romania, where they occasionally engaged the enemy. On a fateful November 6th, an explosion buried him under rubble. An aide, Ivan Dubina, dug him out in the nick of time. For the rest of his life on each anniversary of the narrow escape, Rojankovsky raised a toast in gratitude to his rescuer. Years later he said ironically and coolly of his adventures in the military, "I saw many interesting things."

While recuperating at the military hospital in St. Petersburg in the winter of 1914-15, he drew scenes of the hospital buildings and grounds and, from memory, the first of many war sketches. In May of 1915 the first of these drawings—his first published work—appeared in *Lukomor'e*. Named for a famous phrase in a poem by Pushkin, the magazine was a prestigious weekly journal of literature, art, and satire. The magazine ceased publication at the end of August 1917, as the Old Order was collapsing on the eve of the October Revolution.

Returning to active duty, he went on to draw many more wartime scenes for *Lukomor'e*. Between 1915 and 1917, he contributed at least seventy six drawings and ten covers to the magazine—shaded pencil sketches, pen-and-ink drawings, and watercolors, some reproduced in color halftones. Rojankovsky was one of the journal's key illustrators of the war period and shared the pages with the work of Grigoriev, Narbut, Mitrokhin, Dobuzhinsky, Bilibin, Kustodiev, Lancéray, Yakovlev, and Goncharova. In 1916 he also made illustrations for a few short stories in the more popular magazine *Ogonek* and, after the liberal February Revolution of 1917, painted a patriotic cover for the magazine *Solntse Rossii.*

The wartime drawings for *Lukomor'e* are a little known but significant body of his work. The realistic, reportorial drawings recall newspaper illustration of an earlier day, a medium and style that were the precursors of wartime photojournalism. Occasionally, Rojankovsky drew impressions of the devastating aftermath in abandoned positions. But mostly he portrayed noncombat activities—such as interrogations of prisoners, food canteens, repairing of vehicles, deployment of surveillance balloons, construction of bridges, military field hospitals, soldiers resting in camp, or refugees stranded near the front.

The non-military scenes are idyllic views of villages and towns or city parks with well-dressed strollers—all images in occasional respite from the magazine's pictorial emphasis on the war. The last drawings of early 1917 record the growing revolutionary unrest in Moscow and Petrograd (as St. Petersburg was renamed in 1914), following the February Revolution and abdication of the Tsar.

The Russian Civil War

After the First World War and the Russian Revolution of 1917, Rojankovsky settled briefly in the city of Poltava in the Ukraine, in the same Governorate as Priluki, the country home of his older sister's husband. Aleksandra and her husband had settled on his family estate to be far from the turmoil in St. Petersburg and the enmity raging against all those who had been prominent in the Tsar's government. Rojankovsky's brother Pavel had also gone to the Ukraine before the Revolution, where he became president of the professional artists union in Poltava and worked in a publishing house in Kharkov. The Ukraine had formed its own government in June 1917, first as a republic of federated Russia under the Provisional Government. After the Bolshevik's October Revolution, the Ukraine became an independent country in January of 1918, and so must have seemed out of harm's way.

Rojankovsky worked there briefly in 1918-1919 as an artist for the Poltava Zemstvo (the local district council) of the new Ukrainian Republic. Among the Poltava projects were illustrations for a newly translated literary anthology for the local schools and a new Ukrainian edition of Flaubert's *Salammbô*. But the books may never have been published owing to the turbulent times. The Ukraine was destined to have its own troubles.

In the chaotic civil war of 1918-1920 that followed the October Revolution, Poltava and its region was an area contested by four warring factions—independent Ukrainians, Whites, Reds, and Poles—who swept in and out of control. The Poles had gained Lvov (West Ukraine) in 1919 and the Reds took over central Ukraine, eventually making it a Soviet Republic in 1922. In this brief but bewildering period, Rojankovsky lived through changes of rule by each of the four factions. Ukrainian forces—the hetmans—seized him briefly with the intent of pressing him into military service. At another time under Red control, he was ordered "to draw pictures of their leader," which he thought the better assignment of the two.

In 1919 General Denikin was in Ukraine near Poltava forming his

"White Army"—the well-organized "Volunteer Army" formed from the Tsar's old military establishment that Rojankovsky served in the First World War. Rojankovsky was drafted again in 1919, returned to officer rank as first lieutenant, and assigned to the camouflage corps. In a year of rough service under harsh conditions, he suffered further war injuries as the Whites were battered by the Reds and driven westward.

The great typhus pandemic of 1919-1920 was raging in the war-devastated region and Rojankovsky fell seriously ill to the disease, probably infected by ubiquitous body lice. He was carried unconscious on a litter as the Red Army pushed his unit west into Poland. Here in 1920 he ended the war, his health recovered, but behind barbed wire in a detention camp for Whites near the city of Lvov in eastern Poland. The new Polish government, also fighting the Reds, favored the Russian Whites in 1920 and Rojankovsky was allowed to stay in Polish territory. There was now no possibility of safe return to Russia.

3

Exiled in Poland

After his release, he did not wander far but went to nearby Lvov and searched out employment as a graphic artist. The region was still war-torn and devastated but economic life in the cities persisted, and magazines and books were being published. By mid-1920 he had sold, in quick succession, a dozen drawings and captioned cartoons to *Szczutek*, a Polish humor magazine. He had transliterated his name into Polish and signed the drawings *Teodor Różankowski*, an eminently Polish form.

In Lvov, he also met the Polish bookseller and publisher Rudolf Wegner, who had in 1917 founded the publishing house of Wydawnictwo Polskie in Lvov. Wegner (c.1876-1941) was just then opening new offices for his growing business in Poznan in western Poland and invited Rojankovsky to join him there to design book covers and, eventually, to illustrate whole books. Even after the artist left Poland and settled in Paris, the professional relationship with Wegner continued until the outbreak of the Second World War in 1939.

The experience of war was never far behind him. In spare time, perhaps over several years, he drew from memory a notable series of twenty watercolors, impressions of things he saw in the two wars, and collected the drawings in a yet unpublished album titled *The War Sketches, 1914-1920.* Taken together with the eighty or so war sketches in *Lukomor'e* during the first conflict of 1914-17, these remarkable paintings and drawings are original documents of historical events that are compelling in their eye-witness immediacy. And war was not through with him yet.

During the disastrous aftermath of the Revolution in Russia, he lost contact with his family and had no news for years. Only after moving to Paris in 1925 did he learn the fates of his mother and one of his brothers. Pavel had shot himself in 1921. His mother, Lydia, died in Petrograd during the famine and turmoil. Twenty years later, two of his other siblings died in the Siege of Leningrad. Rojankovsky came to share with millions of other Russians the destruction of his entire family, save his beloved younger sister, Tatiana.

Rojankovsky remained in Poland for five years, until 1925, never returning to live in the new Soviet Union. After the Rapallo Treaty of 1922, when most west European countries recognized the legitimacy of the Soviet government, Rojankovsky's Tsarist papers were no longer valid. He officially became a stateless person, a refugee, living as a guest in host countries. Under the auspices of the League of Nations, most countries issued to the Russian refugees in their midst the so-called Nansen passports, which served as identity papers, travel documents, and proof of residency status. Rojankovsky was now among the legions of Russian émigrés scattered in cities across Europe. The Russian communities in exile—and ensuing events in Europe—were in many ways to shape his life and career.

The handsome old city of Poznan had been made part of new and independent Poland in 1919. After a century of Prussian rule its citizens looked forward to a rosy and prosperous future. The Polish book trade flourished, and Rojankovsky was the chief cover artist for the Wegner firm. But covers and occasional book illustration and magazine cartoons and drawings were modestly paid as piece work, part-time work at best, and the artist sought additional sources of income, anywhere, in any kind of art work. During the next five years, he sometimes had titled positions, such as "art director," with Wegner and other employers, some apparently simultaneously.

Poland in the early 1920s was a small, compact country. Though based in Poznan and living in a modest pension, Rojankovsky moved about the region in search of work opportunities. He searched in Gdańsk and more than once in the capital city of Warsaw, a major publishing center that no graphic artist in Poland could ignore. He eventually found some work with Warsaw-based publications, but secured the most work of every kind in Poznan.

From about 1920 to 1923, Rojankovsky was employed as head of the decorative department in the newly formed Grand Theater in Poznan, the Teatr Wielki. He was primarily associated with the opera component of the theater and apparently among its first staff. The dramatic theater was founded in 1919, concurrent with the repatriation of the city of Poznan itself, and the opera a year later. Both have had a distinguished history in national Polish culture and still flourish in today's Poland.

Not surprisingly, none of the exhaustive official histories of the Teatr Wielki mention Rojankovsky. He was, after all, not a Polish artist of standing but a newcomer and a foreigner, a displaced Russian with useful skills in stage decoration. Nonetheless, he presumably had a hand in the creative execution of stage sets and costumes from maquettes by Polish and other famous artists. And he may have contributed some original but formally uncredited design work of his own.

In handwritten notes for a memoir, from a distance of forty years, Rojankovsky clearly remembered the theater and his work there. He accurately recalled the classical, columned portico, with the wide stairs leading up from the street. And he remembered the two pedestaled, cast-metal figures of heroic peasants, each leading a lion, which flanked the broad staircase. He was, naturally, impressed with "the rotating stage and marvelous technical equipment that would be the envy of many theaters in capital cities." He recalled the atmosphere of the auditorium as "controlled and subdued, decorated in the style of the Maryinskii Theater—in silver and sky blue."

But little physical record remains of the artist's work for the

Teatr Wielki and possibly other theaters in Poznan. A few sketches of costume designs accompanied a magazine review of Rojankovsky's one-man show in 1924 at the Salon Garliński in Warsaw. Hints of the appearance of the theatrical work can be taken from the artist's other modern designs of this period. In the 1920s, Polish theater design was directly influenced by painting and the graphic arts, used many folk motifs, and was quick to take up modernism—all compatible with Rojankovsky's outlook and talents.

The commercially optimistic city of Poznan held the second of its annual spring trade fairs in 1922—and Rojankovsky's starkly modern posters and brochure covers were commissioned to promote the event. Two years later he was again invited to design the poster for the 1924 Trade Fair. All the while he was illustrating books and designing covers for Wegner, drawing magazine covers and cartoons, and painting stage sets. And like many graphic artists, he took commissions to design personal book plates, some of which made their way into reference books on Polish ex libris. He designed one for Stanisław Wasylewski (1885-1958), the prolific Polish author who published with Wegner and for whose books Rojankovsky designed at least three covers.

The artist worked on a few projects in Poznan with his German friend Ernst Czerper (1899-1933) from Mannheim, a graphic artist of Expressionist bent who also worked for Wegner. They collaborated in the illustration of one book, *Sonety Krymskie* in 1922. Both men had been in the world war, though on different sides—and on different fronts. Czerper was in the horrific trenches on the western front, and late in his short life wrote of his war experiences in newspaper articles after returning, ill, to his home city of Mannheim.

The two friends joined in another collaboration to paint a modern mural, commissioned by a local distillery to decorate the private office of the Director, Józef Grabowski, in a grand old building at 15 Mostowa Street in Poznan's Old Town. In three large panels around the walls, the mural depicted the story of Polish brandy from its origin in the sunny vineyards in the south to its joyous consumption in evening cafés. Photographs of the striking new murals were published in *Świat*, the Polish national news magazine, to accompany an article

(March 18, 1922) about the distillery. The old building still stands today, long since converted to residences; the murals are gone.

The popular Polish magazine of humor and satire, *Szczutek*, eventually published thirty nine of Rojankovsky's stylish covers and cartoons. After an initial twelve drawings in 1920, he began contributing again a year later, placing twenty seven more in 1921 and 1922. Founded in 1918 in Lvov, the magazine's editors and writers became increasingly critical of the government and their satire more political. The new Republican constitution adopted in 1921 had not reduced the extremes of poverty and wealth, and the liberal press, including *Szczutek*, were relentless in their criticism. Though Rojankovsky was not central to this fray, his saucy political, social, and sexual humor in many cartoons added to the adversarial reputation of the magazine. In 1926, three years after his last contribution to the magazine, a military coup made the national leader, Pilsudski, a virtual dictator, and the irritating *Szczutek* was shut down. A new and more accommodating humor magazine, *Cyrulik Warszawski*, took its place.

Rojankovsky's drawings for *Szczutek* satirized comfortable bourgeois attitudes and the public life of the city—women preoccupied with fashion, men flirting with women in cafés, bourgeois couples puzzling over abstract sculptures in galleries, the follies of theatrical personalities, and of course scheming, corrupt financiers. The captions are full of double entendres and innuendo, and the figures and situations in these drawings foreshadow his work a decade later in the French counterpart magazine of sex and satire, *Le Rire*.

His first illustrated book in Poland and his first published children's book was Zbierzchowski's *Oczyma dziecka*, 1921, a modest production for which he made the cover and small pen drawings for the text. Next, two small illustrated volumes of Adam Mickiewicz's *Sonety Krymskie* (with Czerper) and Antoni Malczewski's *Marja* were published together in 1922. Both books were illustrated with delicate pastel lithographs, drawn in a style that seemed advanced for their day. The book illustrations were critically praised and included in exhibits in Warsaw, Leipzig and New York as representatives of contemporary Polish book arts.

In 1922, his career now budding after two years in Poland,

Rojankovsky traveled west to nearby Berlin. He probably intended to settle and elevate his career in that exciting center of Russian émigré art and culture. In any case, he arrived too late. The German hyperinflation peaked in 1923, with the ensuing collapse of the German economy and the decline of the Russian émigré community in Weimar Berlin. Almost all the Russian publishing houses in Germany collapsed in 1924, and the émigrés scattered again, many to Paris.

Information is sketchy on Rojankovsky's work in Berlin. He might have assisted in the stage decorations for the 1922 second season at Yascha Yushny's Der Blaue Vogel, the Russian-German theater cabaret. The stage sets and costumes for the 1922 season were designed by Pavel Tchelitchew, Ksenia Boguslavskaia, and Andrei Khudiakov. It was here, we think, that Rojankovsky made friends with Khudiakov. When both were in New York in the 1940s and 1950s they worked on small projects together. And the Rojankovsky family visited the Khudiakov home at 524 Riverside Drive and their dacha near the Russian Village at Southbury, Connecticut.

Rojankovsky recalled illustrating two children's books in Berlin, one of them Sasha Chernyi's *Detskii ostrov*, the other unnamed, both probably for a Russian-language press in Berlin. We find no trace of either book and assume they were drafted but never published, in part because of the economic collapse. But more likely because *Detskii ostrov* would have had to compete with Grigoriev's illustrated edition of the same book (Gdansk, 1921) and almost at the same moment. In a few years Rojankovsky would illustrate other books by his friend Sasha Chernyi, and these would become the favored illustrated editions. The outing to Berlin lasted only a year, before he returned to Poznan.

With fresh experience, he resumed seasonal work in the Poznan opera house and returned to Polish book illustration, now seeking publication beyond the Wegner firm. The illustrations for a Polish edition of Frances Hodgson Burnett's *Little Lord Fauntleroy* were precise line drawings emulating an older English style. Years later Rojankovsky told the story of how he illustrated the book and submitted the drawings to a Warsaw publisher. The editor thought the drawings looked too authentically English and sent them off to Britain to determine if they had been derived from the work of an English illustrator. But of course they had not, and the Polish edition was published in 1925. In the early 1970s, Nina Rojankovsky recalled for a visitor that this book—of all the illustrator's many successes—was a sentimental favorite.

Monochrome lithographs for a Polish edition of Mark Twain's *Tom Sawyer*, also published in 1925, were in a different illustrative style and well-imagined for the American theme. A bold color design for the cover has young Tom, a broad white-wash brush in hand, standing in front of Aunt Polly's fence.

About this time he also illustrated Ewa Szelburg's Polish children's book *Renine Wierszyki*, a whimsical book of verse about a little girl named Rena. The brightly colored lithographs had a new lightness and humor. Years later in 1938 his last Polish-language book for children was pen drawings for *Słoń Birara*, illustrated from Paris.

During the time in Poland, he also worked as an art director for an unidentified fashion magazine, or possibly for a Sunday fashion supplement in a local newspaper. This is, too, an elusive episode of his career. Years later in America, a few jacket blurbs and articles about the artist mention his "fashion background," evidently taken from his own résumé. Art directors in that era often contributed finished drawings, as well as coordinating concept, text, lettering, and layout. At any rate, in 1924 he drew at least one monochrome Cubist-style cover for *Pani*, the prominent fashion magazine based in Warsaw, and in 1925 drew jubilant jazz-age illustrations for a short story in the same magazine.

In 1925, Rojankovsky was commissioned to paint thirty watercolors of historic sites in the Poznan region and of other well-known places in Poland. The scenes were made into popular full-color lithographed postcards. Ten of the cards were collected into a Poznan city viewbook; others were reproduced in magazine articles about the Polish sea coast. Several were included in the 1995 postcard exhibit at the National Museum in Poznan and reproduced in their catalog.

Another group of watercolors of historic places in Poland decorated the covers on nine of eighteen Polish travel guides, a series first issued in the 1930s. These books have been recently reissued with the original cover paintings. Both the guides and their cover art are valued as vintage images of pre-war Poland.

The thirty-three-year-old artist was in 1925 becoming known and respected in Polish graphic art circles, when he left Poland in favor of Paris, after only five years in the country. He may have been resident in Warsaw during his last year or so in Poland, but keeping work links in Poznan. In 1924 he was given an exhibition at the prominent Salon Garliński in Warsaw. Thirty two of his paintings, woodcuts, and illustrative drawings filled one room. The several reviews of the show were highly favorable and singled him out as a versatile modern artist of note and promise.

In Poland today, Rojankovsky is noted in national museum curatorship as a watercolorist of precise, small-scale studies of Poznan's architecture, historic aspects of the city, and its regional landscapes. In histories of Polish graphic art, he is noted for his magazine drawings and satirical cartoons. He is also remembered for the modern posters he designed for the early Poznan Trade Fairs and the lost murals in the city's Old Town—created in the exhilarating first years of Polish independence.

For the postcard paintings, his last job in Poland, he was paid in strong American dollars, which financed his trip west. On the way to Paris by train, he visited friends along the way, probably his friend Ernst Czerper in Mannheim and perhaps other friends in Strasbourg, before going on to the great city and a new life.

4

Becoming a Children's Illustrator
Paris, 1925-1941

Rojankovsky arrived in Paris—his first sight of the great city—in late 1925, probably in November, a "soft but cold grey day, the kind of weather I had left in Poznan." He took a taxi from the Gare de l'Est to the Hotel Molière in the rue de Vaugirard at the heart of the Latin Quarter. A room had been reserved for him by an artist friend from Poznan who had preceded him to Paris by a month.

Years later in his notes he recalled that first day in Paris when he sat at a little table in a corner café. Setting his suitcase to his side, he thought "I am living, not simply existing," taking a line from Pushkin. "I am in Paris!" He was thrilled to be at the center of the art world and soon to see the social life that swirled around it, the "wild tempo of life" in Montparnasse, and to visit the neighborhoods and galleries that had fostered the Cubists and Surrealists. He was to sit in the famous cafés and watch now fabled times in the making. "I can imagine Picasso here talking with his friends, sitting in the same café as me."

Gathering himself, he took a few days to marvel at the physical grandeur of the city, its public life, and the dramatic contrasts of

Paris before assessing his situation. The rest of the several hundred American dollars received for the Polish postcard paintings was in his pocket. This, he calculated, might sustain him for up to a year, if he lived frugally enough. The money probably ran out sooner and he ended living "half hungry in a fleabag hotel on the outskirts of Paris, without heat or light in my room, except for a kerosene lamp—and I could not afford the kerosene." He was, as he wrote, "obliged to put my teeth on the shelf"—a Russian saying for stopping eating.

But he skimped and got by, more than once taking bread and tea at the homes of friends. All the while he sought work opportunities and new contacts in the large Russian émigré community. A friend advised him to go back to Poznan and work again for Wegner, for "here in Paris you will die of hunger." But the possibilities of the art scene in Paris scintillated for him; he was still a young man and relished life. Rojankovsky remembered his feeling at the time, that it was preferable to be hungry in Paris, a simple physical condition he could alleviate by working and buying a piece of bread, than to perish of spiritual ennui in Poznan. By early 1926 various kinds of modestly paid art work appeared—sometimes in surprising places and through lucky encounter—just enough to encourage him to stick it out through a difficult first year.

One of the first bread-and-butter jobs in Paris was painting sets and props for a French silent film starring the popular Russian actor Ivan Mozzhukhin. *Casanova* (or *The Loves of Casanova*), directed by Alexander Volkoff, was released in 1927. Boris Bilinsky designed the sets and costumes for the production and may have provided the work for a Russian colleague with considerable theater experience in Poznan. Rojankovsky assisted on the sets, painting fake marble and other effects, and he also painted portraits to decorate the sets. In his spare time, he sketched behind-the-scenes activities of the movie-making, including impressions of Bilinsky's elaborate 18th century costumes.

One day on the street, Rojankovsky was surprised to meet his old friend Sasha Chernyi, thinking the writer was still living in Italy. Their chance meeting was auspicious. Chernyi proposed that Rojankovsky re-illustrate the writer's Russian-language alphabet book of simple verses about animals for the children in the large Paris émigré community. N. P. Karbasnikov, the former Petersburg publisher and now in Paris, took on the project, and the charming *Zhivaia azbuka* of 1926 was the prompt result. Years later he wrote to a friend that the chance encounter with Chernyi all but saved him in a time of need and was the event that began his career as a children's illustrator in Paris.

This Cyrillic abecedarium was Rojankovsky's first true picture book for children. It featured a brilliant color cover of animals and art-deco Cyrillic letters of his own design that set the stage for superior ink drawings throughout. This new version eclipsed the earlier Berlin edition illustrated in 1922 by Mikhail Aleksandrovich Drizo, the Russian caricaturist who signed as "MAD." Rojankovsky was fond of his new edition of Chernyi's verses and later designed a new color cover featuring a sitting bear reading a book, apparently in an unrealized hope of yet another Russian-language edition.

Sasha Chernyi, the pseudonym of Aleksandr Glikberg (1880-1932), was the renowned émigré Russian poet and storyteller. Rojankovsky illustrated four books by Chernyi in the 1920s, all with Russian-language publishers serving the émigré community. Today they stand as some of the artist's most remarkable but least known children's-book illustrations. Tragically, Chernyi died a few years later from the exhaustion of fighting a fire at a neighbor's house in the south of France. In a moment of reflection many years later, Rojankovsky left in his papers a touching and highly personal eulogy to the dead poet, thanking him for the rarest of friendships.

Another remarkable book with Chernyi followed in 1927, a year after the alphabet book. *Dnevnik foksa Mikki* told a story in the voice of a literate and indignant fox terrier. Mikki was loved by his overly attentive mistress, a young girl, but was put upon by obtuse humans who did not appreciate his special intelligence. Chernyi imagined a chapter in the interior life of his pet dog. Rojankovsky, in complete sympathy, made drawings resembling the real Mikki—who may be seen looking out from photographs in Chernyi's family album. And there soon came a cat book, too. Chernyi's *Koshach'ia Sanatoriia* in 1928 is illustrated with skillful line drawings for the story of a strong-minded feline who has a plan to escape from the captive and dependent society of cats abandoned in the Roman forum of Trajan.

By 1927 Rojankovsky was breaking into the French commercial art market and doing less illustration work for the émigré presses. For the rest of his time in Paris, contributions to Russian-language children's illustration were fewer and more modest.

Many years later in 1954 he illustrated Natal'ia Kodrianskaia's dream-like fantasy *Globusnyi chelovechek* with brilliant color lithographs—his last major Russian-language children's book. But it was not the first he had planned to illustrate for his good friend in Paris.

In 1946 Kodrianskaia had asked Rojankovsky to design a cover and initials for each chapter of her new book, *Skazki*, with a foreword by their mutual friend, Aleksei Remizov. At this time Rojankovsky was under exclusive contract with the Western Publishing Company in the U. S. and needed explicit permission to do other work. Hoping for a waiver, he painted a tentative cover in rich earth tones, a garland of images from the Russian tale of the witch Baba Yaga, with animals and children—all in an oval around the title and the author's name in his own Cyrillic letter forms. He expected that sacrificing work on the many initials would somehow allow the project. But the waiver was denied anyhow, and he withdrew in 1949. Kodrianskaia's book was nonetheless published in 1950, illustrated throughout by Natal'ia Goncharova, who stepped in and did nice work on short notice.

The first magazine illustrations he drew in Paris—all in 1926—were numerous color covers and drawings for the general-interest weekly magazine *Illiustrirovannaia Rossiia.* Rojankovsky understood the Paris émigrés' taste for nostalgia and their sentimentality about pre-Revolutionary Russia. Some of the pictures were romantic scenes of Old Russia, village and market scenes from the view of the great estates—as the émigrés wanted to remember them in the bitterness of their exile. His peasant girls are always young, pretty and plump, the markets always gay, colorful, and mouth-wateringly provisioned. Several of the pictures clearly show the influences of the popular Russian artists Kustodiev, Sudeikin, and Nikolai Remizov and their idealized depictions of pre-Revolutionary provincial life.

The covers and drawings for *Illiustrirovannaia Rossiia* also included fetching modernist illustrations of émigré life and street scenes in the Russian quarters of Paris—and so balanced the worlds of yesterday and today. For these urban scenes, he worked in the fashionable semi-cubistic style of the 1920s, much like the contemporary work of the Russian artists Yurii Annenkov and Aleksandr Jakovlev. But all the drawings have the singular eye and wit of Rojankovsky.

In 1931 Rojankovsky had a brief association with *Satyricon*, a Russian-language émigré magazine of satire. An attempt to revive the famous pre-Revolutionary Russian magazine of the same name, the new Paris *Satyricon* lasted less than a year. He contributed only one large drawing to the magazine, but his growing reputation in Paris was signaled by his name on the masthead among the most prominent Russian artists then in Paris. One of these, Alexandre Benois, the famous art historian, critic, theatrical artist, illustrator, and painter, soon became a strong supporter of the younger artist's career and praised his children's illustrations in several reviews and articles in the major émigré newspaper in Paris.

Benois also noted and favored Rojankovsky's illustrative contributions to the stories in *Ogon'ki*. This Paris émigré children's magazine was the namesake of the Soviet children's magazine briefly published in Moscow, from 1927 to 1932, though the Soviet magazine was for older children and of different ideological slant. The Paris *Ogon'ki* had an even briefer life, appearing in only nine issues in 1932 and 1933. Several issues have one or more of Rojankovsky's dense ink drawings or woodcuts, to illustrate the Russian stories and articles. All are atmospheric of Russian folk tales and deep in their illustrative traditions. Later in the 1930s some of the stories, verses, and their drawings were reprinted in another short-lived children's magazine, *Sverchok*.

French Advertising Art

The illustrator's arrival in Paris fell several weeks too late for the illustrator to visit the *Exposition Internationale des Arts Décoratifs et Industriels Modernes*, which ran from April to October of 1925. The legendary exhibition of the "Art Deco" style, postponed until after the war, attracted many artists to the city and spread the influence of the already established *Moderne* style. Rojankovsky had been long familiar with the style and understood its import. In Poland, he had worked in the modern graphic styles of the late 1910s and early 1920s, all much influenced by images flowing from French fashion magazines and other fields of French graphic art and design.

Soon after arriving in Paris Rojankovsky adopted the mononym "Rojan," a simple shortening of the French transliteration of his longish surname. In French it has an easy soft *j* sound, similar to the Russian *zh* of his name. He designed a professional letterhead with a modern typeface emblazoning "**ROJAN**KOVSKY"—the first two syllables in boldface. It was also a tactful accommodation of a foreign artist to a new working environment in France. Much of his advertising and magazine illustration in the late 1920s and 1930s is signed "Rojan," and he carried the monicker into some of his early work on the Père Castor series for Flammarion. In the late 1930s he used "Rojan" less often in favor of signing his full name, and dropped the signature soon after coming to the United States. Over the years he told certain of his American friends that he no longer liked the abbreviated form. In France today he is still known informally as "Rojan," whereas in the United States he is known as "Feodor Rojankovsky." But often as not old friends who knew him back when still refer to him as "Rojan."

By early 1927 the newly fashioned Rojan found three years of steady work as an art director with the Lecram Press, a Paris studio for commercial art that employed eleven graphic designers. He got the job through a friend working in Paris for the international McCormick reaper company, whose lucrative advertising work was done by Lecram. The Press specialized in the design of magazine ads, posters, brochures, and catalogs for French businesses. Several of the graphic artists in the studio became good friends, and he found digs with two other bachelor illustrators in a shared flat at No. 11 rue Madame, on the Left Bank. The job at Lecram ended in early 1930 when the Great Depression began to descend upon Paris. Lecram merged with another design studio, became Lecram-Vigneau, and now emphasized the international trend of photography in advertising.

Rojankovsky's best known production for Lecram Press is a masterful art deco promotional piece, *Quand la bise fut venue* (c. 1929), a small portfolio made for La Grande Maison de Blanc, a luxury linen and clothing shop in the Place de l'Opéra, Paris. A French curator of graphic design recently called it still "ravissant." This was the work that caught Esther Averill's attention and, indirectly, led to their working relationship and to the publication of *Daniel Boone* in 1931. He also designed stunning *moderne* catalog covers for the great Paris department store, Bon Marché, and drew advertising art for French magazines.

La Fontaine—Fables (c. 1930), the striking tall booklet decorated with color lithographs of the fabled animals, was a giveaway promotional item designed for Les Laboratoires Rosa, a French pharmaceutical manufacturer. The high quality of the artwork caught Paul Faucher's eye, and he set out to recruit the artist for his Père Castor series of children's picture books. Today, examples of all these early advertising designs are prized by collectors and historians of *la publicité*.

In 1929-30, Rojan also contributed designs for projects at La Maison Tolmer, the renowned commercial art studio founded by the publisher Alfred Tolmer and continued by his sons. The firm specialized in book covers, modern consumer product packaging, and commercial graphic designs of every sort. The art work for Tolmer was bought outright from artists and usually issued unsigned and uncredited, unless of course an artist's name was known well enough to add prestige to the product. FR's correspondence suggests that he worked for Tolmer at least until late 1937. In the 1986 exhibition catalog *Tolmer: 60 ans de création graphique dans L'île St Louis*, Rojankovsky is listed among the early artists for the firm, specifically in 1929 and 1930. His graphic designs may be among the hundreds of anonymous catalog entries for the exhibit or, in any case, among the many other designs that Tolmer commissioned around 1930.

Indeed, many of Rojankovsky's graphic designs of the late 1920s and early 1930s remain unidentified. But signed examples are occasionally found. For example, an outstanding Russian Constructivist-style book cover with art deco lettering was made for Marc Chadourne's *L'U.R.S.S. sans passion* (1932).

The Russian Revolution in French Children's Books

French publishers had fallen behind trends in British and American children's books and in the 1920s were still reprising their glories of past decades. Little new was happening by way of innovative theory and design in children's illustration, despite the modernist inroads in other fields of French graphic art and design. One bright spot in French children's books was Jean de Brunhoff's stories of Babar, beginning with *Histoire de Babar, le petit éléphant* (1931). All were about a charming family of cartoon elephants with a French bourgeois style of life.

A. L. de Saint-Rat describes how around 1930-1931 the look of children's books in France was changed—the lag from modernism closed—by three publishers in Paris, all employing émigré Russian artists. In 1930 Gallimard published Nathalie Parain's *Mon chat*, a gorgeous folio-size picture book with direct influences of Russian Constructivism. Gallimard soon issued Marcel Aymé's *Les contes du chat perché*, a children's book of startling design for its day, illustrated by the Russian artist Nathan Altman. In October 1931 the Domino Press released Rojankovsky's *Daniel Boone*. And later in 1931 Flammarion launched its innovative Père Castor series, an enterprise engaging a number of Russian artists living in Paris; the series was soon to include the stellar contributions of Rojankovsky.

A deeper influence from Soviet Russia lay behind all these innovations. Many Russian émigré artists did not come to France until the mid-1920s, and some had earlier participated in the Russian avant-garde. Cultural exchanges between the Soviets and the émigrés in western Europe were still open in those years. The artists in Paris were well aware of trends in Soviet children's picture book illustration and the new educational philosophy behind them. In 1929 many in Paris saw the landmark exhibit of Soviet children's books, arranged by the French poet Blaise Cendrars. And articles on the new Soviet trends were widely discussed. The Soviet children's books of the 1920s were the inspiration to the new avant-garde look in French children's books.

The Soviet government had set about in the early 1920s to educate an illiterate rural population and was determined to use art, books, and education to mold the new "Soviet man." The government publishing houses produced many hundreds of soft-cover picture books with bold modern designs, some in editions of hundreds of thousands, and sold them for a pittance to assure the widest distribution into the remotest corners of the empire. For many Soviet intellectuals, the 1920s was a period of idealism and great artistic creativity, but it was also a time of political naiveté. The best of the artistic work ended with the Stalinist terror and oppression of the 1930s. Then only the most politically accommodating were allowed to work, increasingly along the lines of Socialist Realism and patriotic themes, including in children's books.

During the heyday of the 1920s talented Soviet artists channeled their efforts in practical directions, revolutionizing the decorative arts in every field—fabric design, fashion, ceramics, and architecture. Some of the most talented carried their ideas into children's picture books, also seen as a practical art with a positive social influence. Even discreet political dissenters were allowed to work on children's books. Some of the artists employed the radical Constructivist approach in their illustrations, while others were more realistic in their depiction. Intended to break the old mold and its ways of seeing, the new pictures were bold and imaginative, with a strong visual appeal to both children and adults.

The leading Soviet illustrator of children's books was Vladimir Lebedev, whose picture books of the 1920s were often in the Constructivist style. In *Tsirk* (1925) the figures are simple and semi-abstracted forms, sometimes broken into separate pieces, and seemingly released from gravity. The layout of the page creates a dialog between the brightly colored forms, the white background, and the minimal text. While Lebedev often worked with planes of bold solid colors, some of his most striking books, such as *Prikliucheniia Chuch-lo* in 1922 and *Okhota* in 1925, are soft-crayon lithographs—the medium that

Rojankovsky also used so effectively. Several of Lebedev's books were translated and issued in France after 1929.

Rojankovsky absorbed the lessons of the Constructivists in general and of Lebedev in particular, though the style and its theory had no great or lasting influence on him. The look of the Russian avant garde is seen far more in the Père Castor books of Nathalie Parain and Hélène Guertik. Yet the back cover of Rojankovsky's *Poudre* (Domino Press, 1933) seems inspired by Lebedev's *Tsirk*. The floating images in Père Castor's *Histoire du nègre Zo'bio* (1942) surely owe much to Lebedev's *Slonenok* of 1922. And some of the pictures in *Scaf, le phoque* (1936) seem moved by Lebedev's *Okhota*, also a picture book about seals. In other respects, Rojankovsky's drawings reflect the Soviet artists Nikolai Tyrsa and Evgenii Charushin who illustrated animal stories in soft-crayon lithographs. But Rojan's taste, it was to turn out, was toward a dynamic naturalism of his own.

The Domino Press

Close on the heels of the Russian turn in children's illustration, *Daniel Boone* was simultaneously published in English and French in October 1931 by Esther Averill's and Lila Stanley's fledgling Domino Press. In several memoirs in the *Horn Book* magazine, Averill recounted founding the expatriate press and Rojankovsky's role in its most successful publications. In 1929 the young American woman, Vassar class of '23, was working in the Paris agency of Thérèse Bonney, whose office was a "kind of clearing house of information on contemporary arts."

Averill noticed Rojankovsky's crisp art deco designs in the little advertising portfolio for La Grande Maison de Blanc and brought the piece to her boss's attention. Bonney summoned the artist for an interview. Averill, who "toiled in the wings" of the office did not meet him that day. But the secretary, knowing that Averill had first spotted his work, came and told her, "The man is nice. Oh, really nice. And you should go and see." Averill walked softly to the rear of the front office where Rojankovsky was being interviewed but came away with only a view of his back.

Bonney in the 1920s was well known as a writer, fashionable portrait photographer, friend of avant-garde artists, and arranger in the art world. Alexander Calder and Stuart Davis were among her sitters. Robert Delaunay painted Bonney in 1925 draped in one of the geometric clothing designs by his wife, Sonia Delaunay, the prodigious Russian émigré artist. Bonney engaged Rojankovsky to design the covers for her new *Shopping Guide to Paris*, issued in English by an American publisher in 1929, and perhaps had him do other work, too. The Guide has Rojankovsky's comical and brightly-colored isometric sketch map of central Paris on the wraparound covers and end papers.

Averill met Rojankovsky only several months later in 1930 when she and another young American woman in Paris, Lila Stanley, had formed their own small business. Their chief account was an American stationery manufacturer who wanted to modernize the design of his paper, boxes, and Christmas cards. The two women recruited Rojankovsky for this work. Averill remembered that he "furnished us with drawings that enchanted us. They had color, gaiety and humor, and revealed how thoroughly he understood the graphic possibilities of the medium." But the manufacturer had trouble reproducing the designs with his usual printing method and did not use them.

In 1930 Rojankovsky was more eager to establish himself as a children's-book illustrator. So far he had addressed only the Russian émigré audience in the several books authored by Sasha Chernyi. Averill and Stanley agreed to produce a picture book with Rojan, intending to find an American publisher and so needing an American subject—and one with appeal in the French market too. They settled on the eminently American story of Daniel Boone and his wilderness adventures, surely aware of the long French and general European fascination with the frontier of North America and *les Peaux-Rouges.*

When Rojankovsky set about the project, the book's design grew more elaborate, grand, and of course more expensive to produce. No American publisher could be found for such an innovative and costly project. The two women decided to publish the book themselves and set about to learn the French publishing trade—about which they knew nothing. The Domino Press was born and *Daniel Boone*, its first title, was published in English and French folio editions with sixteen pages of direct lithographs in the unusual richness of five colors.

The pages were pulled on heavy, high-quality paper by Mourlot Frères, a firm noted for their superb color work. Rojankovsky copied the drawings onto the stones himself and advised on the inking, assuring lithographs of remarkable crispness and depth of pure color. In 1932 the critic R.-L. Dupuy, praising the book in *Gebrauchsgraphik*, commented on the radical, modernist juxtaposition of color. "Who but a Russian would ever adventure to beset a grass-green meadow with violet trees, heighten the effect by introducing a chrome-yellow tree, and crown the whole by perching a red squirrel in the branches."

A book with minimal text, *Daniel Boone* is a dramatic sequence of *mises en scène*—all reflecting the artist's interest and work experience in theatrical design, tableaux, and pictorial narration. The modernist influence of film was apparent to some reviewers. Stage design and children's art are easily fused in the hands of gifted artists. Maurice Sendak established himself brilliantly in children's books before turning to stage designs that evoke the same madcap atmosphere. Rojankovsky, on the other hand, was an experienced stage designer who carried those ideas into children's books.

Barbara Bader, the historian of children's picture books, points out the corollary influence of modern advertising layout and illustration. *Daniel Boone*, she writes, was begun as a book without words and "remains a collection of tableaux vivants—one does not so much enter into its narrative as into its spirit." A totally designed book, its pictures create a spatial interplay with the irregularly shaped blocks of text.

Today, the audacious *Daniel Boone* is credited with setting a new direction in modern children's picture books. Yet the book was not a great commercial success, in part because it was a large, expensive luxury production in the *beau livre* tradition and of unfamiliar appearance for a children's book. And it was issued in the Great Depression when purse strings were tight. But *Daniel Boone* was a great critical success, reviewed in the most prestigious venues in France, England, and the United States.

An identical British edition of *Daniel Boone*, also printed in France by Mourlot Frères, was issued by Faber and Faber under their own imprint. The London *Observer* on December 3, 1932, declared it "our choice among all the children's books of the season." The London *Week-end Review* declared: "Here is the technique of film applied to the child's book [which] marks a new era in the history of children's books."

In Boston, Bertha Mahoney's Bookshop for Boys and Girls became the U.S. distributor. The influential critic Anne Carroll Moore of the New York Public Library, noted for her demanding and uncompromising taste, praised the book with superlatives. And so Rojankovsky's innovative art was introduced to a privileged few American children who already knew the story of Daniel Boone but now had the great legend newly inscribed.

In 1932 two prestigious European graphics journals, *Arts et métiers graphiques* and *Gebrauchsgraphik*, devoted special articles to innovations in book design. One reviewer said Rojankovsky's only peer was now the older and esteemed French illustrator André Hellé, a daring and highly complimentary comparison. A. L. de Saint-Rat writes that the publication of *Daniel Boone* "was a revolutionary event which launched Rojankovsky into his new career and ushered in the renaissance of French children's books."

The artist went on to illustrate four other books for the Domino Press. The handsome, though more modest English and French editions of the horse story *Powder (Poudre)* were published in 1933 and its sequel *Flash (Éclair)* in 1934, again with direct color lithographs by Mourlot Frères. Anne Carroll Moore was equally ecstatic about *Powder*.

In 1934 Averill left Paris and reestablished the press in New York, while Rojankovsky, her chief illustrator, stayed in France. From New York, the Domino Press published his handsome, highly-designed interpretation of *The Voyages of Jacques Cartier* (1937), displaying the illustrator's strengths in line drawings. Nearly twenty years later, Harper & Brothers published a greatly altered edition in a smaller format, retitled *Cartier Sails the St. Lawrence* (1956). Averill revised the text for this edition, Rojankovsky supplied a dozen new drawings, and some of the original drawings were either cropped or dropped.

In the late 1930s and still in Paris, Rojankovsky planned to publish *Cortez, the Conqueror* with the Domino Press. He conceived *Cortez* as a larger and more elegant production than Cartier. He sent the drawings to Averill in New York, writing to her of his enormous creative effort and enthusiasm for the illustrations. But Averill delayed its publication in favor of pressing him to work on *Tales of Poindi* (1938), a book of lesser artistic merit, a commercial failure, and destined to become his last book with the Domino Press. Averill's small press went out of business before his magnificent *Cortez* could be published, and the book was never realized quite as Rojankovsky had conceived it.

After several years Averill sold the drawings to Random House who published *Cortez, the Conqueror* in 1947. The publisher recruited Covelle Newcomb to write the text. Anne Carroll Moore, writing in the *Horn Book*, described the author's narrative as "denatured for young readers," believing that boys ought to have a "more vigorous and historical presentation." Though large and handsome, with drawings much like those in *Cartier*, the Random House edition was not the integrated book design Rojankovsky had in mind. Yet the line drawings, some embellished in dull gold ink, are still among his best work. Though romanticized, the rendering of Aztec physiognomy and costumes from secondary sources is bold and the designs are handsome. A cursory look makes clear the missed potential of the book. Barbara Bader wrote, "what he might have done had circumstances been different, *Cartier* continues to attest."

The now unfashionable subjects of heroic exploration and colonial conquest greatly interested the artist and, before present times, many parents and young readers. In 1937 he proposed a new book, "The Voyages of Captain Cook," for the Domino Press, but Averill never took it up. In 1943, he proposed to Random House a "History of Exploration," prompted by his thinking through plans for "Captain Cook" and his work on *Cartier*, *Cortez*, and perhaps future plans for *Balboa*. But it was never realized either.

After Rojankovsky came to the United States in 1941, he stayed in contact with and occasionally visited Averill for the rest of his life.

Each year she faithfully sent him a small royalty check for sales from her private stock of Domino Press books. Through the years they remained good friends but oddly formal in their interactions, perhaps only because of Averill's temperament or preference. He always referred to her by her surname or as "Miss Averill" and she to him as "Mr. Rojankovsky" in writing and probably in person. Yet we know she was always proud of helping to launch his career and wrote warmly of the artist in her articles in *The Horn Book*.

The Père Castor Series

Published by Ernest Flammarion in Paris and under the direction of Paul Faucher (1898-1967), the Père Castor series set another new direction in modern children's picture books. The first was published in December 1931—at the same moment of *Daniel Boone*. But Rojankovsky's first contribution to the series did not come until 1933, launching the next major and overlapping phase of his career in France.

Paul Faucher was the person behind the mask of *Père Castor*, "Father Beaver," the kindly storyteller and teacher of children. Faucher and his wife were inspired by the teachings of the Czech educator Frantisek Bakulé. Faucher was an educational theorist and founded the French section of the International Bureau of Education at Geneva and, to carry out his ideas, the École du Père Castor in Paris, a progressive kindergarten.

The small, colorful and inexpensive books of the series expressed Faucher's theory of modern child education and put it into publishing practice. The books integrated bold, modern images with stories, games, or projects for little hands—all designed to stimulate a child's curiosity and imagination. Faucher believed graphic images should not be mere illustrations of a text, but carry an independent message and way of seeing.

The Russian émigré influence on the Père Castor series was direct and considerable. Faucher's wife and co-theorist, Lida Durdikova-Faucher, was Czech and authored a number of the books. Over half of the series issued in the 1930s were illustrated by Russian artists living in Paris, most notably Rojankovsky, Nathalie Parain, Hélène Guertik, Nathan Altman, and Alexandra Exter. Ivan Bilibin was also among them, but kept steadfastly to the earlier Style Russe of the World of Art. A. L. de Saint-Rat writes that "the Père Castor series owes its initial brilliance to the talented team of Russian artists whom Faucher attracted to this enterprise." The Père Castor books applied Russian developments in avant-garde art, propaganda posters, and picture books—all towards a new understanding of child education. Like many Russian émigré artists, Rojankovsky was almost unknown in the Soviet Union. Today, however, there is considerable Russian interest in his work. A Russian publisher is planning to issue Russian translations of his Père Castor books, and has already published one of his later American books.

After the success of Rojankovsky's first two large-format wild animal picture books, *Les petits et les grands* (1933) and *En famille* (1934), and with the charming *Panache l'écureuil* in hand, Faucher in late 1934 signed the illustrator to an exclusive five-year contract to expire on September 25, 1939. Rojan agreed to illustrate two books a year of the quality of *Panache*, or a minimum of ten books, and agreed not to illustrate French-language children's books for other publishers."

The contract also specified that Rojan would copy his drawings directly onto Flammarion's zinc plates for offset lithography. It was here, as he wrote thirty years later, that he learned the techniques of offset lithography and personally created the drawings for color separation on "six or seven" zinc plates for each design. He became involved in the handwork of reproduction and often touched up drawings, sometimes changing them in major ways or even substituting new drawings between early press runs of the animal stories. The late picture books in the Père Castor series after about 1939, however, were reproduced from watercolors by photomechanical offset methods.

By the time he left France in 1941, Rojankovsky had illustrated twenty seven books for *Père Castor*, and most displayed Faucher's theories. Eight of the finest are in a subseries titled *Le roman des bêtes,* written by "Lida." The oblong, soft-cover books, de Saint-Rat remarks, "gave us a whole course in natural history." Beginning in 1934 with *Panache l'écureuil*, each book is a nature story of a single animal: a squirrel, a hare, a wild duck, a brown bear, a seal, a hedgehog, a kingfisher, and a cuckoo. Rojankovsky also planned a similar book on the marmot in the early 1930s, perhaps drafting it, but it was never published. A pet marmot, the artist's drawing model, wandered around his suburban Paris household, chewing on the furniture, once causing a chair to collapse when a visiting heavy-set friend sat down.

The stories in *Le roman des bêtes* anthropomorphize the animals, giving them personal names and depicting conversations and human motivations. But in a novel approach for the early 1930s, the stories and, especially, the drawings depict the behavior of real animals in natural settings. The drawings are "at once warmly sympathetic and unsentimental," Bader writes. The soft-crayon lithographs of the animals and their habitats, drawn in a romanticized realism, invited the child to identify with the creatures and to understand and appreciate their lives in the wild. For these qualities, Alexandre Benois publicly praised the illustrator for books that encouraged children to observe nature.

The Père Castor books were a great commercial and critical success. The high quality of the first books in the series elevated Rojankovsky's reputation even further. Beginning in 1936, many of his titles were also published in the United States, first by Georges Duplaix's Artists and Writers Guild and soon by Harper and Brothers, with translations by either Georges or Lily Duplaix. In England, they were translated by the children's author Rose Fyleman and published in faithful editions by George Allen & Unwin. The Père Castor series in some ways prompted the educational ambitions of the early Golden Books in America. But more directly they inspired the nature-study and how-things-work English Puffin Books of the 1940s.

Several of Rojankovsky's most popular Père Castor books remain in print—eighty years after their first publication. The illustrator's key role in the establishment of the Père Castor books is also emblemized in his creation of the first logo for the series. His design of a beaver holding a book remains the Père Castor logo today.

Other French Graphic Art and Illustration

A number of independent drawings and paintings of landscapes, portraits of friends, and female figure studies were plentifully produced in France in the 1920s and 1930s and are among Rojankovsky's most engaging work. At the same time, he was creating an abundance of other graphic art and illustration for public consumption, but on more intimate scales of production than the children's books.

Theater, both amateur and professional, was an interest from the overture to the closing acts of his artistic life. He delighted in making costumes and decorations for even modest amateur productions. Over the years, he decorated small theatrical productions in France and the United States, from simple family and neighborhood events to larger community productions.

Before the war, he may have proposed or even realized a few designs for French theatrical productions. For example, he made finished costume designs for Eugène Scribe's comedy *L'ours et le pacha* and for other plays. When he returned to live in France in the early 1960s, he created the maquettes for the scenes and costumes for the student ballet recitals in 1960 and 1964 of Nina Tikanova's École de Danse, staged in various Paris theaters. In previous seasons its designers had included the prominent Russian artists Yurii Annenkov and Lev Zak.

Other than book illustrations and posters, Rojankovsky made but few fine art prints for reproduction in multiples. We know of only one such print, a female ballet subject. One of the artist's favorite models in Paris was Anastasia Minsekova, a young ballet student of Russian background. She was called "Nasten'ka," the diminutive of Anastasia. In the 1950s Nasten'ka herself became a published illustrator, signing with her married name, Chassay. For several sketches and watercolors in the late 1930s, Rojankovsky drew Nasten'ka, Degas-like, in a tutu, usually standing and viewed from the rear, and sometimes spied in informal moments. At least one of these images was issued in a small number of lithographed prints, both in colors and in black and white.

In 1930 Rojankovsky and a friend from his time in the Ukraine after the Revolution, the Russian sculptor, Lev Schultz, took a trip to

Algiers, then a French colony and popular destination for tourists and artists. The casbah or "native" quarter was in the 1930s romanticized for French moviegoers as the fictional setting of *Pépé Le Moko* and later, for Americans, in the remake titled *Algiers*. Like Casablanca, Algiers had the exotic appeal of the cultural "other" that attracted European artists and writers.

Rojankovsky kept snapshots of himself and Schultz in a local green park with a pretty *algérienne* model, she obligingly in native costume. It was surely she who posed in a harem outfit, bare-breasted, baggy pantaloons and all, for Rojan to paint her as several reclining odalisques, a popular subject of erotic appeal inspired, among other things, by Henri Matisse's odalisques of the 1920s. Rojankovsky reworked one such figure study for his 1937 illustrated edition of Béranger's *Chansons galantes*.

Soon after leaving the Lecram Press in 1930, Rojan drafted the first of fifteen covers and full-page cartoons for *Le Rire*, the ribald weekly French humor magazine, and continued in this work through 1932. Each week *Le Rire* had an amusing color cover, either risqué or satirical of social manners. The articles inside were short and the cartoons pointed—easy amusements in idle moments—often as not about loose, slim and naked young women being ogled and chased about by equally loose but older, portly, and married businessmen. The color covers and pen drawings inside were by many artists, some of them well known as illustrators. Rojankovsky's highly-finished contributions were among the best in that period of the magazine.

A 1944 article about the illustrator in *Publishers Weekly* and Fritz Eichenberg's 1957 article about his friend in *American Artist* puzzlingly mention Rojankovsky's illustration of "new editions" of three French literary classics by Diderot, Prévost, and Voltaire. And Rojankovsky himself mentions illustrating these titles in private notes and letters. In fact, these are not new editions but uniquely embellished single copies of books published with the illustrations of other artists. Such unique embellished and extra-illustrated copies of luxury editions were commonly made by many graphic artists in the 1920s, 1930s, and even after the war. The Paris publisher René Kieffer, for example, retained artists for this work and matched them with collectors. Other artists took commissions on their own.

In 1931 and 1932, Rojankovsky embellished one copy each of three books published a few years earlier in large, luxury editions on expensive paper by Javal et Bourdeaux, a Paris firm that specialized in pricey editions of amorous literary titles. The titles are: Abbé Prévost's *Histoire du chevalier des Grieux et de Manon Lescaut* (1927); Denis Diderot's *Les bijoux indiscrets* (1928); and Voltaire's *La princesse de Babylone* (1928). These particular French texts lend themselves to semi-erotic illustration, and over the years many such editions have been published.

Rojankovsky decorated the three copies with additional pictures, sometimes elaborate ones, drawn on their wide margins and blank pages, and he interspersed new sheets with his own additional color drawings and paintings, overwhelming the other illustrator's work. In a letter to a friend, Rojankovsky mentions that he would be paid 10,000 to 12,000 francs for two of these books and that the unnamed "publisher" expected to sell them for 35,000 to 45,000 francs—a lot of money in the early 1930s. In the late 1990s, a New York rare book dealer offered the unique copy of *La princesse de Babylone* for $25,000. Single copies of other such embellished books are in private collections, though the Javal et Bourdeaux editions are his main efforts. The risqué work for *Le Rire* and the Javal et Bourdeaux editions also prefigured several more explicit books in the 1930s.

Like many other figurative artists in Paris, Rojankovsky made elegant erotic book illustrations—picture books and fairy tales for grownups. A fashionable market in literary and artistic "curiosa" thrived in Europe between the wars and engaged some of the most talented illustrators of the day, both men and women, including some of the most prominent Russian illustrators working in Paris. Rojankovsky illustrated half a dozen new editions of old and modern erotic French literary texts, such as the 19th century bawdy chansons of Pierre-Jean de Béranger and the posthumously published erotic verses of Pierre Louÿs. All were published on the model of limited, luxury editions (some copies with extra suites of plates and signed original drawings) and were expensive in the 1930s. Most were published with the illustrator supposedly anonymous, but are now firmly attributed to Rojankovsky's hand. As erotic illustration goes, the work is of high quality, sprightly and brightly colored, extending to the explicit the spirit and style of the risqué drawings in *Le Rire.*

This small and generally amusing body of work has long been known, valued, and collected. Certain of the books are today considered classics of the genre and fetch handsome prices in the rare book market. Rojankovsky lavished his best draftsmanship and color work on these illustrations and they are among his most accomplished work. The only complete and cataloged institutional collection of these editions is held by the Kinsey Institute at Indiana University, Bloomington.

Since the early 1980s choice illustrations from the two most popular works, the wholly original portfolio *Idylle printanière* (1933) and the two editions of Radiguet's *Vers libres*, have been reproduced in British and American anthologies of erotic art. An expensive facsimile edition of *Idylle printanière* was recently published in London and advertised to an upscale market. In 1993 a leading British fashion magazine, *Harpers & Queen*, reproduced a tiny but explicit image from *Vers libres* in an article about the surging market in erotic art. Its appearance caused no public stir and only amused comment in the British press.

The several naughty books are a minor but noteworthy aspect of the illustrator's long and varied career and round out the picture of a man in and of his time and place. The drawings are best viewed in the cultural setting of Paris in the 1930s and, in the much harsher world of today, appreciated for their gentle period style and what they reveal of our social and cultural history.

Graphic Design and Book Illustration in London

While working and living in Paris, Rojankovsky traveled to London several times in the 1930s to visit friends, especially his British agent Leslie V. Cusden, and to arrange work with British publishers and other clients. Cusden and the illustrator became great friends and correspondents and visited again, for the last time, in the 1960s. Much of his British advertising work was done through the firm of Harding & Giles, London.

Rojankovsky created several handsome British travel posters, all signed "Rojan," that were displayed in highly public places and were part of Britain's stylish graphics environment in the years before the war. In 1933 he designed foreign travel posters and brochures for the British Orient Line, including an atmospheric dockside scene promoting North African tours.

In the 1920s and early 1930s, London Transport's Frank Pick had commissioned a stunning series of posters by distinguished artists, such as E. McKnight Kauffer, all lettered with Edward Johnston's classic 1916 Underground typeface. London Underground posters "For the Zoo" were the most frequent topic, with two a year commissioned in the 1920s. In 1935 Pick delegated the commissioning of posters to Christian Barman, and apparently Rojankovsky was among Barman's first choices.

Rojankovsky's 1935 poster for the Underground, "For the Zoo," was garlanded with wild animals and directed users of London Transport to the London Zoo. The same design was used on pictorial information leaflets for visitors to the suburban Whipsnade Zoo. The British Zoological Society today sells various items reproducing the 1935 poster, such as posters, postcards, and bookmarks. Rojankovsky also designed travel posters in 1935 and 1937 for the Southern Railway Company. Examples of the posters are today held in Britain's London Transport Museum, the National Railway Museum, and the Victoria & Albert Museum.

The British Post Office engaged him to design a humorous telegraph form for special use on St. Valentine's Day; it was popular enough to be picked up and parodied by a London tabloid. And bright covers on circus, aviation and other themes were painted for a high-end British magazine, *The Bystander.* He also did graphic design work for product packaging. Much to the artist's surprise and amusement, Mother Goose drawings he made for a British paper manufacturer were used to decorate the wrapping for their brand of toilet tissue. The unsigned designs were later made into a promotional booklet for the necessary product.

The British reading public was already familiar with the Domino Press and Père Castor books in their London editions. Rojankovsky later illustrated directly for British publishers. The pictures for Anne Scott-Moncrieff's *The White Drake* (Methuen, 1936) were naturalistic drawings of ducks in the wild. The charming fairy-tale drawings for J. W. Dunne's *An Experiment with St. George* (Faber & Faber, 1939) were submitted and then obligingly revised according to precise instructions from Dunne himself to bring the picture details into complete harmony with the word of the text. Dunne was a pioneer aircraft designer whose popular books of the 1920s delved into the concept of time.

Among the last book illustrations Rojankovsky drew in France, before his departure for New York in 1941, were pen sketches of the mischievous parrot and cat in *The Adventures of Dudley and Gilderoy* (New York, 1941). This venerable British tale was also published by Faber & Faber in London later in the same year. The slim book is Marion B. Cothren's adaptation for juveniles of Algernon Blackwood's much longer 1929 novel, *Dudley & Gilderoy: A Nonsense.*

5

Paris Friends and Places

In the course of sixteen years in Paris, Rojankovsky came to know most of the prominent illustrators and artists in the Russian émigré community where social relations and professional support were extensive. Beyond émigré circles, he also mixed with many other people in the Paris art and cultural world.

During the first years in France, 1925-1931, Rojankovsky lived in central Paris and kept company with a great variety of people, especially in the fields of graphic arts and publishing. Friendships grew with several of the artists and illustrators at the Lecram Press, including the French illustrators François Hirschler and Gaston de Sainte-Croix and the Hungarian artist László Fircsa. Outside the Lecram group, Rojankovsky also met the American artist George Alexander in 1928 and they too became fast friends. Another good friend in Paris was the noted Russian woodcut illustrator Valentin Le Campion (1903-1952), whose birth name was Valentin Nikolaevich Bitt.

In the several years around 1930, Rojankovsky, Alexander, and Hirschler shared a flat at 11 rue Madame, in the Artists' Quarter on the Left Bank. The three bachelors were a mutual support group, borrowing money from each other in hard times and paying back when art was sold. When not working, they lived a carefree life, sitting for long hours in sidewalk cafés and sketching the scene at the Dôme, the Coupole, or the Select.

The three men remained friends through the 1930s, until the war scattered them. Hirschler, a Jew, survived the Nazi roundups in Vichy by hiding in the basement of a French farmhouse. Alexander went to England in 1939 with his British wife, but Rojankovsky met them again in the United States and exchanged many visits over the years. Upon the first visit back to France in 1951, Rojankovsky looked up several old friends who had remained in France during and after the war.

Rojankovsky knew Nikolai N. Evreinov (1879-1953), the playwright, director, and an historian and theorist of Russian theater. He pursued a lively correspondence with the writer and artist Aleksei Remizov, from the 1930s in Paris through the 1940s and 1950s in the U.S. In 1938, Rojankovsky had illustrated one of Remizov's children's stories in Paris-Soir, one of the many stories he illustrated for the newspaper in the late 1930s. Rojankovsky also knew the artist and stage designer Mstislav Dobuzhinsky, and they exchanged humorous letters in the 1940s and 1950s when both were in the United States. And it was in Paris that Rojankovsky probably first met and became friendly with the Russian critic Marc Slonim; in the 1950s the two men and their families were neighbors in Bronxville, New York, and exchanged social visits.

About 1931 Rojankovsky met Yvette, an attractive and well-composed Frenchwoman in her middle to late thirties, permanently separated from her husband, and with a nearly grown son. Rojankovsky and Yvette set up housekeeping and remained together for ten years, until he left France in 1941. By all reports they were a happy couple. They settled first into the bachelor flat at 11 rue Madame. After a year or two they moved to an apartment in Plessis-Robinson, and in 1937 to a duplex house in Meudon; both places were suburbs nine or ten miles from the center of Paris and well-connected by rail.

Yvette's surname is lost to us and we know little about her, except for a few photographs and distant recollections of several people who met her in the 1930s when they were children or young adults. Yvette was probably of working-class or lower middle-class background but of higher, middle-class aspirations and manners. She may have been of Alsatian provincial descent and earlier have worked in the couture trades, an industry employing 30,000 French people between the wars.

The writer Olga Andreyev Carlisle met the couple in the mid-1930s when they were neighbors at Plessis-Robinson. Through the eyes of a Russian child, Carlisle remembers Yvette as "exotically French with lots of Paris chic." Elizabeth Alexander, the English wife of Rojankovsky's American friend, George Alexander, also recalls Yvette from a distance of sixty years. She and her husband had lunch with the couple in 1939 at their home in Meudon, just before they returned to England on the eve of the war. She remembers Yvette as a gracious woman, an amiable petite bourgeoise, quite the *maîtresse de maison*—and an excellent cook. François Faucher, the son of Paul Faucher, remembers Yvette in 1940 as a woman of quiet temperament, but eclipsed in the young boy's eyes by the picture-book artist's panache and energy.

In early 1933 Rojankovsky and Yvette left central Paris and moved into a more spacious apartment and studio overlooking the woods in the *cité jardin* in the Paris suburb of Plessis-Robinson. Appropriately for the life-long fan and aspiring illustrator of *Robinson Crusoe*, the name *Plessis-Robinson* derives from the title of Defoe's novel—also a popular favorite in France after its publication in 1719.

The Ville du Plessis-Robinson was named in 1909 for its proximity to the popular outdoor pleasure gardens of "Robinson." An inspiration of a mid-nineteenth century restaurant-owner, Gueusquin, the early theme park was designed on a fantasy of Robinson Crusoe's and Friday's improvised life on their desert island. The main feature of the old summer-time pleasure garden was numerous outdoor restaurants of platforms built high in the heavy branches of giant chestnut trees, with names such as "Le Vrai Arbre de Robinson" and "Le Grand Arbre," all honoring the tree where Crusoe first sought shelter from the wild animals. These dining spaces with tables and chairs for small parties were reached by rustic staircases on which waiters dashed up and down. Rojankovsky and Yvette soon visited one of the old tree-house restaurants and he wrote to a friend of his delight in the absurd theatrical atmosphere.

The couple's new apartment in Plessis-Robinson was on the fifth floor at No. 3 on the main avenue Payret-Dortail. The modern, Corbusier-like garden city was designed in the early 1920s by the architect Maurice Payret-Dortail (for whom the main avenue was named) and intended as an improved suburban environment for French workers. (After the war, the wide avenue was renamed Avenue Jacques Duclos, after the French Communist Party leader during the Resistance.) By the early 1930s the apartments had proven too expensive for most French workers, leaving many vacancies, and an informal colony of émigré Russians and others in barely better circumstances had moved in. Here in the wooded suburbs the couple's new social life blossomed among the Russian and other artists and intellectuals.

Olga Carlisle recalls her first encounter with Rojankovsky while on a walk with her mother in the woods directly behind their apartment building. The mother and young daughter came upon the artist as he was intently sketching squirrels that were running up and down trees and perching on branches. The strollers stopped to chat and were delighted to learn that the artist was also Russian and lived in the same apartment building; a life-long friendship with the Andreyev family began.

In a 1962 memoir, Carlisle recalled her visits to Rojankovsky's studio and the little events staged to entertain the children who visited the couple in Plessis-Robinson. And she amplified for us, recalling the squirrel and hedgehog he kept for drawing models and her delight with the impropriety that the animals had the free run of the apartment. She especially savors the memory of late one night stealing into an adult costume party in the Rojankovsky's apartment. Making her way alone in the dark up two flights of stairs and appearing at the door, she was invited in to marvel at the costumes. Some people were dressed as playing cards, costumes likely of Rojankovsky's own design; he had used the theme in satirical magazine cartoons. Carlisle came to know the artist again in the 1950s and 1960s when both were in the United States, and they remained fast friends through his last days.

Ruth Sandemann, another neighbor child at Plessis-Robinson and the daughter of an exiled German Social Democrat, also became great friends with the artist. Ruth was invited to set up paint pots on her own table in Rojankovsky's studio. She became his work companion, his student on nature walks, and occasional model. Sketches of young Ruth appear, reworked, in several of his children's books and related art. The Sandemann family came to the United States in 1941 and Ruth remained friends with Rojankovsky until the end of his life.

In August of 1937 Rojankovsky and Yvette left Plessis-Robinson in favor of a rented, shared, duplex house with a garden at No. 10ter rue Herault in the western suburb of Meudon, only a few kilometers from Plessis-Robinson and nine kilometers by rail to the center of Paris. A social attraction of Meudon was its comparatively large and established Russian émigré community and the presence of an active Russian cultural center and its seasonal arts activities. In Meudon, the couple continued their rich social life among new and old friends, living there until the summer of 1940 and the Occupation of Paris.

Rojankovsky was generous to all around him, a comment heard over and over from people who knew him through the years in France and the United States. He threw costly parties when he got paid for art work and was free with small personal loans, really gifts, to friends. And kindnesses and favors others extended to him were never forgotten. Over the years, he was known to give shelter and support to Russian friends in need. N. P. Karbasnikov, who published his *Azbuka* in 1926 when the artist was struggling, himself fell on hard times in the early 1930s and came to live for a while, sleeping in the kitchen of the Rojankovsky's flat.

Rojankovsky had summered since the late 1920s and through the 1930s on the southern coast of France at La Favière, either renting or visiting in a summer colony of Russians that came to be called "Russian Hill." Rojankovsky had many friends there, including the artist, Ivan Bilibin, who early on had built a tiny one-room hut on Russian Hill. Rojankovsky's friend, the writer Sasha Chernyi, had a year-round family house on the other side of La Favière.

In the early 1950s, Rojankovsky and his new family returned and built a comfortable house, about a kilometer from Russian Hill, and used it as a summer residence for the rest of his life. The French artist Alexis Obolensky recalls, from when he was a young boy living in La Favière, meeting Rojankovsky and how the illustrator thrilled him and encouraged his young art interests.

Beginning in 1935, Rojankovsky and Yvette began vacationing, both summers and winters, in Argentière, a resort community nestled in the French Alps near Chamonix Mont-Blanc in the Savoie region and near the Swiss and Italian frontiers. For several years they rented with a farm family named Couttet, but soon entertained plans for a house of their own. On a nearby property, Rojankovsky built a tiny Alpine-style house, named "Villa Rambles," intended as a respite from workaday Paris and the suburban house in Meudon. He wrote from Argentière in early 1939 of having worked recently for extra money for his "architectural project." The house was not completed until sometime in 1940, that fateful year when Paris fell to the Germans. Rojankovsky was to live in it only a few months, in 1940-41 before leaving for America.

Rojankovsky loved this mountainous spot, wrote fondly of it to friends, and thought about it a good deal after coming to America. He included a nostalgic picture of the house in *The Tall Book of Nursery Tales* (1944) to illustrate "The Wee Little Woman." The Alpine countryside and its people had also inspired *Cigalou* (1939), one of his last and most ebullient books for Père Castor, and it pictures a similar little mountain house. Years later the region—and again its vernacular architecture—inspired Rojankovsky's drawings for Bishop's *All Alone* (1953).

Leaving France

Against all difficulties of economic depression and political trouble in France, the late 1930s and the first years of the war were productive times for the illustrator. From 1937 through 1939, he illustrated many juvenile stories for the Sunday children's page in *Paris-Soir*, the popular newspaper. Two books with London and New York publishers were published in 1939 and 1941. Some of his most enduring Père Castor books were published in these first years of the European war, such as *Cigalou* (1939) and *Michka* (1941). All his books in the wartime *Les "Petits Père Castor"* series were published after the Occupation of Paris in 1940, most in 1941 and 1942. Finally, two little-known illustrated books, Dumas's *Tom, Jacques & Cie* and a completely redrawn and full-text version of Mariotti's *Les contes de Poindi*, were published by Librairie Stock, Paris, in 1941.

Since the early 1930s Rojankovsky had expressed to friends a wish to work in America, and he began to cast about for prospects. Part of his incentive was financial. In his work for Flammarion he was always paid a flat fee, which he considered to be too low, and never did he receive any royalties from Flammarion for the enormously successful Père Castor books. In letters to Esther Averill about their projects in the late 1930s, he expressed hope to join her in New York, and wrote of concerns about the coming war in Europe. One letter in 1938 is illustrated with a drawing of Nazi bombs he expected to fall on Paris—as they had already fallen on the Spanish city of Guernica in April 1937. Later he expressed hope to visit the 1939 World's Fair in New York and, moreover, to see a bit of bosky America—the country of Daniel Boone. But he did not make the trip in time to see the great fair. The European war began in 1939 and France fell the next year.

In the days before the Germans occupied Paris on the 14th of June, several million people left the city and its suburbs, at least temporarily, in favor of the provinces, especially to the south, where they felt safer. They filled the exit roads on whatever conveyances they could manage, many of them walking and others pulling a few belongings in carts. On bicycles, Rojankovsky and Yvette made their way southward out of Paris and took refuge in the family home of his editor, Paul Faucher.

Faucher set up a progressive school for Paris refugee children in his home at Forgeneuve and Rojankovsky helped entertain the children with antics and organized games. Faucher's son, François, remembers that Rojankovsky cooked on occasions and treated all present with samples of his specialty dishes. Today, Faucher revels in memories of the startling stunts, boisterous games, and colorful shows that the artist staged for the displaced children. And during that uncertain time, Rojankovsky painted landscapes of the Haute-Vienne region for gifts to his hosts.

The Faucher house was at Forgeneuve, near Meuzac, in the region of Limousin, about halfway between Vichy and Bordeaux, and lay well within the Non-occupied Zone when the Vichy government was established a month later. France was now divided into an Occupied Zone, including Paris and the northern part of the country, and to the south, a Non-occupied Zone controlled by the Vichy collaborators. The Alpine village of Argentière and the little house, luckily, were a few miles south of the line. The couple retreated here in the winter of 1940-41, and Argentière was the artist's last official address in France. For the rest of his time in France, Rojankovsky cautiously kept to the Non-occupied Zone and never returned to Occupied Paris.

Rojankovsky's contract with Faucher had expired in late 1939 and his last prewar Père Castor book was published in that year. The turn of events in the summer and fall of 1940 may have set the stage for, or only hastened, thirteen more children's picture books for the series. *Michka* and *Pic et Pic et Colégram*, both published in 1941, and the eleven wartime *Les "Petits Père Castor"* were illustrated for Faucher's series during this denouement of the illustrator's career in France.

While the occupying Germans and their French collaborators in Vichy had no particular interest in Rojankovsky, the White Russians were generally a suspect foreign element in France—and now more marginal than ever. Just after the war when Rojankovsky was applying for permanent residency in the U.S., one of his sponsors testified that before the war the illustrator had drawn anti-fascist cartoons in unnamed magazines or newspapers and in 1940-41 was on a Nazi blacklist of intellectuals and artists living in unoccupied France.

And the brutal Nazi persecution of the French Freemasons began in the summer of 1940. Rojankovsky had joined the Grande Loge de France in November 1933 and in 1934-37 designed several covers for Russian-language books on Freemasonry. In October of 1940, the Nazis staged the anti-Masonic *Exposition Maçonnique* at the Petit Palais to display "conspiratorial" art, books, and documents taken from Masonic lodges. In any case, the artist could not look to a bright future in France and wasted no time in making arrangements to get out of the country.

Georges Duplaix, the French editor and occasional children's author and illustrator, had been in the United States since 1931 and, since about 1935, had known Rojankovsky from trips to Paris. In early 1940 Duplaix, now for several years in New York as an editor with the Artists and Writers Guild, was put in charge of production and was hatching plans to produce Golden Books for Simon & Schuster. Duplaix worked through a New York agent, Josef Riwkin, and French intermediaries to engage Rojankovsky to come and work in New York.

The deal to get Rojankovsky sponsorship out of wartime France and a job in the United States, and so a U.S. visa, was all business. The artist was offered a two-fold contract in which Riwkin would seek non-book illustration and advertising work in American magazines and, to supplement this, the Guild promised at least two illustrated books a year. All income for any kind of art work, including that for the Guild, would be paid directly to Riwkin, who would keep an unusually large twenty five percent for his fee, paying the balance to the artist.

A preliminary bargain was struck and the first general advance of $1,000 was paid in the fall of 1940, helping Rojankovsky to break the dependence on Faucher and sustaining him in France for several more months. Rojankovsky renewed his Nansen passport on January 29, 1941, permitting him to travel out of France. The final contracts were signed on March 1, 1941. The general contract with an American agent and the Guild's specific contract providing modest employment were enough to meet U.S. immigration requirements. Rojankovsky was issued an American visa at Lyon on May 13, 1941 and that summer set out alone for New York. Yvette, a French national, had to stay behind in the house in Argentière.

Rojankovsky's declared intention was to return to France and to Yvette. But he could not have anticipated the war's nearly four more years or how, separated by distance and even more time, his life would change in America. During the war and in the hard times in France afterward, he gave Yvette financial help and they exchanged letters. His U.S. immigration status did not permit him to travel until 1948. By then everything had changed for him, and it was not until 1951, after ten years in America, that he returned to France—now with a wife and young child.

In the summer of 1941, Rojankovsky made his way southward through the "Free Zone" of Vichy France and across the frontier of Spain to the port city of Cadiz. He had booked passage on a Spanish ship scheduled to sail on July 10th, with New York as its final destination. The passage was delayed nearly a month and, low on funds, he became stranded in a small hotel. Always resourceful, he struck a deal to paint murals for the hotel's owner in exchange for rent, meals, and a daily bottle of vino fino—and waited.

6

A New American Career

The tiny 5,743-ton Spanish freighter, the *S. S. Navemar*, which had been hastily and crudely outfitted for passengers, picked up people at Cadiz and finally sailed from Seville on August 6, 1941. The ship took on more passengers at Lisbon and set out across the Atlantic on August 16. Aboard were nearly 1200 people, refugees from Germany, France, Switzerland, Romania, and Poland, most of them Jewish. In a dozen articles, the major New York newspapers recounted details of the difficult journey.

Among the passengers were about 400 Berlin Jews who had been allowed to leave by train, each with the equivalent of only four dollars in hand, bound for Seville and then, they hoped, escape from Europe. After a crowded and generally squalid voyage, the ship called briefly at Bermuda on August 30 before going on to Havana, Cuba, where they landed on September 5 and left off the 400 Berliners. The continuing passengers gave them a shipboard party, but it must have been less than joyous. Six elderly passengers had died of typhus during the crossing, and many of the 400 surely had failed hopes for U.S. visas.

Rojankovsky knew a few of the passengers from Paris and made some new and lasting friendships on the crossing. Israel G. Rausen, a Russian Jew, was escaping "the fire of Europe," as he recalled it in a 1970 letter of sympathy to the Rojankovsky family. The two men found common ground in their service in the Russian military fighting the Germans in the First World War. Rausen also settled in New York and, with his firm of Rausen Brothers, was for the next thirty years a printer of Russian-language and émigré books, including at least two with Rojankovsky's cover designs.

The now notorious *Navemar* left Havana and set out for New York, landing with 769 souls at the Columbia Street pier in Brooklyn at 4:30 p.m. on Friday, September 12, 1941. *The New York Post* of that date carried news photos of the landing, dubbing it "the hell ship." In one picture of three unnamed waving, smiling passengers at the rail, Rojankovsky and a Russian friend from Paris, Irene Lebedeva, are clearly recognizable. Arrival records show that, as Rojankovsky was processed through Immigration, he declared $60 in cash and said he would go directly to stay with the agent Josef Riwkin at 48 Charles Street in Greenwich Village until he found his own apartment.

Years later, Rojankovsky mythologized his crossing and mused that his journey recapitulated Columbus's voyage to the New World—and took longer, following a similar transatlantic route to a personal discovery of America. While attending art school in Moscow, 1912-1914, Rojankovsky had met the poet Vladimir Mayakovsky, a fellow student at the school and just then forming the Futurist group. Mayakovsky teasingly called the young artist the "Frenchman" because of his early determination to go to Paris one day and his interest in the styles of Gauguin, Matisse, and Marquet. Rojankovsky valued this brush with the great Russian poet and now evoked Mayakovsky's poem on Christopher Columbus, saying his own experience in America was echoed by the poet's lines: "But I would close America, clean it a bit and then/ Discover it again!"

Rojankovsky also liked to tell the crossing story of how, again resourceful, he painted the ship captain's portrait in exchange for permission to sleep in a lifeboat and, so, escape the crowded quarters below deck. The next best thing to a "drawing room" on the crowded ship, he said of the lifeboat. From this perch, he organized the small contingent of Russians and became, in effect, their shipboard social director, staging little events and entertainments to lift the spirits of the weary passengers. To amuse himself on the tedious voyage, he sketched flying fish and portraits of the passengers, often without their knowledge.

Among his subjects was a Russian émigré from France, the prominent historian and political essayist Georgii Fedotov—who five years later, as it would happen, became Rojankovsky's father-in-law. Fedotov's daughter, Nina, and her mother had gone to New York by an earlier passage from France. Fedotov was charmed by the ebullient fellow Russian passenger, and after they arrived introduced the artist to his wife and daughter. Actually, Rojankovsky had first met Nina fleetingly in the 1930s in the Russian colony at La Favière when he helped the blonde, strikingly attractive young woman design her Valkyrie costume for a Russian ball.

Though now in America, the war in Europe was not yet behind him. Four years later and just after the war, Rojankovsky would learn that his older sister Aleksandra and older brother Sergei and Sergei's wife, Zina, had perished in the Siege of Leningrad early in the War. Only his younger sister, Tatiana—the last of his immediate family—escaped the Siege; she had been exiled to Arkhangelsk in the Arctic Circle for political indiscretions. The attachment to his sister now became all the more precious, though she was farther away than ever, and their hopes of visiting delayed by the emerging Cold War.

Settling In and the Climb to Success

The newcomer found his first apartment in a substantial, relatively expensive middle-class building at 45 West 11th Street in Greenwich Village. The neighborhood was the closest thing in America to the Left Bank of Paris and only a fifteen minute walk to the Guild offices at 200 Fifth Avenue on Madison Square. So at age 50, Rojankovsky here began a new life and long second career, during which he would illustrate most of his children's books.

Rojankovsky lived on West 11th for only six months or so, perhaps because it was a sublet or was too expensive, and spent the summer of 1942 with friends in Westport, Connecticut. When he came back to the city in the fall, he moved into an apartment in a run-down tenement building at 50 West 8th Street, between Fifth and Sixth avenues, also in the Village. He lived here until 1944, complaining and joking all the while in letters to friends about the brazenness of New York cockroaches. The old residential building still stands, much as it was then, and perhaps still harbors struggling artists.

Rojankovsky was quickly welcomed into the American graphic arts community where his artistic reputation had preceded him by a decade. He was widely admired as the creator of *Daniel Boone*, and since 1935 Harper and Brothers had translated and published ten of his Père Castor titles. In 1943, he became an active member of the American Institute of Graphic Arts. One of his first new friends in America was the German-American illustrator Fritz Eichenberg, then a key figure in the AIGA. They and their families became great friends over the years, and Eichenberg was one of his most ardent supporters and sponsors in the world of graphic art and illustration.

Among the Russian artists and illustrators who were also working in the United States, Rojankovsky knew Constantin Alajalov, an occasional house guest, and Alexandre Serebriakoff, the son of famous artist Zinaida Serebriakova. The Italian illustrator Valenti Angelo was also a neighbor in Bronxville in the 1950s and exchanged visits with the Rojankovskys. From the years in Paris, he remained friends with Mstislav Dobuzhinsky, who also settled in the United States. And from the early 1920s in Berlin, he continued his friendship with Andrei Khudiakov, also now settled in New York.

The upheavals of two world wars brought several waves of talented European graphic artists and children's illustrators to the United States. Among them were Boris Artzybasheff, Fritz Eichenberg, Ludwig Bemelmans, Roger Duvoisin and many others—whose artistic examples and ideas changed the look of the American picture book and brought children's illustration resoundingly into the twentieth century. Of the several Russian illustrators who immigrated, Rojankovsky was preeminent in productivity and influence in the field of children's art.

From Paris, he brought modern illustrative idioms from advertising and poster art and his experience with the Domino Press and the Père Castor books, and of course Russian folk themes. The European illustrators introduced to American children's books a distinct new note of international cultural variety. American children saw in positive contexts images of children who lived in other countries and had different experiences and values. But just as importantly, the European illustrators made the American picture book brighter and bolder—more visual fun. In the hands of strong artists like Rojankovsky, graphic values competed seriously with the literary texts and brought the two mediums into dynamic balance.

The war years and just afterwards was a golden time for the illustrator, both professionally and personally. Rojankovsky was soon well known in American children's illustration, enjoying rave reviews in national magazines, one-man shows in New York and other cities, and profiles in *Harper's Bazaar* and *Publishers' Weekly*. Even his advertising art and story illustrations, highly visible in top-line national magazines, recalled the children's books. Prime examples of the advertising work were included in several annual exhibits of the New York Art Directors Club and reproduced in their yearbooks. Most famous were the twelve fairy tale pictures painted for John Morrell & Company's 1948 advertising calendar, an extremely successful project, and they were also published in book form as *Favorite Fairy Tales* (1949). A second Morrell calendar came out two years later on a circus theme.

Though several of the American ads won awards from the Art Directors Club, little of his advertising art in the 1940s matched the artist's more innovative and modernist commercial work in Paris. The designs were now in the prevailing American styles of the 1940s and most featured whimsical cartoon animals and story-book scenes. The ads and story illustrations appeared in the *Saturday Evening Post*, *Life*, *Harper's Bazaar*, *Esquire*, *Readers Digest*, *McCall's*, *Woman's Day*, and elsewhere. In the *Saturday Evening Post*, where most of the drawings were seen, he shared the ad pages with illustrators such as Arthur Szyk,

Peter Arno, Reginald Marsh, and Constantin Alajalov. Prominent clients, such as Ford Motor, Kaiser-Frazer, Whitman Sampler boxed candies, Carter's Ink, Manhattan Shirt, Lee Hats, and The Travelers, engaged him through advertising agencies, often the J. Walter Thompson Company.

As success and money accumulated, despite paying twenty five percent of everything to Riwkin, in 1944 Rojankovsky moved one block north to a better apartment in a converted brownstone at 20 West 9th Street, still in the Village. In the mid-1940s, he summered in Bar Harbor, Maine and skied in Stowe, Vermont. Nina Fedotova, whom he had first met years earlier as a young woman in France, he now met again in New York and they became engaged. They married in April of 1946 and resided in the brownstone apartment on West 9th Street. Two years later the couple's daughter Tatiana, called Tanya, was born in New York. For at least one summer in the 1940s, Rojankovsky rented a house near Wardsboro, Vermont, near where Nina's father was staying at the dacha of the Russian historian, Michael Karpovich. Rojankovsky decorated three doors of the Karpovich's kitchen with pictures of birds and animals, which remain in the house to this day.

The newlyweds treated themselves to one of the first 1946 Buick convertibles made after the war and drove it into the sun of Florida. On the elegant Gold Coast of Palm Beach, near the house owned by Rojankovsky's affluent editor Georges Duplaix, the couple bought a seaside lot and built a modest house and studio. And, so, the Rojankovsky family began wintering, working, and entertaining friends in their new Palm Beach home. The little house, rather incongruously, was in the row of estates owned by Joseph Patrick Kennedy and other rich and famous residents.

Catherine Lodyjensky, Nina's good friend from Paris, also settled in the U.S., and in the 1940s became a fast friend of the Rojankovsky family. A physician, Dr. Lodyjensky was for many years a pediatrician in New York, and she knew and remained close to four generations of the Fedotov family. Dr. Lodyjensky recalled for us a 1940s visit to her friends' Florida home and its elegant neighborhood in Palm Beach. The Duke and Duchess of Windsor, who were visiting wealthy neighbors, strolled through the Rojankovsky's beach front and nodded politely to the young doctor who was taking the sun.

But Things Began to Change

After the war and the demobilization, with the return of millions to civilian life—including many professional graphic artists—advertising and publishing began to change. The re-gearing of the postwar consumer economy, responses to new consumer tastes, and new demands of competitive business were coming into play by 1946. Photography in magazine advertising became all the more ascendant over drawn images and continued to change the field of graphic design. All these things, added to Rojankovsky's unfortunate contractual situation, worked silently to threaten his financial security in all his endeavors.

Throughout the 1940s the illustrator worked hard under a series of overlapping and exclusive contracts with the agent Riwkin and the Artists and Writers Guild under Duplaix's direction. The first Guild contract of March 1, 1941 ran for five years and was renewed, to expire in late 1951. Through favorable modifications to the contracts, the work for the Guild turned out to be more and better paid than first promised. The magazine work provided by Riwkin may have been less than expected—and the artist wondered what the agent was doing for his huge fee. Still Riwkin took his handsome one quarter cut of everything, whether or not he found or brokered the work.

Riwkin effectively owned the illustrator's career and Duplaix generally refused waivers for non-Guild book projects. The contracts, especially the one with Riwkin, troubled Rojankovsky from the beginning and he was chafing under them by the mid- 1940s. In retrospect, the contracts seem draconian, though they had made possible his leaving war-torn Europe and provided him with a comfortable income during the war years. But enough was enough.

When the first contract with Riwkin was to expire in late 1946, Rojankovsky tried to escape its renewal for three more years. But a clause, until now unnoticed, stipulated that both parties had to agree to cancel. Riwkin refused to cancel and sued, but both sides eventually compromised and settled. The contract was renewed through late 1949. Riwkin reduced his take to a standard 15 percent of income from all sources, but stipulated that he would no longer find work for the illustrator, just take the money. Riwkin died a few months later, but payments continued to his widow until the end of the contract.

Also at issue in the dispute with Riwkin was work that Rojankovsky had since about 1943 contracted independently—outside their supposedly exclusive contract. All this work was published anonymously and some, perhaps most, has not been located. These projects may have included the two ten-foot long panoramic toy books, *Grandfather's Farm Panorama* (1943) and *Choo-Choo Panorama* (1945) and several picture jigsaw puzzles (1945) published by Platt and Munk. Neither of the panoramas credit an illustrator, but the publisher apparently identified Rojankovsky on the publicity sent out with review copies. The reviews of the two panoramas in the *New York Times* named Rojankovsky as the illustrator and did not mention their otherwise anonymous publication. The illustrator's style was apparent in any case. In 1947, Rojankovsky also designed a pull-toy, "Woofy Wagger," one of five new toys issued by Fisher-Price in that year.

By 1948 Rojankovsky was in financial trouble, heavily overdrawn on his account of advances from the Guild. The accountants demanded he tighten his belt and bring his account into better balance. He complied, and stepped up production of Golden books under special arrangements to reduce the debt; he produced four books in 1948 and three in 1949. In late 1949 his contract with Riwkin expired, giving him more income to pay back the Guild, and the account was soon brought into an acceptable balance. He also left expensive Manhattan in 1949, taking his wife and infant daughter to a rented house in the semi-rural Russian ethnic enclave in Lakewood, New Jersey.

He now sought non-book commercial work on his own to relieve his diminished income. The major project was to design a series of Christmas cards for Irene Dash Greeting Cards in New York. Rojankovsky painted twenty four or more pictures that were reproduced in full color by high-quality lithography and signed in the plates. Originally issued in the early 1950s, some of the cards have been reissued over the years and are still being sold by American Artists Group. All the cards, firmly in the manner of his best children's art, are among his most charming work. Most of the scenes depict small wild animals in snowy, woodsy settings, but several snug house cats and dogs too—all celebrating Christmas. The cards, popular ephemera decades ago, are now collected by enthusiasts.

The illustrator's relationship with Duplaix had been strained since the mid-1940s and remained so until the editor retired in 1958 and moved back to Paris, and the more ameliorative Lucille Ogle took over as editor of Golden Books. Rojankovsky felt that Duplaix rode herd on him and pressed him into projects he did not want to do. The first break with his naturalistic style in the Golden books came during the financial crunch of 1948-49 when he was being pressed to illustrate sure money-makers. The cartoonish *Gaston and Josephine* (1948) and *The Big Elephant* (1949) were perhaps concessions to Duplaix. At least Rojankovsky told friends that he resented having to reillustrate Duplaix's own pig story of *Gaston and Josephine*, though both books are quirkily charming. After Duplaix retired and the source of conflict was gone, the two men became friends again and in the 1960s visited most amicably in Paris.

In 1950 he sold the heavily mortgaged and now overly burdensome Palm Beach house in an arrangement with Duplaix and the Guild. By late 1951 Rojankovsky had finished with the last of the exclusive contracts with Duplaix, the Guild, and Western Publishing. He continued working with the Guild on a book-by-book contract basis for many more years, but was now released to pursue free-lance work. And in 1951 he made his first post-war trip back to France and stayed more than a year. This time he crossed the Atlantic on the French Line's Liberté, a far cry from the voyage on the Navemar ten years earlier.

Rojankovsky had never cut emotional ties in Europe, where he left many friends and interests. And he greatly missed and was nostalgic for the aesthetic stimulation of Paris, a world much changed after the war but still attractive to the artist who had spent the last ten years in corporate harness. The worst post-war hardships in Paris had now lessened, and old Paris friends and places were beckoning. With the family, he began to travel to France every year, staying a year or more on two trips in the 1950s, and he went to Russia every two years or so until the end of his life.

In the early 1950s, the Rojankovskys bought land and built a second home near the old and familiar Russian colony at La Favière on the French Riviera. He had visited the colony many times in the 1920s and 1930s, once had friends there, and it was where he and Nina Fedotova had first met before the war. They named the house *Maoun Repaou*, "My Rest" in the Provençal language, and the family summered there for many years until the onset of his last illness in the late 1960s.

After returning from their second trip to France in late 1953, the couple bought a house at 17 McIntyre Street in Bronxville, New York, just north of New York City. Their daughter, Tanya, was about ready to enter school. They chose the village of Bronxville at the suggestion of a friend, the Russian émigré critic and writer Marc Slonim, whom Rojankovsky in the 1930s had known in Paris and who was now teaching at a college nearby.

Only six years later, in 1960, they sold the house in Bronxville, and the family of three moved to France—with no present plans to returnand stayed five years. Tanya, now about twelve, was enrolled in French schools. In this later French period of his life between 1960 and 1965, he produced several Golden Books and projects for other American publishers. He also created maquettes for small Paris ballet productions.

From this time in France, Rojankovsky left behind an impressive cycloramic mural in a Russian orphanage housed in an old estate in Montgeron, an outer suburb of Paris. The main building later sheltered the former Musée Russe en Exil, and the buildings and grounds are today held by a Russian organization. The mural is in the circular tower room over the gate house for the old estate. The room had been converted into a playroom for the children, and Rojankovsky turned it into all but a stage-set in the round, with benches for the children around the walls. From the benches to the ceiling, the circular painting is in full and brilliant colors and evokes Russian fairy tales in settings of village life in old Russia, with pictures of children dancing around a Maypole and other scenes. The mural completely surrounds viewers once they step into the small room high in the tower and has all the charm of an unexpected thing found in an unlikely place. The mural is still extant but begging of preservation—the only known surviving example of Rojankovsky's several murals.

After five years in France and now in his seventies, Rojankovsky brought the family back to the United States. Eye surgery done in France in 1964 had to be repeated a year later in the U. S., and as a result his work had been slowed. And it was clear that he could no longer work at such a distance from his American editors. The Rojankovskys settled again in Bronxville, buying a roomy house at 91 Cassilis Avenue, where he spent his last years.

Rojankovsky always and above all considered himself a Russian, though one in exile, and so an accidental citizen of the world. He did not become a naturalized U.S. citizen until 1968, only two years before his death in 1970, and then more for practical reasons than indicating a new national identity.

The Artists and Writers Guild

The story of the founding of Western Printing Company's Artist and Writers Guild and, eventually, the Golden Books industry is key to Rojankovsky's coming to New York and the course of his career. The story of the Guild begins with Samuel E. Lowe. Trained as a social worker at the Henry Street Settlement in New York City, Sam Lowe was a young man in the 1920s working for a social agency in Racine, Wisconsin. When Western Printing in Racine started the Whitman Publishing Company, Lowe was hired to direct the new subsidiary and carried it to success.

Whitman published inexpensive juvenile books sold in ten-cent stores, including the popular Little Big Books. Between 1935 and 1947, Whitman also produced over 300 books for trade publishers, such as Grosset and Dunlap. Lowe had ideas about progressive child education and inexpensive children's books, and was familiar with the theories of Paul Faucher. On a trip to France in 1932, Lowe contracted for

Whitman the American rights to Flammarion's Père Castor books for translation and publication in the U. S. The rights eventually included Rojankovsky's eight animal stories in the series *Le roman des bêtes*, as well as his other Père Castor titles.

Western Printing also acquired the property of the Artists and Writers Guild, a printing firm at Poughkeepsie, New York, which had manufactured a line of playing cards and, later, greeting cards. The success of Lowe's work at Whitman led to his appointment as editorial head of the newly reorganized Artists and Writers Guild. The new Guild was not, as the name suggests, a craft guild of writers and artists working for their common welfare. Rather it was an arm of a corporate publisher, a production unit and printing plant.

The Guild's first list of children's books, 1935-36, had twenty eight titles, including seven Père Castor titles from Paris. Rojankovsky's two large animal books by Rose Celli and Marguerite Reynier, were translated and published as *Wild Animals and Their Little Ones* and *Wild Animals at Home*. Other Père Castor titles on the first Guild list were illustrated by Paris Russian émigrés Hélène Guertik and Nathalie Parain, including Parain's *Baba Yaga* and *Picture Play Book*, as well as a twenty cent reprint of Maxfield Parrish's *Knave of Hearts*—all from the printing plant at Poughkeepsie.

In 1936 the Frenchman Georges Duplaix, then 41 years old and in the United States since 1931, and the American editor Lucille E. Ogle (1904-1988), in her early thirties, joined the Artists and Writers Guild. Their alliance was to prove fateful for Rojankovsky's life and career. Ogle was trained as an artist, had been a teacher, and had editorial experience. Eventually she would become his editor at Golden Books and lifelong friend.

Between 1936 and 1942, the Guild produced American editions of the eight animal stories in *Le roman des bêtes* for Harper and Brothers. Georges Duplaix translated the first three of the animal stories, and the rest were set over from the French by his wife Lily Duplaix. Margaret Wise Brown translated Lacôte's *Calendrier des enfants* as *The Children's Year*, and it was published with Rojankovsky's outstanding illustrations in 1937.

Sam Lowe left the Guild in 1940 and went into business for himself and published inexpensive children's books for the next 30 years. Duplaix was put in charge of production at the Guild. Soon, Duplaix and Ogle successfully proposed to Simon & Schuster a new line of inexpensive, mass-marketed children's books that were to become the famous Golden Books. The two editors were well acquainted with Rojankovsky's work in France and saw its commercial potential in their new imprint.

The First Guild Projects

As soon as Rojankovsky landed in late 1941, he set furiously to work on children's books—and 1942 was a remarkably productive year. His American career began significantly with *The Tall Book of Mother Goose* (1942)—less than a year after setting foot on a Brooklyn pier. A Guild project, the innovative book was published by Harper and Brothers under the general editorship of Ursula Nordstrom. It was an immediate success and stirred an unusual amount of critical comment.

Roger Duvoisin had broken with traditional Mother Gooses in his colorful version of 1936 and introduced, as Barbara Bader wrote, "gaiety and mischief." But Rojankovsky, she continues, "scuttles" the tradition entirely and draws real people and children. "It is not a modern Mother Goose so much as a human one." The children's literature historian John Goldthwaite more recently affirms that Rojankovsky's version broke the mold of a century of illustrated Mother Goose rhymes by making the characters in the book look like the children who read it. With a historical view of its color printing, editor Grace Hogarth in a 1989 article in the *Horn Book* cites the book as a "perfect example" of the "fascinating period of transition from letterpress to photolithography" and praises the high quality of the offset color reproductions.

The rapidity of Rojankovsky's picking up the American pictorial idiom is stunning. The saucy, realistic, and wholly contemporary illustrations of urban American children in *The Tall Book of Mother Goose* stirred wide praise as well as a little sniffy criticism. In a review article, two librarians pulled long faces over Humpty Dumpty drawn with Hitler's forelock and mustache, and wrote that it was "a mistake because Hitlers are only passing phenomena and Humpty is immortal." But in 1942 funny pictures of Hitler were the rage among American children. Boys held black pocket combs to their upper lips and shouted "Sieg heil!"—exactly as Max Kunten's cover for the *Saturday Evening Post* of January 23, 1943, depicts a kid clowning as Hitler. Rojankovsky had made a quick and sure cultural reading. The librarians also disapproved of the cigarette dangling from the mouth of the naughty boy of "Ding, Dong, Bell." But how better to stigmatize a bad boy? To leave no doubt, the illustrator even painted a red "X" over the sullen boy's face.

The picture on page 49 of a pregnant mother standing in the rain under an umbrella, her four-year-old's head pressed to her belly, and the gaily dressed West Indian nanny on a New York street on page 63 might also have raised a few unplucked eyebrows in the better children's libraries of 1942. Adult readers wrote to Rojankovsky objecting to his depictions of the children, one citing with disapproval the expression of surprise and disgust on the face of Little Miss Muffet as she spied the spider—one of the best pictures. Encouraged arachnophobia, it seems.

The text as well as the pictures troubled the waters in children's libraries. In the first printing of the book, the last line of the rhyme "They That Wash on Monday" (p. 31) read "Oh! they are sluts indeed." Undoubtedly responding to complaints, the publisher altered *sluts* to *bad* in subsequent printings so there would be no misunderstanding about the behavioral problem of Saturday's slovenly children. Never mind that the unwashed children were indeed "sluts" in the older, nursery-rhyme sense of that word. And the cultural cleansing of the book was not finished.

In 1965 when Harper & Row was preparing to reissue *The Tall Book of Mother Goose*, the black nanny fell to the newly emerging social forces of avoiding ethnic offense. The nanny, with a small pig in a basket and her little white charge in tow, was banished from the illustration of "To Market, To Market." Ogle wrote to the illustrator that the picture was to be dropped because of new sensitivities in the country, that the nanny would be seen as a Negro stereotype—and of their plans to include the book in a "basket" for public schools. Ogle instructed him to make the nanny "white," or to draw some other market scene.

Though unstated by Ogle, the nanny more likely had to go because of the ethnic slur a concerted mind might imagine in the old rhythmic phrases of the nursery rhyme, "Jiggety-jig, Jiggety-jog," especially in the presence of the black nanny. Firing the nanny was less controversial than purging the traditional rhyme, and the more prudent course. Rojankovsky grumbled, actually tried putting the nanny into white face, but gave up and drew a large pink pig, which in the new editions sprawls in the middle of the page.

The editors of *Mother Goose* might have done as well to catch a major interpretive error in the illustration for "Ladybird, Ladybird" (p. 99), which readers quickly noticed. In British English the common lady*bug* beetle is called a lady*bird*, and British schoolchildren regard finding one as an omen of good luck. The beetle is named after Our Lady, the Virgin Mary, in tribute to the beetles' good work in devouring harmful insects. The beetles often winter over in crevices of old houses and emerge in the warmth, and this is perhaps their association with a house afire in the rhyme. The illustrator, whose English was not perfect, either assumed or was instructed that *ladybird* referred to a female perching bird. In any case, Rojankovsky painted her as a song bird on wing, wearing a dress, and carrying two tiny buckets of water to extinguish the fire in her tree nest where her distressed hatchlings are calling for help.

Two years after *Mother Goose*, the publication of *The Tall Book of Nursery Tales* (Harper and Brothers, 1944) provided a companion volume of the same size and format, though the illustrations were now less eccentric. Not as many grown-up allusions are apparent, unless temperance forces objected to the corked bottle of wine in Little Red Riding Hood's basket. Several years later, the traditional bottle did become a little brown jug of unspecified contents in a similar picture in *Favorite Fairy Tales* (1949). Rojankovsky left his personal mark on *The Tall Book of Nursery Tales* in another way, with the picture on page 49 of his former vacation home in the French Alps.

The other major Guild project during his first year in the country was the series of little books illustrating Kipling's *The Just-So Stories* for Garden City Publishing. The first four books were published in 1942 and the set was supplemented in 1947 with two additional volumes, making a uniform set of six. Kipling's original drawings were put aside—unforgivably in the minds of purists. Rojankovsky's new illustrations are of a different, more comical disposition with outsized characters. And in *The Butterfly That Stamped*, an outdoor nude bathing scene and the see-through skirts and the on-again, off-again blouse on the most beautiful harem wife were not your usual children's fare. Brian Alderson writes that the Garden City series was the first to make "dramatic incursions" into Kipling's classic. And he describes Rojankovsky's pictures as "typical examples of the artist at his gaudiest and most vulgar." But Alderson admits that of all the later illustrators of the stories none brought "any greater sensitivity to bear."

The 1942 publication of the first four books of *Just-So Stories* occasioned an unusual project—Rojankovsky's only known drawing for a pop-up construction. For an early promotion, the four books, stacked two high and two wide, came packaged together in a folding box and were collectively titled *Four Famous Just-So Stories* (1942). The pop-up design for the lid of the box incorporates the chief story characters and is a composite scene from the four books. The outside of the closed yellow box is decorated with yet more drawings, top and bottom. Evidently, not many of the pop-up boxes were manufactured, for they are now rarely seen. The only known copy in an institutional collection is at the Morgan Library in New York.

Rojankovsky's first major title with the Golden Book imprint was *Animal Stories* (Simon & Schuster, 1944), and it was a singular triumph. Duplaix celebrated the publishing event by also seeing to a special limited edition of 300 copies in a special cloth binding, signed by himself as the author and by Rojankovsky as the illustrator.

Animal Stories and the two *Tall Books* for Harper and Brothers, were projects of a single artistic turn, both stylistically and in their new spirit. The three books were often compared by critics and were exhibited together in book displays. These three wartime books, along with Garden City's first four volumes of the *Just-So Stories*, launched Rojankovsky's American career and once again swayed the course of modern children's illustration.

What he did for French children's illustration in the early 1930s, he did for American illustration in the early 1940s, though in a new and more popular direction. The picture books for Domino and Flammarion, themselves departures from older European styles, were nonetheless steeped in an elite, modernist aesthetic of hand lithography and fine bookmaking and appealed to a sophisticated European audience of parents who chose tasteful and uplifting books for their children. The European books were intended to civilize the young ones. Rojankovsky's American books, some critics thought, barbarized their immature tastes. But it was only the adults who were offended.

In the view of many critics and collectors, the restrained style, studied layout, and direct lithographs of the early 1930s books remain more interesting as graphic design than the more exuberant, less expensive books of Rojankovsky's American career. But an illustrator must work within the limitations imposed by the publishers, and American mass-market publishing of juvenile titles was a demanding business with little room for personal experimentation. Yet Rojankovsky achieved surprising versatility within these constraints and produced good work by any standard.

By 1952 the exclusive contracts with the Guild had run their course and Rojankovsky became free to work directly for other publishers as well. While he continued to illustrate Golden Books for the rest of his life, the illustration work for other publishers returned to some of the handwork and techniques reminiscent of his work for Domino Press and Père Castor. He began working in lithographic crayons again and learned to make color separations on acetate. On one occasion he was able to use the more expensive French hand-printing and production processes of his early work to make intensely colored lithographs for his friend Natal'ia Kodrianskaia's Russian-language children's book, *Globusnyi chelovechek* (1954). These designs have a 1930s look and are printed with the same high quality as the first Domino Press titles—by the same printer, Mourlot Frères.

The Little Golden Books

The Little Golden Books series is one of publishing history's great success stories, and Rojankovsky had an important role in the enterprise. Lucille Ogle and Georges Duplaix, both now with the Artists and Writers Guild (Western Printing), were the co-creators of the series. In 1940 they approached Leon Shimkin of Simon & Schuster with a proposal to jointly publish a line of children's books to retail at twenty five cents. In October 1942, the first twelve titles were issued in 125,000 copies each (none of these by Rojankovsky), and this publishing phenomenon was launched.

By the early 1950s, according to Albert Leventhal, vice president of Simon & Schuster, first print runs of 500,000 for Little Golden Books were considered small and some first printings approached two million copies. The twenty five cent books quickly spread from book stores and department stores into the chain variety stores, newsstands, toy stores, infant wear shops, and finally into their biggest new outlet of all—the new supermarkets in the burgeoning suburban shopping malls of the 1950s. The little mass-marketed books required big investments and yielded big dividends. Other firms quickly entered and crowded the field. The total potential market in the forty eight states was about sixteen million pre-schoolers—today's baby boomers. The whole industry of several mass-market publishers sold these children an annual average of seven books—or about 100,000,000 books a year.

In 1958 Simon & Schuster sold its one-half interest in Golden Books to Western Printing and Lithographing Company (Racine, WI) and Affiliated Publishers, the latter of which was to become Pocket Books, Inc. The new company name and imprint became Golden Press, and in 1960 Western Printing and Lithographing became Western Publishing Company. In 1964, Western Publishing bought out Pocket Books' interest in Golden Press, and the Golden Press imprint became solely owned by Western Publishing Company of Racine, Wisconsin. The creative book division finally dropped the confusing and incongruous word *Guild* from its title and became the Artists and Writers *Press.*

In the reorganization of 1958, Georges Duplaix left the group and returned to France, though Lucille Ogle stayed on as vice president of Golden Press until 1968. Upon Duplaix's departure, Ogle took Rojankovsky strongly in hand and guided his further work with Golden Books. She was his editor and friend for nearly thirty years, and remained in close contact with the artist and his family, visiting and exchanging many letters, until she left the firm two years before Rojankovsky's death. Half of the illustrator's Golden Books were produced under Ogle's supervision and he was grateful for her intervention. From retirement, she worked with Nina Rojankovsky to produce a memorial anthology of illustrative art for Golden Books, *F. Rojankovsky's Wonderful Picture Book* (1972). Ogle also wrote the eulogy prefacing the unfinished, posthumously-published picture book *A Year in the Forest* (McGraw-Hill, 1973).

Rojankovsky's popular reputation in the United States is closely associated with his many Golden Books—and popular acclaim is liable to bring critical disclaim. On the occasion of his Caldecott Award in 1956, Esther Averill, his editor and publisher at Domino Press in Paris in the 1930s, peevishly chose the venue to lament the artist's neglect of high-minded children's books during his Golden Book years. "Rojankovsky was typed, and let himself be typed, just as an actor in Hollywood often gets poured into a mold. And certainly this was at the expense of his great lyric qualities and his own brand of gentle humor which springs from nature rather than from the world of man." Yet she went on to commend him for breaking away and going back to "a more traditional kind of bookmaking."

This line of criticism, made by others too, overlooks several realities of American popular culture and its consumption. Compared to Europe, American children more often chose their own books, and their tastes reigned. In France the success of the cartoon-like Babar books and the enduring popularity of the comic strip characters Bécassine and Tintin suggest the tastes of French children were not all that different. At any rate, Rojankovsky's new American style proved a great commercial success, helping make Golden Books one of the publishing phenomena of the twentieth century. Kids reached for them by the tens of millions.

The Disney Nexus

Rojankovsky had entered the American field at a time of cultural revolution in the mass media—the confluence of comics, movies, and radio—and it was to engulf children's-book illustration, too. During the Depression years of the 1930s, the animated images from Walt Disney's Hollywood studio—bright, comic, and kinetic—were extremely popular in the U.S. During the 1930s Whitman Publishing had an exclusive on Disney books. The spin-offs of picture books and pop-ups from Disney's animated cartoons had been successfully tested in the marketplace and were high in the esteem of American children. In 1940 the executives at Simon & Schuster, seeking a mass market for their inexpensive Little Golden Books, emulated the popular and proven Disney look and formula.

The blatant Disney style has always stirred criticism among children's-book professionals. They objected then—and today—to Disney's animated vulgarizations of children's literary classics. With regards to the graphic art from the Disney Studios, they objected to the animal caricatures, with their cloying and banal sentimentalism, and to the crudely comic and garish images. Today, the list of complaints includes multicultural excess, on the one hand, and rank commodification, on the other. Disney's animal cartoons in the 1930s and 1940s were but animated comic books and, indeed, were spun off as actual comic books. Rojankovsky did not like the Disney style either.

The Artists and Writers Guild sponsored exchanges of personnel and kept other interpersonal contacts with the Disney Studio in Hollywood—and influences from Disney were expectable at Golden Books. Several former Disney artists, notably Gustaf Tenggren, J.P. Miller, and Martin and Alice Provensen, became major artists for the Guild. And Duplaix, who had his considerable connections in Hollywood, liked to introduce some of his best artists to the Disney Studios by way of temporary loans.

In the late summer of 1943, Duplaix arranged a paid trip to Los Angeles for Rojankovsky to work about two weeks in the Disney Studio. The illustrator was treated as a guest of honor, put up in a luxury hotel, and picked up each morning in a limousine and delivered to the Disney Studio where he worked on assigned projects. But he wrote to Nina that the work was mundane and boring. Rojankovsky was never sympathetic with the Disney aesthetic and never capitulated to it as much as did, say, Tenggren in the Golden Books.

Under pressures from Duplaix, Rojankovsky did develop a bright, popularizing illustrative style of his own for a few of his Golden Books, such as *Gaston and Josephine* (1948) and *The Big Elephant* (1949), and it was unlike anything he had done before. Here and in certain others the characters and scenes are more comic and the bright pictures are filled with action and playful things going on. The animals are not naturalistic, but cute, wearing clothes with accessories, speaking funny lines, having silly human habits and motives. His popular cartoon animals show up, too, in the advertising designs for American magazines in the 1940s. Some of his Golden Book pictures were, as the critics said, "vulgar"—a concept that began to disappear, incidentally, about the time of the illustrator's death and is now considered quaint and elitist by cultural egalitarians.

We are less disappointed that Rojankovsky, to some small degree, capitulated to this commercial aesthetic than amazed at how well he did it, how originally. Barbara Bader wrote that to be a Golden Book artist was "a career and discipline in itself." Rojankovsky, with his usual adaptivity and discipline of long experience, brought his own look to the cartoon aesthetic and made a distinct niche within it.

"A Career and Discipline in Itself"

At their best, Rojankovsky's Golden Books are highly creative and among the best children's books of their time. His work for Golden Books over nearly thirty years falls into two broad periods. The stronger work was from the early 1940s to the early 1950s and roughly corresponds to the decade when he was under exclusive contracts with the Artists and Writers Guild and pouring all his creative energy into those projects. After he was released from that obligation—at age sixty it bears noting—his best work may be seen in the books he did with various other American publishers. His Golden Book illustrations, with exceptions, now became more ordinary.

Among the early projects, *The Golden Bible* (1946) was hugely popular. Religious instructors and parents, both Protestant and Catholic (with an approved, alternate edition), found in the bright and dramatic illustrations a way to reach young people with stories from the Old Testament. The companion volume of stories from the New Testament by other illustrators, also in a Catholic edition, made the teaching unit complete. The Old Testament is a highly designed book, the text and artwork integrated, and each chapter begins with initials of inventive thematic design.

Rojankovsky made sketches for *The Golden Bible* in 1944 when visiting Bar Harbor, Maine and southern California, and certain features of their landscapes may be seen in the book. He sought ideas around Carmel, palm trees and other topical details, which he thought must resemble the Holy Land. Apparently, his editors instructed him to include the countenances of Anglo-Saxon children in the Bible drawings, for he mentioned this necessity in letters and took it seriously. "I wanted to sketch people, too, visit the zoo, observe many Anglo-Saxon children," he told a reporter for a Monterey newspaper. But the finished book, after all, did not show the fair faces of America's Golden West.

Readers poured over details in the artwork. A British academic at Hammersmith College in London and a German researcher at the Leitz optical firm in Wetzlar queried Rojankovsky on his paintings of rainbows, for their study of unusual—or rather inaccurate and idiosyncratic—rainbow paintings in art. Rainbows similar to Rojankovsky's in *The Golden Bible* appeared chiefly, it seems, in early medieval paintings. But artistic license was probably the better explanation for the whimsical rearrangement of hue and order in Rojankovsky's personal spectrum.

From France, Rojankovsky illustrated three large Golden Books, sequentially, of *Cat Stories* (1953), *Dog Stories* (1953), and *Horse Stories* (1954), all authored by Elizabeth Coatsworth. In the cat and dog books, the artist was in fine form and clearly liked the subject, and in letters to Ogle mischievously referred to the author of so many cat stories as "Mrs. Catsworth." But he was winding down in the book of horse stories, and complained in a 1953 letter that "this animal cannot inspire me for 60-70 pages, I'm afraid not." *Horse Stories* was published in 1954 to the length of only thirty pages, less than half the length of the two previous books.

Some of the gay and colorful Golden Books of the 1940s and early 1950s are very good indeed. Favorites include *The Three Bears* (1948), *Gaston and Josephine* (1948), Georges Duplaix's unlikely story of two determined French pigs making their way to America. *The Big Elephant* (1949) is a kind of American Babar character of wacky appeal and equally bourgeois inclinations. Several years later, the artist was pleased to see these and others appear in France as well. Another outstanding Golden Book is *Big Farmer Big* (1948) with its novelty of a miniature book inserted in a kangaroo-like pocket on the front cover of this tall book. Also very good are *Our Puppy* (1948), *The Kitten's Surprise* (1951), and *F. Rojankovsky's ABC* (1970), published in the year of the artist's death..

Several other Golden Books were drafted, all or in part, but never published. In the 1950s, he made studies and a number of finished drawings for a proposed edition of Robert Louis Stevenson's *Treasure Island*. A reproduction of a single painting intended for the book appears in J.-R. Thomé's 1958 article on the illustrator in *Le Courrier Graphique*, who notes the book as "in preparation." Years earlier he had made a striking cover for a Polish edition of the classic. The book clearly interested him, and we can imagine it would have been the equal of Golden Books' *Robinson Crusoe*. For many years, lastly in 1960, Rojankovsky and Duplaix discussed a children's edition of *Don Quixote*, but nothing came of that either.

Yet other Golden Book projects fell through when Rojankovsky was living in France, 1960-65. Now in his seventies, problems with cataracts and two rounds of eye surgery in the mid-1960s slowed his pace of work. A companion to his illustrations of Ole Risom's *I Am A Fox* (1967) would have been *I Am A Lion*. Rojankovsky delivered drawings in 1964 but the book was never published. In 1967, he delivered pictures for a Golden Book to be titled *The Mice Who Loved Words*, but it was never published either, and Ogle paid him a kill fee. He may also have drafted a book to have been titled *Animal Orchestra*, for he listed it among his completed projects.

Rojankovsky's large body of work for Golden Books engaged him until the end of his life. Despite the frustrations, he had two Golden Book successes in his last years—the new edition of *The Three Bears* (1967) and *F. Rojankovsky's ABC* (1970). His contributions to the series were always bright and engaging, and the best were imaginative and fresh. All in all, he was among the best of the Golden Book illustrators, and this has become more and more apparent over the years.

Return to Free-Lance Illustration

After 1951, Rojankovsky—now free to work with other publishers—produced some of his most successful books and rose to the second peak of his American career, illustrating twenty seven books, numerous stories and other projects—all independent of the Guild and Golden Books.

He returned to his native Slavic themes in juvenile stories with the publication, among other books, of Mikhail Prishvin's *The Treasure Trove of the Sun* (Viking, 1952). This pretty, much-praised book is lavish with fifty color lithographs illustrating the story of two Russian children lost in a great swamp. In 1953 he followed with Claire Huchet Bishop's *All Alone* (Viking, 1953), an uplifting story of two boys who herd the family cows in the French Alps of Savoie, near where the artist had his vacation house before the war. This juvenile title is plush with forty soft-crayon lithographs in black and white.

The sun-drenched illustrations of freckled children at the beach for Dorothy Koch's *I Play at the Beach* (Holiday House, 1955) were a sharp stylistic departure from anything he had done since coming to America and, in retrospect, are among his best work. The Rojankovsky family were fond of ocean-side holidays and the illustrator undoubtedly liked to watch children at play in the sand. The artist's own daughter was about six when these pictures were drawn; the cover picture is modeled on young Tanya. The images inside were taken from his daughter and her playmates at play on the beach not far from their home at La Favière in the south of France. Helen Gentry designed the book for Holiday House and used Rojankovsky's illustrations to best advantage against a weak text of verse.

In the same year, Rojankovsky's whimsical illustrations for John Langstaff's *Frog Went A-Courtin'* (Harcourt, Brace and Company, 1955) were published under the close editorship of Margaret McElderry and in 1956 won the prestigious Caldecott Medal for children's-book illustration. Rojankovsky himself said the award came as a complete surprise to him, and that seems to have been the fact.

The Caldecott was an occasion of great celebration and brought the illustrator a new round of national attention, the first since his Golden Book successes and wide media attention in the 1940s.

The drawings for *Frog Went A-Courtin'* were made in the summer of 1954 at La Favière. This particular book, as Anne Carroll Moore uncharitably pointed out in her column in the special Caldecott Award issue of the *Horn Book*, was perhaps not for all tastes the best illustrated children's book of 1955. And neither was it necessarily the best book he had done in recent years. We share Barbara Bader's view that *I Play At the Beach* is an equally good illustrated children's book of 1955. But all such awards for professional and artistic achievement take into account more than simply the ostensible reason for the award.

Yet the color lithographs in *Frog Went A-Courtin'* are strong and witty, their look something of yet another stylistic departure for Rojankovsky. The book holds a secure place among the Caldecott winners of that period. The book's author, John Langstaff, shared with us his humorous observation that Rojankovsky misinterpreted a colloquial phrase in the lines accompanying the picture of the old gray goose, "She picked up her fiddle and she cut loose!" Rojankovsky's lady goose, just strolling down a path, carries the fiddle under her wing, with a few loose, cut strings trailing behind.

Fritz Eichenberg wrote of his friend that the Caldecott Medal "was long overdue. . . . He has raised on this alien soil a crop of sparklingly gay books which will delight our children for many years hence."

Rojankovsky was now sixty five years old, and would continue to work and produce an impressive array of books in his remaining thirteen years. The 1950s and early 1960s were an especially productive period for the artist. Work with his new editor Margaret McElderry, who was the second strong woman editor in his life, led to four more books—*Over in the Meadow*, *The Little River*, *So Small*, and *A Crowd of Cows*, all superbly produced.

Jane Thayer's *The Outside Cat* (Morrow, 1957) is an appealing story of an ingratiating yard cat who finally got to live inside the house and by the fire. Ann Rand's *The Little River* (Harcourt, Brace and Company, 1959) is an intelligent natural history with an early environmental sensibility. Dimitry Varley's *The Whirly Bird* (Knopf, 1961) is a suburban melodrama of an orphaned baby robin and its rescue by a little girl; the author was a friend and next-door neighbor in Bronxville. Rojankovsky's own *Animals in the Zoo* and *Animals on the Farm* (Knopf, 1962, 1967) are finely-drawn and well-produced ABC books of familiar animals.

Two of the artist's happiest achievements of the early 1960s were Ann Rand's *So Small* (Harcourt, Brace & World, Inc., 1962), a mouse story, and the illustrations for Aileen Lucia Fisher's verses in *Cricket in a Thicket* (Scribner's, 1963), all drawn in France during his last extended residence there. Both books are filled with drawings reminiscent of his early work, the first book with full-color drawings and the second with elegant pencil sketches, and are among Rojankovsky's best work. His re-illustration and novel reinterpretation of *The Three Bears* in 1967 after he returned to Bronxville was, to many tastes, the capstone of his late career.

7

The Complete Artist of Children's Books

In a long career, Rojankovsky illustrated in every genre of books for youngsters: juvenile novels, historical biography, classical stories of adventure, books of verse, song books, nursery rhymes, ABC books, picture books without texts, fairy tales, animal stories, natural histories, counting books for tiny tots, and even Bible stories for children. And he illustrated children's posters, calendars, toys and other playthings with images from the picture books.

Less known and often overlooked by his fans are the many short stories and tales he illustrated in children's magazines and book anthologies in France and the United States. Illustrations for eleven stories and seven covers appear in the Artists and Writers Guild's *Story Parade* magazine between 1951 and 1954. The Nelson Doubleday company, between 1957 and 1961, published a series of forty two books of stories called *The Best in Children's Books.* Rojankovsky illustrated stories in fifteen of the anthologies and drew several pictures for their jackets.

Over the years, he illustrated eight abecedaria, those traditional favorites of children's-book illustrators. He created ABC books for three different languages—Russian, French, and English, and most pictured animals whose names begin with the letters of the Cyrillic or Roman alphabets. The ABC books bracket Rojankovsky's career as a children's illustrator from beginning to end. His first true picture book was his brilliant re-illustration of Sasha Chernyi's *Zhivaia azbuka* in 1926; the last book published in his lifetime was an elaborate alphabet book for Golden Press in 1970.

In all the ABCs, the animals are depicted accurately and naturally. In *Zhivaia azbuka*, his new drawings accompany Sasha Chernyi's short verses and two animals or plants signify each letter of the Cyrillic alphabet. A. L. de Saint-Rat writes that this book was "the fountainhead" of the Père Castor series and "the precursor" of Rojankovsky's *ABC jeux du Père Castor* (1936). The game was to cut out labels at the end of the book and match names of animals with appropriate letters of the alphabet.

A complete alphabet, keyed to the initial letters of the first lines of the twenty six verses by Georges Duplaix, is part of *Animal Stories* (1944). In the late 1940s, Rojankovsky made an unusual ABC for a series of ads for the Puss 'n Boots brand of cat food, published in installments over two years in the *Saturday Evening Post.* The manufacturer also issued the series as a giveaway children's book for product promotion. Years later came Jane Werner Watson's *Animal Dictionary* (Golden Press, 1960) and Rojankovsky's own *Animals in the Zoo* (1962) and *Animals on the Farm* (1967), both published by Knopf.

His last book for Golden Press was *F. Rojankovsky's ABC* (1970), published a few months before his death, one of his brightest and most admired Golden Books. This was originally planned in the 1960s for another publisher, Harper, and was to have been titled "The Tall Book of the Alphabet," to reprise his two *Tall Books* of the 1940s. But he did not take up finishing the project until very late in his life, when he was in rapidly failing health. Research became a family project, with wife, Nina, and daughter, Tanya, searching dictionaries and other books for animals and other things whose names started with each letter of the English alphabet.

In some of the ABC books Rojankovsky displayed his skill in the design and deployment of letter forms, beginning with the stunning art deco Cyrillic characters on the cover of *Zhivaia azbuka.* Certain early Polish and émigré Russian book covers display a variety of innovative block and calligraphic letter forms. In the later children's books, whimsical letters and their witty placement are an integral part of the pictorial designs. On the dust jacket of *I Play At the Beach*, the designed letters of the title—and the author's and illustrator's names on the bathing hat of the little girl—are a good example. The fanciful folk-art letter forms in *Animal Stories* (pp. 21-26) are original with Rojankovsky and reflect a Russian folk aesthetic. Two years later he topped himself with the many similar initials in *The Golden Bible.* Years later, grasses and flowers made up the decorative letter forms on the title page of *Over in the Meadow.*

In America, Rojankovsky felt free to mix American stories and rhymes with Russian ethnic and folk images and to imbue his pictures with the visual feel and colors of rural and peasant Russia. Many of the children in his books have the stereotypical round faces, chunky bodies, and thick legs of Russian country youngsters—and of many American children, too. The colors and details are those of gaily painted and decorated Russian folk arts, they too reflecting the colors of the land.

As half-coded signs of his ethnicity and of Russian folk influences on his work, Rojankovsky whimsically introduced traditional folk objects into his illustrations. In the painting of Little Red Riding Hood in *Favorite Fairy Tales*, a famous eighteenth century *lubok* image of "The Cat of Kazan" (complete with a Cyrillic caption!) hangs on the wall behind the bed now harboring the disguised wolf. A medicine bottle on a bedside table has a label with the Czarist double-eagle design, and even the ticking of Grandmother's pillow has a Russian folk design. In other books, we see a Russian samovar on a table, a kitten wearing an embroidered peasant's smock, or a rabbit strumming a balalaika.

In Rojankovsky's never-never land of story books, the houses often have the exterior decorations and carved trim of Russian wooden architecture and their furnishings have a folk decorative motif, even when the story itself does not have a Russian setting. The first two large pictures in *Frog Went A-Courtin'* depict a classic Russian peasant house, despite the setting in the Southern Appalachians. The "wedding cake" is, in fact, a traditional Russian Easter *paskha.* And near the end, as the frog's and mouse's wedding pie is eaten up, an empty plate of Slavic folk design is revealed to us. Colorful Russian decorative designs and costumes came out all the more strongly when he illustrated books of explicitly Slavic stories, such as Prishvin's *Treasure Trove of the Sun* (1952), Kalashnikoff's *My Friend Yakub* (1953), and Daniel's *The Falcon Under the Hat* (1969).

The artist mischievously worked other kinds of signs and symbols into his pictures, and the game waits to be fully discovered. In Cat Stories (1953), the year of Rojankovsky's birth, 1891, poses as a house number; his daughter's name Tatiana is lettered on the life buoy of the cat's good ship. Published at the height of the Cold War and the McCarthy era, the worshipful cats in various European national costumes gather around a Stalin-esque monument engraved "The Cat of Bubastis." The ancient Egyptian city of Bubastis was the center for the worship of the cat-headed goddess Bast. As a boy in Russia, he may well have read a translation of G.A. Henty's boys' novel *The Cat of Bubastes* (1889).

His anti-fascism is expressed, too. In 1942 he had made Humpty Dumpty in a ridiculing image of Hitler to express hope for his defeat and the impossibility of his resurrection. The Nazi swastika on the forehead of the fallen and destroyed bovine idol on page 105 of *The Golden Bible* of 1946 signifies Hitler's defeat and death in the ruins of Berlin.

In the last picture of *Frog Went A-Courtin'* the frog and the mouse are on their way to France on the S. S. Liberté, Rojankovsky's own ship of choice for transatlantic travel. And what might the letters *EMA* on Old Miss Rat's sewing machine stand for?

Throughout his career some of Rojankovsky's most memorable work focuses on the lives of children. *Calendrier des enfants* (1936) in the Père Castor series contains twelve full-page color illustrations of children engaged in activities of the seasons, each with a verse, one for each month of the year. The pictures are brightly colored in the modern illustration style of the 1930s. The situations and images evoke the everyday domestic experiences and feelings of childhood. These youngsters are not the raucous, irrepressible American kids we see in his later books, but the delicate well-brought-up city children of the French bourgeoisie.

But not all the children in his Père Castor books were subdued and sheltered. Barbara Bader reminds that "when we incline, by habit, to regard Rojankovsky's later work as more exuberant than his Père Castor books as well as more involved with children, we would do well to remember *Cigalou*." The joyous depictions of the little boy who is so loved by the animals on the mountain in *Quand Cigalou s'en va dans la montagne* (1939) prefigure the children in the two Tall Books (1942 and 1944) and the Golden Books. Some of Rojankovsky's most satisfying drawings of children appear outside the influence of the Golden Books, as in Prishvin's *The Treasure Trove of the Sun* (1952), Bishop's *All Alone* (1953), and Koch's *I Play at the Beach* (1955).

The Russian Bears

Baby bears, adolescent bears, adult bears, bear families, bear stories, and even a teddy bear recur throughout the artist's work. And he liked them enough to make them appear in unlikely settings. If by any stretch of the imagination a bear could make an appearance, one does, and seems quite at home. The bears in their various guises are emblematic of Russian brown bears and the traditional symbol of Russia—but are of more personal meaning, too. The drawings of the animals are particularly effective, and we think Rojankovsky had a soft spot for bears and their antics.

Rojankovsky did not, as some think, create the image of "Smokey Bear" of U.S. Forest Service fame. Smokey Bear, who was popularly renamed "Smokey the Bear," was drawn by another artist and was already famous from TV and other ads several years before the publication of Rojankovsky's pictures in *The True Story of Smokey the Bear* (Golden Books, 1955), a book officially endorsed by the U. S. Forest Service. Rojankovsky accommodatingly flattened the face of Smokey to make him appear more like the already established image of the

Ranger bear. Rojankovsky's own bears looked like real bears, though in America they wore clothes.

His first full bear story was *Bourru l'ours brun* (1936), a picture book in *Le roman des bêtes* for Père Castor. The book follows Bourru's life as a young bear, from birth until he leaves his mother and siblings to go off to live as a solitary adult. Bourru and his playmates look like real bears, with small eyes, long muzzles, and formidable claws, and they roll and play like young bears in the wild.

Bourru looks remarkably similar to the bears drawn by Rojankovsky's Soviet contemporary, Evgenii Charushin, particularly in *Kak Mishka bol'shim medvedem stal* (1930) and later books. If there was a direct influence here, it is from Charushin to Rojankovsky. Charushin's *Mishka* was published first and his work was surely known to Rojankovsky in Paris. Charushin probably did not know the work of the émigré artist, whose art was eclipsed in the Soviet Union.

Rojankovsky's other Père Castor book devoted to the bear was *Michka* (1941), Marie Colmont's story of a sentient teddy bear (reissued as *Christmas Bear*, Golden Books, 1966). Michka (the common Russian nickname for any teddy bear) leaves his rich and selfish mistress to find freedom in the outside world. But he soon relinquishes this freedom to fulfill the giving spirit of the season by presenting himself to a poor boy as a Christmas gift. Michka, the teddy bear, is drawn as a toy—soft instead of shaggy, with large ears, button eyes, hinged joints, and almost no claws. This is Rojankovsky's only story of the life and adventures of a stuffed toy. Years later Michka popped up again, of all places, among the cats that populate the pictorial end papers of *Cat Stories* (1953).

The artist with a taste for bear stories was naturally drawn to the old nursery tale of "The Three Bears." Bader describes the first Golden Book version as Rojankovsky's "dramatic opus." All in all, he illustrated five versions: two as full Golden Books, two as shorter versions in books with other stories, and the two-page spread with a short text and its single but wonderful picture in *Favorite Fairy Tales*. All point up Rojankovsky's narrative strengths through pictures alone. His sentiments and moral sympathies clearly lay with the bears.

Many Russians believe—and not a few have said—that "The Three

Bears" is an indigenous Russian folk tale. Actually, it is an old English folk tale first published in 1831 when the human intruder was not yet named Goldilocks and, for the record, was an old woman with grey hair. Years later Leo Tolstoy wrote a famous version that is known to all Russian children, but he did not invent the old tale itself. Fact is not always the most important thing, and Russian story tellers and illustrators have made the tale their own and given it forever a Russian flavor. Rojankovsky, as much as any illustrator has ever done, makes "The Three Bears" a thoroughly Russian tale.

Rojankovsky's first account of the tale appeared as a short-short story in *The Tall Book of Nursery Tales* (1944) and later as a complete Little Golden Book in 1948. In both versions, the depiction of the bears and their attire as they stroll through the woods—Father Bear with vest and cane, Mother Bear with her parasol, and Baby Bear picking mushrooms—are a direct artistic citation of a famous Russian predecessor. Both pictures are an admiring compliment to Yurii Vasnetsov and his illustrations for Tolstoy's version of "The Three Bears," published in the Soviet Union in 1935. Having acknowledged that, Rojankovsky goes on to make the ensuing story and pictures entirely his own. Bader wrote that "Quite unlike the Russian version, which consists of large complete scenes, exteriors or interiors with the appropriate figures, Rojankovsky's [story] unfolds in a fluid sequence of images."

In our estimation, Rojankovsky's best single picture of the Three Bears is on a leaf of the prize-winning Morrell calendar for 1948 and appeared the next year as the sole illustration of the short story in *Favorite Fairy Tales* (1949). Here the three bears stand closely around the littlest bed, staring down curiously at dumbstruck Goldilocks. She is caught sprawled and disheveled on the tiny bed, her fingers gone to her lips with dismay, her blue eyes wide in surprise. These are not Charushin's or Vasnetsov's bears, but pure Rojankovsky in high American form.

The first Little Golden Book version of *The Three Bears* (1948) is a conventional telling of the tale with the brattish Goldilocks at the center of the narrative. The later book version, an entirely redrawn Golden Book of 1967 and a new text by Kathleen Daly, focuses on the quandary of the bears at the girl's intrusion and its appalling presumption. We see little of Goldilocks here, and just her heels as she flees the house. Perhaps Rojankovsky thought of the orderly animal family as ciphers for peasants living in a hut in a forest, suffering the arrogant intrusion of an outsider who had no feeling or respect for their humble way of life. In private notes, he wrote that the 1967 version pleased him most of all and had "more dramatic intensity." His enthusiasm for the story made the books among the most popular Golden Books and the best treatments by any illustrator.

Many editions of *Michka* have been published in France since the first in 1941. By French tastes, *Michka* is the most popular of the earlier Père Castor books and is still in print. The story of "The Three Bears" and especially the French editions of Rojankovsky's two major illustrations of it for Golden Books are today at the center of a sentimental and nostalgic enthusiasm in French popular culture. In 1949 *Les trois ours*, from Rojankovsky's 1948 version of the story, was published in France and reissued several times. The redrawn and rewritten 1967 edition was simultaneously published in Paris and was similarly popular. *Les trois ours* is now emblematic of French children's culture and is a popular theme in nursery appointments, play houses, and even in a fashionable adult fantasy world.

In his 1992 autobiography, Christian Lacroix, the French couturier, reproduces two large pages of color images from Rojankovsky's *Michka* and the house, interior, and furniture designs from *Les trois ours* (1949) and cites the influences of the illustrations upon his own taste and design work. Rojankovsky's fanciful Russian folk designs for the three bears' big, medium, and small beds and their three chairs made of rough branches inspired Lacroix to create similar furniture for some of his couture salons. "Even my own home reflects the same mixture of patterns, motifs, and heart shapes," he writes.

Lacroix joined other admirers to commemorate Rojan's work in catalog essays for a circulating French library exhibit, which opened in October 1998 at Villeurbanne near Lyon. The exhibit, titled *La maison des trois ours: hommage à Rojankovsky*, was presented on the big-medium-small narrative structure of "The Three Bears" and speaks to the immortality of the tale and the extent to which it is emblematic of Rojankovsky's children's art.

Like all artists who have more ideas than time and sponsorship allow them to finish, Rojankovsky left behind several promising but unrealized illustration projects—what might have been—or older readers of classics. In early 1950, he proposed and was invited by George Macy to submit a plan to illustrate a luxury edition of *Androcles and the Lion*, with a text rewritten by Jean Hersholt, for Macy's Limited Editions Club. But Macy, as it worked out, never published this book with any illustrator or author. After a visit to England and the old city of Selborne in 1965, he planned to illustrate a new edition of Gilbert White's *Natural History and Antiquities of Selborne* (1788), which would have been a natural for this artist. And he was drawn to Pushkin's *Eugene Onegin* and made some preliminary sketches.

In the years just before his death, Rojankovsky signed a contract with Simon & Schuster to illustrate a manuscript by Jan Wahl, to be titled "The Bear, the Wolf, and the Vole." He completed at least two illustrations, which remain in Wahl's papers at Bowling Green University, but probably became too ill to finish the book.

Another project he dreamed of doing late in his life was a picture book on "the first five years in the life of a little girl"—his own daughter's, of course. The text was to have been by his old friend Olga Andreyev Carlisle, whom he had known as a child in Paris in the 1930s. When both were settled in the United States, they renewed their longstanding friendship in the 1950s. She visited the artist at his bedside on the evening of his death in October 1970. Rojankovsky's health failed before he could work extensively on any of these projects. But he gave us enough as it is, well over a hundred fine books.

* * *

Feodor Rojankovsky came to America and brightened and enlivened illustrated books for children and young people and gave pleasure to millions. Many are now repaying him with their growing admiration of his books and their illustration art. The best work—and there is plenty of that—is a magnificent achievement and fulfills an artistic life.

II.

Bibliography of Books and Stories for Children

Introduction

In his fifty-year career, Feodor Rojankovsky illustrated 130 books for children and young people and over sixty children's stories in periodicals, and he made a variety of children's prints and playthings. All the while, he was making hundreds of illustrations and graphic designs for other audiences.

The first editions of the children's books were published in Poland, France, England, or the United States with texts in Polish, Russian, French, or English. Several were anonymously illustrated and others are but little known. The early Polish, Russian émigré, and certain of the French books are today scarce and found mainly in private collections and research libraries. No complete bibliography of the books was previously available and no single public collection holds nearly all the books.

For the illustrated books, we specify the first impression or printing of the first edition, with points of issue when known. As a general rule, we omit later reissues and translations of the books, some with the artwork rearranged or attenuated by the publishers, in favor of the primary books in their first editions. But under certain main entries we include significant simultaneous editions, first American and British editions of the French-language first editions, and later editions of any books that have new or additional artwork.

The color illustrations in most of the European books were made either by direct lithography from stones (e. g., Domino Press) or by offset lithography from zinc plates (e.g., Père Castor). The Golden Books and other books produced by the Artists and Writers Guild were made by screened photolithography from watercolors. Certain later illustrations for other American publishers were drawn on acetate sheets for color separation and printed offset.

The covers and illustrations described as *color* are printed by the full- or four-color process (yellow, cyan, magenta, plus black for strength and detail), unless fewer or more colors are noted. Color illustrations often alternate with (usually subordinate) black-and-white pictures, either halftones or line reproductions. In some of the major and strongest books, all the illustrations are made from pen or pencil drawings.

In Rojankovsky's best productions, the illustrations are part of the overall book design. He decorated the covers and dust jackets and often the end papers, half titles, title pages, and even the copyright and contents pages. The illustrations appear as double-page, full-page, and half-page layouts, and often with many smaller pictures, initials, headpieces, and tailpieces.

B1

Polish and Russian Children's Books & Stories

Rojankovsky's career in children's-book illustration may have begun in 1918 or 1919, when he worked briefly in the Ukrainian city of Poltava for the local government publishing house, the Poltava Zemstvo. Many years later, he recalled drawing illustrations for a translated Ukrainian edition of a children's literary anthology for use in the local schools and, of another sort, for Gustave Flaubert's novel *Salammbô*. But we find no publication records for these books, and they may never have been published owing to the turmoil of the times.

The documented career in book illustration began in 1921 after he settled in the city of Poznan in western Poland, where by 1925 he had illustrated four books for children and young people, as well as two adult literary books. The seventh and last Polish-language book was illustrated from Paris in 1938. All were published by R. Wegner and other Polish publishers.

In 1922 Rojankovsky went to Berlin for several months, where he designed at least one literary book cover and, by his account years later, illustrated two children's books, probably for the Russian-language presses in Berlin. He named only one of these books, Sasha Chernyi's

Detskii ostrov. This book had been earlier and most famously illustrated by Boris Grigoriev in 1918, also in Germany. But we find no publication records of his two Berlin books and assume they were drafted but never published due to the economic collapse in Weimar Germany in 1923 and the closing of the Russian publishing houses.

After settling in Paris in 1925, he illustrated several children's and young people's titles for the Russian-language émigré presses in France. He also illustrated stories and verse for the Paris-based émigré children's magazines *Ogon'ki* and *Sverchok*. After the Second World War, he illustrated a few other Russian-language books published in Paris and New York.

Polish Children's Books (PO.1 - PO.5)

PO.1. Zbierzchowski, Henryk. *Oczyma dziecka: opowiadania wierszowane dla dzieci i młodzieży* [Children's Reader: Stories in Verse for Children and Young People]. Lvov: Odrodzenie, 1921. 53 pp. 23 x 15 cm.

Cover design (in black, white, and red) of a young child sitting in a wooded glade, her hand raised to butterflies overhead; a shining sun and clouds in the background. Eleven verses, each with a decorated initial and illustrated with one to three line drawings, for a total of 22 drawings and 11 initials.

PO.2. Burnett, Frances Hodgson. *Mały Lord: powieść dla młodzieży* [Little Lord: A Novel for Young People; i.e., Little Lord Fauntleroy]. Translated by M.J. Zaleska. Warsaw: Gebethner i Wolff, 1925. 272 pp. 18.25 x 12.5 cm.

Color pictorial paper-covered boards. Orange cloth spine, blocked in gold letters, with narrow blind-stamped bands at top and bottom. Cover picture of man, woman, and two children standing on dock, with ship's rigging in background. Sixteen full-page black line drawings.

PO.3. Twain, Mark [Samuel L. Clemens]. *Przygody Tomka Sawyera* [The Adventures of Tom Sawyer]. Translated by Jan Biliński. Series: Świat podróży i przygód, Tom II [World of Travel and Adventure, Vol. 2]. Lvov and Poznan: Wydawnictwo Polskie, 1925. [8] + 325 + [2] pp., plus six unnumbered leaves of plates. 18.5 x 12 cm.

Six full-page monochrome (grey-green) lithographs. White stiff-paper wraps. Full-color cover picture of Tom Sawyer, paint brush in hand, with Aunt Polly's fence in background.

PO.4. Szelburg [Zarembina], Ewa. *Renine wierszyki* [Rena's Little Verses]. Warsaw: J. Mortkowicz, nd [c. 1925]. [22] pp., including insides of covers. 18 x 20 cm.

White soft-paper wraps. The front cover is in effect, the title page; the letter forms (title line in red, rest in black) and small red decorative devices are probably by FR. Dedication on inside of front cover: "MAMUSI RENINEJ poświęcam." Back cover: "BARWNA ROTOGRAWJURA DRUKARNI NARODOWEJ W KRAKOWIE." Twenty-one color lithographs illustrating verses by Szelburg (b. 1899). The girl's hair is yellow, her dress bright red; she wears a yellow hat with a blue ribbon.

The verses and pictures narrate a day in the life of a little girl.

PO.5. Ossendowski, F[erdynand] Antoni. *Słoń Birara: powieść dla młodzieży* [Birara, the Elephant: A Novel for Young People]. Poznan: Wydawnictwo Polskie (R. Wegner), 1938. 173 pp. 22.5 x 18 cm.

Cream, stiff-paper pictorial wraps. Cover design and sixteen line drawings, frontis of hippopotamus.

In the service of a crown prince, an East Indian boy, Amra, and his elephant, Birara, participate in royal hunts, are separated in the jungle, but reunited. Eventually, the elephant gives his life to save his human friend. Realistic drawings of the elephant and other animals. Illustrated from Paris.

Russian Émigré Children's Books (RU.1 - RU.6)

RU.1. Chernyi, Sasha (pseudonym of Aleksandr Mikhailovich Glikberg). *Zhivaia azbuka* [Lively Alphabet]. Paris: N. P. Karbasnikov, 1926. 40 pp. 27 x 22 cm.

White soft-paper, pictorial wraps. Front cover has a color photolithograph of an elephant, a giraffe, and three monkeys.

Cover text: "Sasha Chernyi / Zhivaia / azbuka / kartinki F. Rozhankovskago / izdanie t·va 'N. P. Karbasnikov,' Parizh / 1926." Half title is lettered with the name of the author and the book's title, with a line drawing of seven animals and a book. Full title page is lettered in red and black. Last page: "Imp. L. Beresniak / 12, rue Lagrange / Paris." Back cover: "Sklad izdaniia: / Sté N. P. Karbasnikoff / Paris / Imp. L. Beresniak, 12, r. Lagrange.Tél: Gobelins 42-72."

All of the many illustrations inside are black halftones. Two drawings of (mostly) animals for each character in the Russian alphabet, illustrating short verses by Sasha Chernyi. Pages 36-37 have a poem suggesting to child readers that the pictures may be colored in. The book concludes with a formal presentation of the 36 characters in the old Cyrillic alphabet, arranged on two pages (38-39).

This is the third edition of Chernyi's *Zhivaia azbuka.* The first was published in St. Petersburg (1914) by Shipovnik and illustrated by V. Falileev; the second, in Berlin [1922] by *Ogon'ki* and illustrated by MAD [Mikhail Aleksandrovich Drizo].

Sasha Chernyi, the pseudonym of Aleksandr Mikhailovich Glikberg, is often transliterated to English as *Chernii* or, sometimes, *Chorny.* In France, the author transliterated his pseudonym as *Tchorny.*

RU.2a. Chernyi, Sasha (pseudonym). *Dnevnik foksa Mikki* [Diary of the Fox Terrier Mikki]. Paris: Privately printed by the author, 1927. 51+1 pp. 30.75 x 24.5 cm. **Limited, signed edition**.

Cream stiff-paper wraps, with color cover picture of the sitting dog, Mikki. Thirty- six line drawings (4 full-page and 32 smaller in-text designs). Two hundred copies were numbered and signed by the author.

Cover text: "Sasha Chernyi / Dnevnik Foksa / Mikki / risunki F. Rozhankovskago / izdanie avtora. Parizh 27 g." Copyright page: "Soc. Anon. Impr. de Navarre 5, rue des Gobelins, Paris. Copyright A. Tchorny, 1927, Paris."

Colophon: "*Oblozhku illiustratsii v tekste i vin'etki risoval F. S. Rozhankovskii. Klishe ispolneny khudozhestvennym atel'e Jouffroy et Rochefort (Paris). Tekst nabran i otpechatan v tipografii Navarre. Dvesti numerovannykh i podpisannykh avtorom ekzempliarov knigi otpechatany na bumage Pur fil Lafuma.*"

Copy No. 10 bears the inscription (but is not otherwise signed): "Ot chestnoi sobaki Mikki milomu Sergeiu Sergeevichu / Sasha Chernyi / Parizh 1927" [From the honest dog Mikki to dear Sergei Sergeevich / Sasha Chernyi / Paris 1927].

The text and drawings for this book, in their entirety, are reproduced in the collected prose of Chernyi (Moscow, 1991), which also has photographs of Chernyi and his pet dog Mikki. An excerpt from the book appeared (translated into French) two years later in the young persons' serial publication of *Figaro, Les enfants de France* [B3, FS.1]. An excerpt (in French) also appeared shortly after publication in the Paris children's magazine, *Les petits bonhommes.*

Pencil in paw, the sentient and literate fox terrier, Mikki, writes his diary over a long summer, describing his relationship to his beloved mistress, Zina, and her parents. He ruminates on the stupidity of humans, the hatefulness of cats and fleas, and the perversity of a world that ignores dogs. Recalling his adventures in Paris, at the beach, the zoo, and the circus, and of getting lost, he dreams of fame as an author.

Recently mentioned as one of 100 major books published by Russian émigrés (Seslavinsky, 2012).

RU.2.b. The **trade edition** is the same, except slightly larger (32.5 x 26 cm), in grey stiff-paper wraps and printed on different but high-quality paper. The copyright page states "Copyright by A. Tchorny, 1927, Paris" and the printer appears on the last page: "Soc. Anon. Impr. de Navarre 5, rue des Gobelins, Paris." The back cover verso indicates distribution by: "Société N.P. Karbasnikoff. 23, rue de Richelieu, Paris (1er), Tel.: Louvre 61-96."

RU.2.c. A later edition was published in reduced size by Moskva-Logos, Berlin, nd [1929], 25.5 x 18.5 cm. The text and pictures are the same.

RU.3. Chernyi, Sasha, ed. (pseudonym). *Molodaia Rossiia* [Young Russia]. Zemgor: Paris, 1927. 23 pp. 32 x 25.5 cm.

Eleven line drawings (resembling block cuts) and several vignettes are by FR. One full-page drawing (p. 15) is by Vasilii Shukhaev. Text pages on heavy buff paper.

Brown paper wraps, with a 10-cm image of young Pushkin on front cover. Cover text: "Molodaia Rossiia / K dniu russkoi kul'tury." Title page text: "Molodaia Rossiia / Sbornik dlia detei pod redaktsiei / A. M. Chernago / Oblozhka i risunki v tekste / khud. F. S. Rozhankovskago / Izdanie obedineniia zemskikh i gorodskikh deiatelei / Parizh 1927." Last page: "Soc. Anon. Impr. de Navarre, 5, rue des Gobelins, Paris."

A collection of stories, prose and poems on Russian culture written for young people, all by émigré writers.

RU.4. Chernyi, Sasha (pseudonym). *Koshach'ia sanatoriia* [Cat Sanatorium]. Paris: A. I. Kuprin, Detskaia Bibliotechka "Mikki," 1928. 60 + [2] pp. 16 x 12.25 cm.

Cream stiff paper wraps, with a cover drawing of a rumpled man and four cats. Cover text: "Sasha Chernyi / Koshach'ia sanatoriia." Title page text: "Sasha Chernyi / Koshach'ia sanatoriia / Risunki F. Rozhankovskago / Detskaia Bibliotechka "Mikki" / Parizh 1928."

Five full-page line drawings and two small drawings of cats.

A cat named Beppo is abandoned in the Roman Forum of Trajan. The cats trapped there are fed by an old man and live an easy life. The indolent cats reminisce about their grand pasts and deny their fate. But Beppo, a free spirit, refuses to succumb and escapes by hiding in an outgoing sack of dead cats, taking a city tram to a place of freedom described by a fellow inmate.

An excerpt (translated into French) appeared shortly after publication in the Paris children's magazine, *Les petits bonshommes.*

RU.5. Kodrianskaia, Natal'ia. *Globusnyi chelovechek* [The Little Man Out of the Terrestrial Globe]. Paris: Privately printed by the author, 1954. 68 pp. 27.5 x 21.25 cm.

Tan boards with color designs on paper mounted on front and back of covers. Marked 600 francs. Issued without dust jacket. Cover text: 'Natal'ia Kodrianskaia / Globusnyi / chelovechek / risunki F. Rozhankovskogo." Half-title text: "Globusnyi / chelovechek / skazochnoe puteshestvie." Title-page text: "Natal'ia Kokrianskaia / Globusnyi / chelovechek / illiustratsii Fedora Rozhankovskogo." Text on last page: "Cet ouvrage / a été imprimé à Paris / la lithographie / par Mourlot Frères / la typographie / par L'Imprimerie Union / Tous droits réservés pour tous pays / Copyright 1954 by Natalie Codray / Printed in France."

Twenty-five color lithographs, by Mourlot Frères.

The terrestrial globe in Dixie's bedroom lights up, a small door opens, and a little man steps out, ready to take Dixie and her cat, Blackie, on adventures to all parts of the world—providing Dixie behaves and does her school work. Among other adventures, Dixie and the little man from the globe rescue a girl in Holland who was turned into a china doll by a wicked stepmother, a boy in Normandy who has been living with seals at the bottom of the ocean is returned to his parents, and the trio barely escape a wicked king on a magic star. Finally, the little man shows Dixie enchantment and fascination in her own garden, where the plants and animals talk.

The kindly Little Man in the illustrations was drawn by FR in the likeness of the émigré writer, Aleksei Remizov, a good friend of both the illustrator and the author. Remizov identified with the Little Man in the story and FR accommodated him in the comic physical caricature. Remizov also thought Dixie was a cypher for the author as a little girl and saw other resemblances with émigré personalities of their acquaintance.

RU.6. Smirnova, Tosia. *Zaichata: skazka dlia detei s kartinkami* [Little Rabbits: A Story for Children with Pictures]. New York: Russian Printing House, 1955. 16 pp. 19 x 15.5 cm.

Cream soft-paper wraps. Center stapled. Cover design in black and olive. Six line drawings of clothed rabbit family, with many baby rabbits. FR is not credited as the artist in this memorial edition for the author, Tosia Smirnova.

A story in verse. Mama Rabbit has difficulty keeping her ten children in mended clothes, because they play too roughly. Papa Rabbit solves the problem—the little rabbits shall live and play wearing no clothes.

Russian Émigré Children's Magazines (RS.1 - RS.8)

Ogon'ki (RS.1 - RS.4)

In 1932-33, FR illustrated with black ink drawings at least six stories in a new children's magazine, *Ogon'ki* [Twinkles], edited by Ivan Novgorod-Severskii. Though this Paris magazine was the namesake of the Soviet young people's magazine published in Moscow from 1927 to 1932, the two magazines differed in age level and ideology. Only nine issues of the Paris *Ogon'ki* were published from March 1932 (No. 1) to No. 9 in 1933. All the drawings are in-text on leaves 26 x 18 cm. FR's illustrations appear in Nos. 1-4 and 8, but not in 5 and 6. We were unable to examine issues Nos. 7 and 9.

RS.1. Small drawing of small shed in woods titled "Ovin" [Barn for Drying Crops]. Captioned "Illustration to book, *Sibirskiia skazki* [Siberian Fairy Tales], by Ivan Novgorod-Severskii." No. 1, March 1932, p. 11.

RS.2. Small drawing of head and torso of Russian boy cadet, for A. Kuprin's "Fialki: Otryvok (iz kadetskoi zhizni)" [Violets: Excerpt (Out of a Cadet's Life)]. No. 2, April 1932, pp. 2-3; reproduced from *Molodaia Rossiia* (Zemgor: Paris, 1927) [RU.3], but here illustrating a different text.

In same issue, small drawing of old woman in woods leaning on a staff, titled "Vorozhka" [Little Sorceress], for the first of three stories, "Shchuch'e slovo" [Word of the Pike], by Iv. Novgorod-Severskii, under the general title *Sibirskiia skazki* [Siberian Fairy Tales], pp. 7-8.

RS.3. Small drawing of man in forest, seated before a cooking pot, with a deer in the background and geese flying overhead, for Iv. Novgorod-Severskii's "Pesni moego druga (Votiatskii pesni)"

[Songs of My Friend (Votyak Songs)]. Nos. 3-4 (as one issue), nd [1932], p. 6.

In same issue, horizontal headpiece drawing of old-fashioned train, with engine pulling three cars, for Valentin Gorianskii's "Nakazannyi korol" [The Punished King], pp. 7-9.

RS.4. Larger drawing of three figures in heavy winter garb walking through a forest, one pulling a small sled loaded with a hat box and one candle on top; the other two carry a bouquet and a shovel; for Aleksandr Iablonskii's "Fil'ka" [Little Phillip]. No. 8, 1933, pp. 4-6, 8-10.

Sverchok (RS.5 - RS.8)

The Paris émigré children's magazine, *Sverchok* [Cricket], edited by Ivan Novgorod-Severskii and Boris Kostrov, was published in a run of 15 issues, Nos. 1-15, from October 1, 1937 to July 1939. Five previously published drawings by FR were reproduced in four issues.

Moreover, FR probably drew the many unsigned and uncredited realistic line drawings of wild animals that illustrate the several continued stories "Dnevnik sledopyta" [Diary of a Tracker] in issues 5-11, 13, and 15.

RS.5. Drawing titled "Kadet" [Cadet], head and shoulders of boy in uniform, No. 1 (25 October 1937), p. [5]. Picture reproduced from *Molodaia Rossia* (1927), p. 22 [RU.3], and from *Ogon'ki*, No. 2 (1932) [RS.2], but here illustrating yet a third text.

RS.6. Drawing of two boys in schoolroom, with blackboard, No. 6 (10 March 1938), p. 5. Text and picture reproduced from *Molodaia Rossii* (1927), p. 17 [RU.3].

RS.7. Drawing of toy-like train, No. 8 (30 June 1938), p. 4. Text and picture reproduced from *Ogon'ki*, Nos. 3-4 (1932) [RS.3].

RS.8. Small drawing of shed in woods, No. 15 (1 July 1939), p. 7. Drawing (uncredited and untitled) illustrating Novgorod-Severskii's story, "Ovin" [Barn for Drying Crops]. Reproduction of a credited drawing titled "Ovin" in *Ogon'ki*, No. 1 (1931), where it appeared first but without the text [RS.1].

In same issue, p. 15, old woman in woods leaning on a staff (here uncredited and untitled). Story text and drawing reproduced from *Ogon'ki*, No. 2, pp. 7-8 [RS.2].

B2

The Domino Press Books

Esther Averill (1902-1992), the American editor and children's author and illustrator, was the founder and principal figure behind the tiny expatriate Domino Press in Paris. She collaborated on the early projects with her friend, Lila Stanley, another American in Paris, but later worked alone. The first Domino Press book was *Daniel Boone* (1931). The last were the English and French editions of Jean Mariotti's *Tales of Poindi* (1938, 1939), both published in New York after Averill moved her press there late in 1934.

The Domino Press published only six books, of which Rojankovsky illustrated five. All but one had both English and French editions, and some were also issued with the imprints of other publishers. Because Rojankovsky's work with Domino Press so influenced the history of modern children's picture books, we show separate entries for the trade editions in boards and the limited luxury editions in wraps and for the French, British, and American editions of each book.

The Domino Press's four English, French, trade, and luxury editions of *Daniel Boone* (1931), *Powder/Poudre* (1933), and *Flash/Éclair* (1934) were in fact issued simultaneously, or nearly so, and their primacy is pedantic. Nonetheless, we have given symbolic primacy to the English-language trade editions of *Daniel Boone*, *Powder* and *Flash*. Each book was written in English and translated into French. And all the books had peculiarly Anglo-American themes and were born of American dreamers (including a Russian) in Paris between the wars.

Some copies of *Powder*, *Poudre*, *Flash* and *Éclair* were distributed in Paris by Librairie Fischbacher and bear their label in place of Domino Press's imprint on the title page.

Averill, using the pseudonym "John Domino," also authored *The Fable of the Proud Poppy* (1934), the only Domino Press title not illustrated by Rojankovsky. Illustrated by the Hungarian painter Emile Lahner, this book was issued in both French and English and was the last Domino Press book published in Paris.

Further reading about the Domino Press, including selected illustrations, may be found in the several articles by Averill in *The Horn Book* magazine and in the articles by Beston, Bruller, Dupuy, Frenzel, and "J.B.M."

Editions of *Daniel Boone* (DP.1)

DP.1a. Averill, Esther, and Lila Stanley, eds. *Daniel Boone, Historic Adventures of an American Hunter among the Indians*. Paris: Domino Press, 1931. [16] pp. 36.5 x 29 cm.

Five-color direct lithography from stones. Pictorial paper-covered boards. Blue cloth spine. **English-language trade edition**.

Colophon: "*The text of this book is printed by Robert Coulouma of Argenteuil and the illustrations are printed by Mourlot Frères of Paris. There are twenty-five copies on vélin d'arches including a series of the lithographs printed separately without text, and numbering from 1 to 50. Completed October 17, 1931.*"

The size of the larger, unnumbered printing of this edition is unknown but said to be about 1,000 copies.

A succinct telling of Daniel Boone's life, starting with his early childhood in Pennsylvania, and taking him ever farther south and west to new frontiers, as a scout, explorer, pilot, trapper, river merchant, twice prisoner of the Indians, soldier, commander of the fort in the historic 1778 Battle of Boonesborough, KY, and, in his last years, as a settler in Missouri and a hunter as far west as Yellowstone.

DP.1b. Deluxe English-language edition, numbers 1 to 25.

Same as the trade edition, except issued unbound in a wrapper, printed on *vélin d'arches*, numbered under the colophon and signed "F. Rojankovsky." The cover is a folio sheet folded once to contain the similarly folded loose sheets of the book. A complete corresponding set of color lithograph proofs (including the cover design), printed without text, also numbered by hand but not signed, is loosely inserted at the end of this edition. 38.8 x 29.5 cm.

DP.1c. Averill, Esther, and Lila Stanley, eds. *Daniel Boone, Historic Adventures of an American Hunter among the Indians.* London: Faber & Faber, 1931. [16] pp. 36.5 x 29 cm.

Five-color direct lithography. Pictorial paper-covered boards. Blue cloth spine. **First British edition**.

This issue is identical to the Domino Press, Paris, English-language trade edition, except the front cover bears the imprint line "Faber and Faber, Limited, London" beneath the names of the editors and in the place of "Domino Press, Paris."

We have seen offered for sale, but have not examined, a "1934 original print" from a page of *Daniel Boone*, about two-thirds the size of the original book pages. Below the print, in the center:

"Design by Rojan, c/o Harding & Giles, London"; on the left: "Color blocks by J Swain & Son, Ltd."; and on the right: "Inks by Shackell, Edwards & Co., Ltd.," indicating that new blocks were created in the slightly smaller size for the prints.

DP.1d. [Averill, Esther, and Lila Stanley, eds.] *Daniel Boone, les aventures d'un chasseur américain parmi les Peaux-Rouges.* Paris: Domino Press, 1931. [16] pp. 37 x 29 cm.

Five-color direct lithography. Pictorial paper-covered boards. Blue cloth spine. **French-language trade edition**

Colophon: "*Ce livre, achevé le 17 Octobre 1931, a été imprimé, pour le texte, sur les presses de R. Coulouma, à Argenteuil, H. Barthélemy étant directeur, et pour les illustrations, sur les presses de Mourlot Frères, à Paris. Il a été tiré 50 exemplaires sur vélin d'arches, contenant une suite des lithographies, et numérotés de 1 a 50.*"

The size of the larger, unnumbered printing of this edition is unknown but is generally said to be about 1,000 copies.

The French-language edition omits the names of the two editors on the cover and elsewhere. The title page remains in English, though the cover and other texts are in French.

A facsimile edition was published by Circonflex (Paris 1992).

DP.1e. **Deluxe French-language edition,** numbers 26 to 50.

Same as the French-language trade edition above, except issued unbound in a wrapper, printed on *vélin d'arches*, numbered under the colophon and signed "F. Rojankovsky." The cover is a folio sheet folded once to contain the similarly folded loose sheets of the book. A complete corresponding set of color lithograph proofs (including cover design), printed without text, also numbered by hand but not signed, is loosely inserted at the end of this edition. 37 x 29 cm.

DP.1f. Averill, Esther. *Daniel Boone*. New York: Harper & Brothers, 1945. 60 pp. 28.5 x 21.5 cm. Stated "First edition," i.e., first thus by Harper.

Full-color illustrations. Pictorial paper-covered boards. Red cloth spine. White pictorial end papers. Pictorial dust jacket, with bios of Averill and FR on back panel; $1.50 on front flap.

A new edition, smaller in format, with rearranged pictures and an extended narrative text by Averill. First printing of 50,000 copies. Also library edition by E.M. Hale.

Editions of *Powder/Poudre* (DP.2)

DP.2a. Averill, Esther, and Lila Stanley. *Powder: The Story of a Colt, a Duchess and the Circus*. Paris: Domino Press, 1933. 29 + [3] pp. 26.75 x 17.5 cm.

Direct color lithography. Pictorial red and green paper-covered boards. Yellow cloth spine. Plain white end papers. **English-language trade edition**. Some copies may bear the Fischbacher label on the title page.

Colophon: "*Achevé d'imprimer le 17 Janvier 1933 par Coulouma et Mourlot Frères à Paris. Printed in France.*"

The white colt, Powder (Poudre), lives free with other horses on the estate of the irascible Duchess. Every year the circus comes to the village. The Duchess hates the circus, but cannot go against the will of her people by forbidding it. When the overweight Duchess selects young Powder as her riding horse, Powder runs away with the circus. He becomes a splendid circus horse and returns home every year with the circus.

DP.2b. Averill, Esther, and Lila Stanley. *Powder: The Story of a Colt, a Duchess and the Circus*. Paris: Domino Press, 1933. 29 + [3] pp. 27 x 19 cm.

Direct color lithography. Pictorial red and green wrappers. Plain white end papers. **English-language limited edition**.

Colophon: "*Achevé d'imprimer le 17 Janvier 1933 par Coulouma et Mourlot Frères à Paris. Printed in France.*"

This wrappers edition on vélin is signed by FR and numbered. Limitation unknown, but probably no more than 150 copies.

The Duchess's "purple" umbrella is mentioned rather prominently in the text, but appears in only one illustration, on p. 25. In this gold-and-black illustration, the parasol is uncolored in the limited edition, but appears as shocking pink in the English and French trade editions, and presumably in the American and British editions, as well. On the flyleaf of a copy of the French trade edition in the Rojankovsky archive is a hand-written note in Russian by FR to "please pay attention to the fact that the parasol of the duchess [p. 25] was colored separately in every single book of the entire edition." We speculate that the limited edition had already been completed, when FR decided to color the umbrella pink for the trade editions, requiring the inking of a separate stone.

DP.2c. Averill, Esther, and Lila Stanley. *Powder: The Story of a Colt, a Duchess and the Circus*. New York: Harrison Smith and Robert Haas, 1933. 29 + [3] pp. 26.5 x 17 cm.

Direct color lithography. Pictorial red and green paper-covered boards. Yellow cloth spine. Plain white end papers. $2.00. **First American trade edition**.

Colophon: "*Achevé d'imprimer le 17 Janvier 1933 par Coulouma et Mourlot Frères à Paris. Printed in France.*"

DP.2d. Averill, Esther, and Lila Stanley. *Powder: The Story of a Colt, a Duchess and the Circus*. London: Faber and Faber, 1933. 29 + [3] pp. 26.75 x 17.5 cm.

Direct color lithography. Pictorial red and green paper-covered boards. Yellow cloth spine. Plain white end papers. Five shillings. Printed in Paris. **First British edition**.

Colophon: "*Achevé d'imprimer le 17 Janvier 1933 par Coulouma et Mourlot Frères à Paris. Printed in France.*"

DP.2e. Averill, Esther, and Lila Stanley. *Poudre, l'histoire d'un poulain, d'une duchesse et d'un cirque*. Translated from the English by Jeanne and Jacqueline de Beaufort. Paris: Domino Press, 1933. 29 + [3] pp. 26.75 x 17.5 cm.

Direct color lithography. Pictorial red and green paper-covered boards. Yellow cloth spine. Plain white end papers. **French-language trade edition**.

Colophon: "*Achevé d'imprimer le 17 Janvier 1933 par Coulouma et Mourlot Frères à Paris. Printed in France.*"

Some copies have a 1/2 x 2 inch label, "Librairie Fischbacher / Paris," pasted over the imprint "Domino Press / Paris."

[DP.2f]. If Domino Press published *Powder/Poudre* in the same array of English, French, trade, and limited editions as its sequel *Flash/Éclair*, then a limited, signed, wrappers edition of *Poudre* would have been issued, corresponding to the French-language issue of *Éclair*. But we have not located such an issue of *Poudre*.

Editions of *Flash/Éclair* (DP.3)

DP.3a. Averill, Esther. *Flash: The Story of a Horse, a Coach-Dog and the Gypsies*. Paris: Domino Press, 1934. 32 pp. 26.75 x 17.5 cm.

Direct color lithography. Pictorial tan and blue paper-covered boards. Matching tan cloth spine. Plain white end papers. **English-language trade edition**. Some copies have label,

"Fischbacher," pasted over "Domino Press" on title page.

Colophon: "*Achevé d'imprimer le 17 Mai 1934 par Coulouma et Mourlot Frères à Paris. Printed in France.*"

A sequel to the story of *Powder (Poudre)*. Powder's father, Flash, the fastest horse in the kingdom, ran away, rather than be taken by the Duchess as a stable horse. Powder, traveling with the circus, seeks his lost father. The old Duchess dies, making it safe for Flash to come home. Wig-wag, the coach dog, travels the kingdom looking for Flash and finds him with the gypsies. Flash escapes the gypsies, returns home, and lives free on the open plain with Powder's mother.

DP.3b. Averill, Esther. *Flash: The Story of a Horse, a Coach-Dog and the Gypsies*. Paris: Domino Press, 1934. 32 pp. 27 x 19 cm.

Direct color lithography. Pictorial tan and blue paper wrappers. **English-language limited edition**.

Colophon: "*Achevé d'imprimer le 17 Mai 1934 par Coulouma et Mourlot Frères à Paris. Printed in France.*"

This wrappers edition on vélin is signed by FR and numbered. Limitation unknown, but probably no more than 150 copies.

DP.3c. Averill, Esther. *Flash: The Story of a Horse, a Coach-Dog and the Gypsies*. New York: Harrison Smith and Robert Haas, 1934. 32 pp. 26.5 x 17 cm.

Direct color lithography. Pictorial tan and blue paper-covered boards. Matching tan cloth spine. Plain white end papers. $2.00. **First American trade edition**.

Colophon: "*Achevé d'imprimer le 17 Mai 1934 par Coulouma et Mourlot Frères à Paris. Printed in France.*"

DP.3d. Averill, Esther. *Flash: The Story of a Horse, a Coach-Dog and the Gypsies.* London: Faber and Faber, Limited, 1934. 32 pp. 26.75 x 17.5 cm.

Direct color lithography. Pictorial tan and blue paper-covered boards. Matching tan cloth spine. Plain white end papers. Five shillings. Printed in Paris. **First British edition.**

Colophon: "*Achevé d'imprimer le 17 Mai 1934 par Coulouma et Mourlot Frères à Paris. Printed in France.*"

DP.3e. Averill, Esther. *Éclair: histoire d'un cheval, d'un chien de carrosse et des bohémiens.* Traduit par Jacqueline André. Paris: Domino Press, 1934. 32 pp. 26.75 x 17.5 cm.

Direct color lithography. Pictorial tan and blue paper-covered boards. Matching tan cloth spine. Plain white end papers. **French-language trade edition**.

Colophon: "*Achevé d'imprimer le 17 Mai 1934 par Coulouma et Mourlot Frères à Paris. Printed in France.*"

A slightly variant "issue" bears on the title page the imprint of the Paris distributor, "Librairie Fischbacher, Paris," in place of the imprint of "Domino Press, Paris." This is apparently a specially printed title page. 15 francs.

DP.3f. Averill, Esther. *Éclair: histoire d'un cheval, d'un chien de carrosse et des bohémiens.* Traduit par Jacqueline André. Paris: Domino Press, 1934. 32 pp. 27 x 19 cm.

Direct color lithography. Pictorial tan and blue paper wrappers. **French-language limited edition**.

Colophon: "*Achevé d'imprimer le 17 Mai 1934 par Coulouma et Mourlot Frères à Paris. Printed in France.*"

This wrappers edition on vélin is signed by FR and numbered. Limitation unknown, but probably no more than 150 copies.

The Domino Press in New York (DP.4 - DP.5)

DP.4a. Averill, Esther. *The Voyages of Jacques Cartier.* New York: Domino Press, 1937. 96 pp. 28 x 22 cm.

All black line drawings. Brick-red pictorial cloth. Plain white end papers. Pictorial dust jacket, with $3.00 on front flap.

Colophon: "*This book has been printed by The Marchbanks Press of New York City and this first impression is limited to three thousand copies.*" *On front flap of dust jacket: "This first printing is limited to 3,000 copies.*"

Domino Press's first book published in the U. S. A juvenile title about the three voyages and many adventures in the New World of the French explorer Jacques Cartier and his company, and based on Cartier's own log-books.

DP.4b. Averill, Esther. *Cartier Sails the St. Lawrence.* New York: Harper and Brothers, 1956. x + 109 pp. 26 x 19 cm.

Line drawings throughout, including in all the front matter. First or early issue examined has beige cloth covers, red lettering on spine, and picture of ship on lower right of front cover. Plain white end papers. Pictorial dust jacket, with $3.00 on flap.

A new truncated edition of Averill's *The Voyages of Jacques Cartier* (Domino Press, 1937) [DP.4a]. The text is heavily revised, 11 new drawings and three small devices have been added, many older drawings have been either cropped or dropped, and the book's dimensions are smaller.

DP.5a. Mariotti, Jean. *Tales of Poindi.* Translated by Esther Averill. New York: Domino Press, 1938. xi + 64 pp. 27 x 22 cm.

All black line drawings, three full-page and about 40 smaller drawings and devices. Pictorial dust jacket. $2.50.

The English-language edition was published a year earlier than Domino's French edition, and is the first edition of this eminently French colonial tale by a French author. But see the Stock (Paris 1941) edition [DP.5c].

The author's retelling of the native myths and legends about nature that he heard in his youth in the French colony of New Caledonia. Poindi is the name of a Kanaka hunter who relates the stories to his young son during a long rest deep in the forest. Most of the mythical characters are birds.

DP.5b. Mariotti, Jean. *Contes de Poindi: Légende Océanienne.* New York: Domino Press, 1939. 66 pp. 27.5 x 22 cm.

All black line drawings, three full-page and over 40 smaller drawings and devices; same as English edition, except adding one device (p. 16) and one small bird picture (p. 37). Pictorial green cloth. Plain white end papers. Pictorial dust jacket, with both flaps blank.

FR's contract with Faucher and Flammarion, which prohibited his illustrating any other French-language juvenile titles, expired in 1939, allowing this first French edition of Poindi—a year after the English edition was published.

DP.5c. Mariotti, Jean. *Les Contes de Poindi.* Paris: Éditions Stock, Delamain et Boutelleau, 1941. 211 pp. 19 x 14.5 cm.

All black line drawings, 16 full-page, including frontis, and several smaller drawings. White paper wraps, with color thematic oval garland around lettering on front cover and smaller color pictures on back cover and spine. Mariotti's text is doubled over that used in the Domino Press editions, adding one full story of 92 pages (pp. 113-211).

Many will consider this 1941 Stock edition, published under the German Occupation and on cheap paper, an original edition because of the entirely new 16 full-page pen drawings (many of the specimen animals are identified verso) and the added story. The full-color cover is also different from the garland on the Domino editions. Also listed under other French books [B3, OF.2].

B3

Père Castor and Other French Children's Books and Stories

Rojankovsky illustrated 27 French-language picture books for Flammarion et Cie's *Albums du Père* Castor, the first in 1933. The Père Castor books fall into three sequential groups, each significantly smaller than the group before it: the two large quarto-size animal books of 1933 and 1934; the eight oblong books in the subseries *Le roman des bêtes* of 1934 to 1939 and six other, mostly oblong but slightly smaller, octavo books issued from 1936 to 1941; and finally, the smallest eleven *Petits Père Castors*, 1941 and later, which are about one fourth the size of the large albums in the first category.

The French-language editions published by Flammarion—in their first issues—are the true first editions. In Rojankovsky's lifetime, most of the books had later but significant translated British and American editions, which are shown under each of the French first editions.

Certain of the Père Castor books are difficult to identify in their first states. Between early reprintings, Rojankovsky sometimes revised the designs on the zinc plates, though the books do not indicate a second or later printings. Some books in *Le roman des bêtes* were here and there slightly redrawn in their details or inked a little differently. In one case (*Bourru l'ours brun*), a new full-page color lithograph is substituted. But none indicates a later printing.

Generally, one may reasonably assume an example in hand is a first or early issue, if there is no month and year date (shown as numerals following the printer's credit line on the bottom of the last page and/ or back cover) that is later than the copyright year on the title page. All the books were printed by the firm of M. Déchaux, Paris.

The early books, 1933 to about 1939, were printed by offset lithography from, in the illustrator's words, "six or seven zinc plates" on which he "personally" drew the color separations. Later books, after about 1939, were reproduced by photo offset from watercolors and used the standard four-color process.

Further readings on the Père Castor series in general and Rojankovsky's contributions in particular may be found, especially, in Flammarion's 1982 retrospective catalog and in Bader, de Saint-Rat, Hürlimann, Jan, and Parmegiani.

Albums du Père Castor (PC.1 - PC.27)

Quarto-size Animal Books (PC.1 - PC.2)

PC.1a. Celli, Rose. *Les petits et les grands* [Small Ones and Big Ones]. Albums du Père Castor. Paris: Flammarion, 1933. [24] pp. 32 x 28 cm.

Pictorial yellow, laminated, stiff paper wraps, printed on one side. The front cover has an elephant with her calf, the back a smaller picture of a beaver. Twelve large two- and three-color lithographs alternating with smaller black line drawings of various wild animals and their young.

PC.1b. Celli, Rose. *Wild Animals and Their Little Ones*. Poughkeepsie, NY: Artists and Writers Guild, 1935. [16] pp., plus two printed insides of both covers. 32.25 x 27.75 cm.

Pictorial yellow, laminated, stiff paper wraps. The English version of *Les petits et les grands*, with a shorter text and with fewer and rearranged pictures. **First American edition**.

PC.2a. Reynier, Marguerite. *En famille* [In the Family]. Albums du Père Castor. Paris: Flammarion, 1934. [24] pp. 32 x 28.5 cm.

Pictorial yellow, laminated, stiff paper wraps, printed on one side only. The front cover picture has an orangutan and her young one, the back a smaller picture of a chimpanzee and her young one. Twelve large two- and three-color lithographs alternating with smaller black line drawings of various wild animal mothers and their dependent young.

PC.2b. Reynier, Marguerite. *Wild Animals at Home*. Poughkeepsie, NY: Artists and Writers Guild, 1935. [16] pp., plus two printed insides of covers. 32.5 x 28 cm.

Pictorial yellow, laminated, stiff paper wraps. The English version of *En famille*, with a shorter text and with fewer and rearranged pictures. **First American edition**.

Le roman des bêtes (PC.3 - PC.10)

The eight books of animal stories, *Le roman des bêtes* [The Novel of the Animals], are uniformly about 21 x 23 cm. All have 36 unnumbered pages, counting the illustrated title page and the last page of ads. All are stapled into laminated stiff paper wraps, printed on one side only; the insides of the covers are plain. Each front cover has a different thematic picture in full color; the back covers have a small theme drawing, a full-size picture, or other design. The books are illustrated throughout on nearly every page with a variable mix of color lithographs and black line drawings. The title pages are decorated, usually with black line drawings.

Significant new editions of the eight books (translated by either Georges or Lily Duplaix) were published by Harper and Brothers (New

York) between 1936 and 1942. Four (*Ploof*, *Bruin*, *Scuff*, and *Spiky*) were reissued by the Golden Press in 1966 and only in Goldencraft library bindings. The pictorial layouts in the Harper and Golden Press editions vary from the original Flammarion editions, though all or most of the pictures are present.

George Allen & Unwin (London) also published new editions of all eight titles in late 1930s. All were translated by Rose Fyleman, the noted British children's-book author. The title pages carry the legend "PÈRE CASTOR'S WILD ANIMAL BOOKS"—with that delicate gaiety which shows they come from the French."

All were issued in paper-covered boards, cloth spines, and dust jackets. Otherwise, they are faithful to the French originals—with the same oblong size and same number of pages (35, plus one page of ads); they use the same cover art and layouts, page by page. And they have a comparable high quality of color printing.

PC.3a. Lida [Lida Durdikova-Faucher]. *Panache l'écureuil* [Panache the Squirrel]. Albums du Père Castor. Paris: Flammarion, 1934. [36] pp. 21 x 23 cm.

The mischievous squirrel Panache (Pompom/Mischief) lives happily, eats, and gambols in the forest with his parents and siblings. A hunter shoots Panache in the foot and carries him away. Poor Panache, kept in a cage as a pet, escapes and rejoins his family before winter sets in.

PC.3b. Lida. *Pompom the Little Red Squirrel.* Translated by Georges Duplaix. New York: Harper and Brothers, 1936. [38] pp. 26.5 x 23.5 cm. Stated "First edition".

Pictorial paper-covered boards. Cloth spine. Pictorial end papers. Pictorial dust jacket. $1.00. LC 36-33408. **First American edition**.

PC.3c. Lida. *Mischief the Squirrel.* No. 1, Père Castor's Wild Animal Books. Translated by Rose Fyleman. London: George Allen & Unwin, nd [c. 1938]. [36] pp. 21 x 23 cm.

Pictorial paper-covered boards. Cloth spine. Pictorial dust jacket. Trade edition, 2s 6d. Library edition, 3s 6d. **First British edition**.

PC.4a. Lida [Lida Durdikova-Faucher]. *Froux le lièvre* [Froux the Hare]. Albums du Père Castor. Paris: Flammarion, 1935. [36] pp. 21 x 23 cm.

The little hare Froux (Fluff/Frou) finds a companion, Capucine, to spend the summer with. Separated in the autumn while fleeing hunters, each spends a difficult winter alone. When spring arrives, they are joyously reunited.

PC.4b. Lida. *Fluff the Little Wild Rabbit*. Translated by Georges Duplaix. New York: Harper & Brothers, 1937. [40] pp. 26.5 x 23.5 cm. Stated "First edition".

Pictorial paper-covered boards. Cloth spine. Pink pictorial end papers. Dust jacket. $1.00. LC 37-3096. **First American edition**.

PC.4c. Lida. *Frou the Hare*. No. 4, Père Castor's Wild Animal Books. Translated by Rose Fyleman. London: George Allen & Unwin, nd [c. 1938]. [36] pp. 21 x 23 cm.

Pictorial paper-covered boards. Cloth spine. Pictorial dust jacket. Trade edition, 2s 6d. Library edition, 3s 6d. **First British edition**.

PC.5a. Lida [Lida Durdikova-Faucher]. *Plouf canard sauvage* [Plouf the Wild Duck]. Albums du Père Castor. Paris: Flammarion, 1935. [36] pp. 21 x 23 cm.

Plouf (Ploof), a wild duck, and his siblings are born in the swamp and learn to swim on the pond. Plouf is almost taken by a falcon and first uses his wings escaping a dog. At summer's end, one duckling is attacked by coots and is unable to migrate. But Plouf and his brother fly south with the flock.

PC.5b. Lida. *Plouf the Little Wild Duck*. Translated by Georges Duplaix. New York: Harper & Brothers, 1936. [40] pp. 26.5 x 23.5 cm. Stated "First edition".

Pictorial paper-covered boards. Cloth spine. Pictorial end papers. Pictorial dust jacket. $1.00. LC 36-33407. **First American edition**.

PC.5c. Lida. *Ploof the Wild Duck*. No. 3, Père Castor's Wild Animal Books. Translated by Rose Fyleman. London: George Allen & Unwin, nd [c. 1938]. [36] pp. 21 x 23 cm.

Pictorial paper-covered boards. Cloth spine. Pictorial dust jacket. Trade edition 2s 6d. Library edition 3s 6d. The title alters the spelling of Plouf to Ploof. **First British edition**.

PC.5d. Lida. *Ploof the Little Wild Duck*. Translated by Georges Duplaix. Père Castor Book. New York: Golden Press, 1966. [36] pp. 22 x 23.5 cm. Last page, first printing "A".

Pictorial boards. Plain mint green end papers. Goldencraft binding. Matching pictorial dust jacket. $2.95. LC 66-4430.

PC.6a. Lida [Lida Durdikova-Faucher]. *Bourru l'ours brun* [Bourru the Brown Bear]. Albums du Père Castor. Paris: Flammarion, 1936. [36] pp. 21 x 23 cm.

The bear cub, Bourru (Bruin), and his sister learn basic bear lessons from their mother and older brother in their first summer. But in the second summer they rely less on their mother and venture out alone. As winter descends, they find their own dens and thereafter live as adult bears.

PC.6b. Lida. *Bruin the Brown Bear*. Translated by Lily Duplaix. New York: Harper & Brothers, 1937. [32] pp. 26.5 x 23.5 cm. Stated "First edition. M-M".

Pictorial paper-covered boards. Brown cloth spine. Green pictorial end papers. Pictorial dust jacket. $1.00. LC 37-38861. **First American edition**.

PC.6c. Lida. *Bourru the Brown Bear.* No. 5, Père Castor's Wild Animal Books. Translated by Rose Fyleman. London: George Allen & Unwin, nd [c. 1939]. [36] pp. 21 x 23 cm.

Pictorial paper-covered boards. Cloth spine. Pictorial dust jacket. Trade edition 2s 6d. Library edition 3s 6d. **First British edition**.

PC.6d. Lida. *Bruin the Brown Bear.* A Père Castor Book. Translated by Lily Duplaix. New York: Golden Press, 1966. [36] pp. 22 x 23.5 cm. Last page, first printing "A".

Pictorial boards. Plain green end papers. Goldencraft binding. Matching pictorial dust jacket $2.95. LC 66-4429.

PC.7a. Lida [Lida Durdikova-Faucher]. *Scaf le phoque* [Scaf the Seal]. Albums du Père Castor. Paris: Flammarion, 1936. [36] pp. 21 x 23 cm.

Scaf (Scuff) and his herd of seals live peacefully in the Arctic Ocean, until attacks from sharks, walruses, Eskimos, and white hunters force them to seek new territory. Young Scaf, appointed as the new leader, leads the herd through encounters with a polar bear and whalers, and they reach a safe and happy island.

PC.7b. Lida. *Scuff the Seal.* Translated by Lily Duplaix. New York: Harper & Brothers, 1937. [32] pp. 26.5 x 23.5 cm. Stated "First edition".

Pictorial paper-covered boards. Cloth spine. Pictorial end papers. Pictorial dust jacket. $1.00. LC 37-35652. The title is changed to Scuff. **First American edition**.

PC.7c. Lida. *Scaf the Seal.* No. 6, Père Castor's Wild Animal Books. Translated by Rose Fyleman. London: George Allen & Unwin, nd [c. 1939]. [36] pp. 21 x 23 cm.

Pictorial paper-covered boards. Cloth spine. Pictorial dust jacket. Trade edition 2s 6d. Library edition 3s 6d. **First British edition**.

PC.7d. Lida. *Scuff the Seal.* A Père Castor Book. Translated by Lily Duplaix. New York: Golden Press, 1966. [36] pp. 22 x 23.5 cm. Last page, first printing "A".

Pictorial boards. Plain blue end papers. Goldencraft binding. Matching pictorial dust jacket. $2.95. LC 66-4431.

PC.8a. Lida [Lida Durdikova-Faucher]. *Quipic le hérisson* [Quipic the Hedgehog]. Albums du Père Castor. Paris: Flammarion, 1937. [36] pp. 21 x 23 cm.

The hedgehog Quipic (Spiky) and his family live in the garden, and are counted among the Good People—those animals who eat grubs and other destructive insects. Leaving the garden, Quipic encounters a snake and is captured by Gypsies before returning safely home. Winter comes, and the young hedgehogs hibernate and awake to adult lives in the spring.

PC.8b. Lida. *Spiky the Hedgehog.* Translated by Lily Duplaix. New York: Harper & Brothers, 1938. [34] pp. 26.5 x 23.5 cm. Stated "First edition G-N".

Pictorial paper covered-boards. Cloth spine. Pictorial end papers. Pictorial dust jacket. $1.00 on front flap. LC 38-29787. **First American edition**.

PC.8c. Lida. *Quipic the Hedgehog.* No. 2, Père Castor's Wild Animal Books. Translated by Rose Fyleman. London: George Allen & Unwin, nd [c. 1938]. [36] pp. 21 x 23 cm.

Pictorial paper-covered boards. Cloth spine. Pictorial dust jacket. Trade edition 2s 6d. Library edition 3s 6d. **First British edition**.

PC.8d. Lida. *Spiky the Hedgehog.* A Père Castor Book. Translated by Lily Duplaix. New York: Golden Press, 1966. [36] pp. 22 x 23.5 cm. Last page, first printing "A".

Pictorial boards. Plain colored end papers. Goldencraft binding. Matching pictorial dust jacket. $2.95. LC 66-4432.

PC.9a. Lida [Lida Durdikova-Faucher]. *Martin-pêcheur* [Kingfisher]. Albums du Père Castor. Paris: Flammarion, 1938. [36] pp. 21 x 23 cm.

The kingfisher and his mate build a nest along a stream and raise their young for six seasons until they die. But the next spring brings a new pair of kingfishers to the stream and the cycle of life continues.

PC.9b. Lida. *The Kingfisher.* Translated by Lily Duplaix. New York: Harper & Brothers, 1940. [32] pp. 26.5 x 23.5 cm. Stated "4-40 First Edition B-P".

Pictorial paper-covered boards. Cloth spine. Pictorial end papers. Pictorial dust jacket. $1.00. LC 40-6905. **First American edition**.

PC.9c. Lida. *Martin: the Kingfisher.* No. 7, Père Castor's Wild Animal Books. Translated by Rose Fyleman. London: George Allen & Unwin, nd [c. 1938]. [36] pp. 21 x 23 cm.

Pictorial paper-covered boards. Cloth spine. Pictorial dust jacket. Trade edition 2s 6d. Library edition 3s 6d. **First British edition**.

PC.10a. Lida [Lida Durdikova-Faucher]. *Coucou* [Cuckoo]. Albums du Père Castor. Paris: Flammarion, 1939. [36] pp. 21 x 23 cm.

A young boy makes a flute-whistle to converse with cuckoos. The interloping cuckoo lays her egg in the tits' nest, letting the small tit feed her chick. But the cuckoo fledgling becomes too big to leave the tree hollow and is abandoned when the tits fly south. The boy finds and frees the young cuckoo from her prison.

PC.10b. Lida. *Cuckoo.* Translated by Lily Duplaix. New York: Harper & Brothers, 1942. [32] pp. 26.5 x 23.5 cm. Stated "First edition".

Pictorial paper-covered boards. Cloth spine. Pictorial end papers. Pictorial dust jacket. $1.25. LC 42-36190. **First American edition.**

PC.10c. Lida. *Cuckoo.* Translated by Rose Fyleman. No. 8, Père Castor's Wild Animal Books. London: George Allen & Unwin, nd [c. 1939]. [36] pp. 21 x 23 cm.

Pictorial paper-covered boards. Cloth spine. Pictorial dust jacket. Trade edition 2s 6d. Library edition 3s 6d. **First British edition.**

PC.10d. Lida. *Cuckoo.* Montreal: Les Editions Variétés, nd [c. 1942, or later]. [34] pp. 25.75 x 22.70 cm.

Pictorial paper-covered boards, plain inside. Color lithographs, but some in only yellow and black. On title page: "Brentano's/ New York, N. Y."

This French-language Montreal edition is the only title from the *roman des bêtes* series we found published in French Canada. The pictures are rearranged and the one on page three of the original edition is omitted. The Montreal edition has the same end papers, a forest scene, as the Harper's edition.

Other Albums (PC.11 - PC.16)

PC.11. *ABC du Père Castor* [ABC of Père Castor]. Albums du Père Castor. Paris: Flammarion, 1936. [32] pp (26 pp., plus three sheets or six pages of game cards and instructions at the end). 28 x 24 cm.

Pictorial paper-covered boards. Yellow cloth spine. Pictorial grey-green end papers, continuous from front to rear, with ABC schemes used in one of the games. The cover (green background) has a color picture of three animals in a box, on the front and a rear view of the box, on the back, both with FR's letter forms. The title page reads "ABC jeux du Père Castor" [ABC games of Père Castor].

An ABC book, each page has capital and lower-case letters and a color lithograph of an animal, from A for âne to Z for zèbre. One of the games is to match the tear-out tabs with names of animals with corresponding pictures. The last page of the book is instructions (to adults) for playing the games.

PC.12a. Lacôte, Y. *Calendrier des enfants* [The Children's Calendar]. Albums du Père Castor. Paris: Flammarion, 1936. [28] pp. 17 x 18.5 cm.

Pictorial cream limp paper wraps, originally under glassine. When complete, this book has an illustrated, three-panel folding "Calendrier 1937" laid in. Twelve color lithographs, each facing a page of verse with a black line initial—one such double-page spread for each month of the year. Pictures of boys and girls doing a seasonal activity of each month.

Reissued as: Y. Lacôte. *Petites joies de chaque mois* [Small Joys of Each Month]. Albums du Père Castor. Paris: Flammarion, 1964. [22] pp. 18 x 21 cm.

PC.12b. Lacôte, Y. *The Children's Year*. Translated by Margaret Wise Brown. A Père Castor Book. New York: Harper & Brothers, 1937. [26] pp. Oblong octavo. Stated "First Edition".

Pictorial paper-covered boards. Pictorial end papers. Pictorial dust jacket. 75 cents. LC 37-21953. **First American edition**.

PC.13a. Andersen, H. C. *Ce que fait le vieux est bien fait* [What the Old Man Does is Well Done]. "Adaptation de Marie Colmont." Albums du Père Castor. Paris: Flammarion, 1939. [24] pp. 16.5 x 18.5 cm.

Twelve color lithographs alternating with 12 black line drawings (including title page). Pictorial buff (front) and green (back) laminated, stiff paper wraps, plain inside. Color picture of old couple on front cover; a cow with a bag of apples on the back.

A rendering of Andersen's tale of an old farmer who foolishly keeps trading his animals down for less valuable animals, but with dumb luck comes out in the end with a bushel of gold.

PC.13b. Andersen, H. C. *The Old Man Is Always Right.* New York: Harper & Brothers, 1940. [28] pp. 24 x 22 cm. Stated "First edition, I-P".

Pictorial paper-covered boards. Cloth spine. Pictorial end papers. Pictorial dust jacket. 75 cents. LC 40-34279. **First American edition**.

PC.14. Colmont, Marie (pseudonym of Marie Collin Delavaud, née Anne-Marie Moréal de Brevans). *Quand Cigalou s'en va dans la montagne* [When Cigalou Goes to the Mountain]. Albums du Père Castor. Paris: Flammarion, 1939. [24] pp. 16.5 x 18.5 cm.

Pictorial laminated stiff paper wraps, front with color picture of Cigalou, the back with his large dog and a smaller picture of Cigalou's head, both against black backgrounds. Twelve full-page full-color lithographs and three black line drawings.

The small boy Cigalou and his dog wander up the mountain, encounter wild animals, such as a snake, but are befriended by the various domesticated animals of the mountain pastures.

PC.15a. Colmont, Marie. *Michka.* Albums du Père Castor. Paris: Flammarion, 1941. [24] pp. 16.5 x 18.5.

Eight color lithographs (some double-page) alternating with black line drawings. Pictorial stiff paper wraps. Front cover has a color picture of Michka with an armload of toys, the back a color picture of a winter bird, both against grey backgrounds. First or early printing has on last page (with final drawing of Michka in shoe): "DÉCHAUX PARIS-7-41." Back cover: "IMP. M. DÉCHAUX.PARIS."

Michka is a sentient teddy bear, who leaves his spoiled mistress for a life of freedom. Learning of an ill and poor boy, Michka is taken by the spirit of Christmas and gives himself as a present to the boy and becomes a toy again.

FR originally illustrated this story for *Paris-soir dimanche* in 1936 [FS.12].

PC.15b. Colmont, Marie. *Christmas Bear.* "A Père Castor Book." A translation of Michka by Constance Hirsch. New York: Golden Press, 1966. [24] pp. 18.75 x 21.5 cm.

Pictorial paper-covered boards. Plain yellow end papers. Goldencraft binding $1.95. LC 66-6197. **First American edition**.

PC.16. Colmont, Marie. *Pic et Pic et Colégram* [Peak and Peak and Colégram]. Albums du Père Castor. Paris: Flammarion, 1941. [24] pp. 16.5 x 18.5 cm.

Pictorial stiff paper wraps, illustrated front and back (smaller drawing) in color against black. Each page has either one or two small color in-text lithographs. First or early printing on last page (with ads): "Déchaux Paris-7-41."

The sprite Colégram tries to help people but overdoes everything, creating disaster in his enthusiasm. The forest creatures advise him to reflect and go slowly. Today, simple but pleasurable things, like soft summer breezes, are the result of Colégram's more restrained good deeds.

Les "Petits Père Castor" (PC.17 - PC.27)

After FR left France in 1941, Flammarion used drawings made in 1940-41 and left with Faucher to issue 11 miniature picture books in the wartime subseries, *Les "Petits Père Castor,"* most issued in 1941 and

1942, but the last in 1948. The covers uniformly are 15 x 12.5 cm. All the books have 10 leaves or 20 unnumbered pages, counting the title and last pages. All are center-stapled into laminated stiff paper wraps, printed on one side only; the insides of the covers are always plain. The cover of each book is of a different background color. Each front cover has a different color thematic picture; the back covers have a small thematic color picture.

The illustrations are either all color or a mix of color and black line drawings. Ten to 20 illustrations are in each book and are spread throughout. The title page of most books (except *Mes amis* and *Drôles de bêtes*) are illustrated with a black line thematic drawing or with a vignette. The last page of most contains ads for other Père Castor books.

All the books were printed by M. Déchaux, Paris, whose credit line in capital letters usually appears on the bottom of the last page and on the bottom of the back cover. The printer's line on the last page of the books published in 1941 and 1942 indicates the last two digits of the year of publication, and the full line reads such as: "IMP. M. DÉCHAUX. PARIS. 41." The last book, published in 1948, has a longer, now standard credit line.

PC.17. François, Paul. *Mes amis* [My Friends]. Les "Petits Père Castor," No. 1. Paris: Flammarion, 1941. [20] pp. 15 x 12.5 cm.

Yellow covers with picture of a puppy in front of a doghouse on the front. Ten color illustrations of various other animal friends, concluding with a picture of three children in a donkey cart. The minimal text is printed in brown ink.

PC.18. Lida [Lida Durdikova-Faucher]. *Les animaux du zoo* [Animals of the Zoo]. Les "Petits Père Castor," No. 2. Paris: Flammarion, 1941. [20] pp. 15 x 12.5 cm.

Tan covers with a picture of a bear, a giraffe, and a caribou on the front. Ten color lithographs of various zoo animals, with a brief text about each.

PC.19. Nelly-Roussel, Mireille. *Les oiseaux du zoo* [Birds of the Zoo]. Les "Petits Père Castor," No. 3. Paris: Flammarion, 1941. [20] pp. 15 x 12.5 cm.

Yellow covers with picture of two toucans on the front. Ten color lithographs of various zoo birds, with a brief text about each.

PC.20. François, Paul. *Drôles de bêtes* [Strange Animals]. Les "Petits Père Castor," No. 4. Paris: Flammarion, 1941. [20] pp. 15 x 12.5 cm.

Brown covers with a color picture of an elephant shrew on the front. Ten color lithographs and eight black line drawings. Various small and exotic wild animals, with a brief text about each.

PC.21. François, Paul. *Une histoire de souris* [A Story of a Mouse]. Les "Petits Père Castor," No. 5. Paris: Flammarion, 1942. [20] pp. 15 x 12.5 cm.

Blue covers with a picture of a mouse and cheese on the front. Ten color lithographs and one black line drawing.

A hungry baby mouse, Caroline, against mother's orders, ventures out of her hole, is harassed by the cat and caught by the housewife, but finally escapes and returns to mother.

PC.22. François, Paul. *La maison des oiseaux* [The Birdhouse]. Les "Petits Père Castor," No. 6. Paris: Flammarion, 1942. [20] pp. 15 x 12.5 cm.

Covers with color picture of birds in a feeder on the front. Ten color lithographs and eight black line drawings.

An instructional book for making bird houses and feeders and a pictorial guide to some common European birds.

PC.23. Perrault, [Charles]. *Cendrillon* [Cinderella]. Les "Petits Père Castor," No. 7. Paris: Flammarion, 1942. [20] pp. 15 x 12.5 cm.

Red covers with color picture of Cinderella fleeing the ball. Ten color lithographs and 10 black line headpieces. The text begins on the title page and ends on the last page of the book, precluding the usual ads.

PC.24. Grimm, Jacob. *Les musiciens de la ville de Brême* [The Musicians of the Town of Bremen]. Les "Petits Père Castor," No. 8. Paris: Flammarion, 1942. [20] pp. 15 x 12.5 cm.

Black covers with a color picture of the four musicians—a donkey, a rooster, a dog, and a cat. Ten color lithographs and eight black line drawings.

PC.25. Nodier, Charles. *Histoire du chien de Brisquet* [Story of Brisquet's Dog]. Les "Petits Père Castor," No. 9. Paris: Flammarion, 1942. [20] pp. 15 x 12.5 cm.

Yellow covers with a circular design on the front (framing the title) of two children and of a wolf attacking the dog. Ten color lithographs.

Traditional French folk story of a heroic dog who gives his life protecting two children from a savage wolf in the forest. The woodsman father, Brisquet, arrives in the nick of time and kills the wolf with an axe.

PC.26. Colmont, Marie. *Histoire du nègre Zo'hio et de l'oiseau Moqueur* [Story of the African boy Zo'hio and the Mocking Bird]. Les "Petits Père Castor," No. 10. Paris: Flammarion, 1942. [20] pp. 15 x 12.5 cm.

Dark grey covers covered with small pictures of many African animals. Ten color lithographs, each including a figure of the African boy Zo'hio. Re-illustrated by Gaston de Sainte-Croix in 1959.

Zo'hio goes into the bush where he is threatened by wild animals and harassed by the mocking bird of the title. He cuts off a lion's tail and returns home a hero, severed tail in hand.

PC.27. Anonymous (text). *Le royaume de la mer* [The Kingdom of the Sea]. Les "Petits Père Castor," No. 26. Paris: Flammarion, 1948. [20] pp. 15 x 12.5 cm.

Yellow covers with pictures of marine creatures. Ten color lithographs, with black line drawings on title pages.

Child's natural history of sea life, describing the appearance and behavior of marine plants and animals.

Other French Books and Covers (OF.1 - OF.4)

OF.1. *La Fontaine—Fables* [Fables of La Fontaine]. Laboratoires Rosa, nd [c. 1930]. [12] pp., including insides of covers. 27 x 21 cm.

Pictorial soft paper wraps. Center stapled. Album of 12 fables, each with a large three-color illustration in black, gold, and rust. Though issued as a promotional premium [listed also as B8, EA.4], this children's book contains only oblique advertising matter, on the inside of the back cover. Mentioned by René Thiébaut in *L'art publicitaire pharmaceutique* (Thiébaut, 1939).

OF.2. Mariotti, Jean. *Les contes de Poindi* [The Tales of Poindi]. Paris: Éditions Stock, Delamain et Boutelleau, 1941. 211 pp. 19 x 14.5 cm.

New redrawn, expanded-text edition of *Les contes de Poindi* (Domino Press, 1939). See full description under Domino Press [DP.5c].

OF.3. Dumas, Alexandre. *Tom, Jacques & Cie* [Tom, Jack, and Co.]. Adaptation of *Capitaine Pamphile*, by T.O. [Tatiana Ossorguine?]. Paris: Stock, [c. 1941] 2nd ed., 1942. 184 pp. 19 x 14 cm. *Collection Maïa*, Série B.

Ten full-page black pen and ink drawings, often depicting the antics of a bear and a monkey. The cover design is also by FR, and is used on other books in Stock's Maïa series.

OF.4. *Collection Maïa*. Librairie Stock, Paris, c. 1927-1950.

FR designed a generic front and back cover (and spine images) used on many of the books issued in Stock's *Collection Maïa* of children's and young people's books, beginning about 1927.

Paper covers mounted on boards or paper covers. Different pictures on the front and back covers; the bi-color images (black and a single color that varies by book) are arrays of boys' adventures, mostly of human figures and animals in action scenes. The spines are similarly decorated. Signed "Rojan" on front and "FR" on back (on fuselage of airplane).

Visual examination of two other, unattributed cover designs used in the Maïa series suggests they also may have been done by FR, based on the style and similarities to designs he used elsewhere.

French Children's Magazines (FS.1 - FS.43)

Les enfants de France (FS.1 - FS.5)

The Paris newspaper, *Figaro*, published a magazine for young people, *Les Enfants de France* [The Children of France], to which FR contributed a few illustrations from 1929-1933.

FS.1. Black-ink illustrations for "Les Pages du journal de Fox-Mikki chien" [Pages from the Diary of the Fox Terrier Mikki] by Sacha Tchorny in No. 25, 1 March 1929. Presumably an excerpt from the Russian-language book published two years earlier [B1, RU.2a].

FS.2. Two illustrations, one color and one black ink, for a Christmas story, "Le rouble perpétuel" [The Perpetual Ruble], in the Noël 1931 issue.

FS.3. Color cover, with action picture of smiling boy skiing downhill. No. 94. 15 January 1932. Two-page spread of skier's going uphill on skis, on left, and skiing downhill, on right. Vignette on back cover of skiers going uphill on skis.

FS.4. A large drawing for Jean Mariotti's "La légende des cloches: savez-vous pourquoi elles viennent de Rome?" [Legend of the Bells: Do You Know Why They Come from Rome?]. Easter issue in early 1930s, probably 15 March 1932. Two-page spread with a garland of color drawings of Easter-themed images. FR reworked this design for pp. 78-79 in *Animal Stories* (1944) [B5, GB.2].

FS.5. Black ink and color illustrations for a serialized story, "Histoire d'une girouette" [Story of a Weather Vane], in several issues in 1933, at least from No. 118, 15 January 1933 through No. 138, 15 November 1933.

Pour les enfants (FS.6 - FS.43)

From 1936-39, FR illustrated 38 children's stories that appeared on the Sunday children's page, *Pour les enfants* [For the Children], of the Sunday supplement, *Paris-Soir Dimanche* [Paris-Soir Sunday], to the popular Paris newspaper, *Paris-Soir*. Starting in January 1938, the independent supplement appeared on Saturdays instead of Sunday and was included as part of the regular newspaper.

FS.6. Eight uncredited drawings of exotic animals, each with a short text on how the animal is unusual, titled, "Dans le monde entier" [In the Whole World . . .]. 15 March 1936.

FS.7. Three drawings of a girl with a wolf for Marie Colmont's "Marlaguette." 2 August 1936.

FS.8. Two drawings, of boys sitting in a group in the woods, and of boys throwing stones at another boy, for Gaston Tesseyre's "L'aventure de Jolicœur, le voleur volé" [The Adventure of Jolicœur, a Robber Robbed]. 23 August 1936.

FS.9. Two drawings, of heads of three girls looking in amazement, and of lioness with five cubs, for Georges G.-Toudouze's "Les six lions dans la brousse"[Six Lions in the Bush]. 20 September 1936.

FS.10. Two drawings, of an adult watching toys come to life and leaving toy cabinet, and of a sleeping child with toys pulling at bedcovers, for Christian Schewaebel's "La révolte: conte pour mon jeune cousin Philippe . . . et les autres" [The Revolt: Story for My Young Cousin Philippe . . . and Others]. 11 October 1936.

FS.11. Two drawings, of a family sitting at the dinner table, and of boy looking at pastry display in window, for André Lichtenberger's "Une nouvelle aventure de Trott: Éclairs et tonnerre" [A New Adventure of Trott: Lightning and Thunder]. 29 November 1936.

FS.12. Two drawings, of toy bear walking out of house with footprints in snow, and of Santa putting toys in chimney with reindeer and sleigh nearby, for Marie Colmont's "Michka, conte de Noël" [Michka, a Christmas Story]. 27 December 1936. FR illustrated this story as one of the Albums du Père Castor in 1941 [PC.15] in a similar style, but with different drawings.

FS.13. Four uncredited drawings, each slightly different, of a dense crowd at a carnival, in a game for children to find the differences in the pictures. Titled "Que manque-t-il?" [What is Missing?]. 24 January 1937.

FS.14. Two drawings, of a boy standing at open door of dentist's office, and of the boy walking beside his mother, for André Lichtenberger's "Trott et le dentiste" [Trott and the Dentist]. 4 April 1937.

FS.15. Two drawings, of a girl sitting, and of the girl standing and watching boy constructing a playhouse of pieces of boards, for André Lichtenberger's "Trott se marie" [Trott Gets Married]. 8 May 1937.

FS.16. One drawing, of an old peasant woman sitting on log and looking at a deer and two rabbits, for Marie Colmont's "Le balai fleuri" [The Flowered Broom]. 12 June 1937.

FS.17. Two drawings, of a boy standing by front tire of truck, and the boy with dog and magpie, for André Lichtenberger's "Trott, la pie et le Guatemala" [Trott, the Magpie, and Guatemala]. 11 July 1937 .

FS.18. Two drawings, of two small boats, and of a boy holding a fish, for Georges G.-Toudouze's "L'extraordinaire sauvetage d'un matelot de treize ans" [The Extraordinary Rescue of a Thirteen-year-old Sailor]. 12 September 1937.

FS.19. Two drawings of a boy in knickers at doorways, for André Lichtenberger's "Trott et le gangster" [Trott and the Gangster]. 10 October 1937.

FS.20. Two drawings, of a boy in a tree, and of the boy with animals, for Marie Colmont's "Histoire de Jean Méchant" [Story of Jean Méchant]. 31 October 1937.

FS.21. One uncredited drawing of a boy in knickers looking at portrait of Louis XIV hanging over antique table, for André Lichtenberger's "Trott et Louis XIV" [Trott and Louis XIV]. 14 November 1937.

FS.22. Pictorial border for entire page, uncredited, and two drawings, of a hunter loading a crossbow, and of the hunter lying on ground with several animals hovering over him, for Marie Colmont's "Guttri le chasseur" [Guttri the Hunter]. 1 January 1938.

FS.23. Two drawings, of a boy in knickers leaning against wall, and of a girl sitting on wooden bench, for André Lichtenberger's "Trott et les étrennes de Crabotte" [Trott and the New Year's Gifts of Crabotte]. 22 January 1938.

FS.24. One drawing, of a boy in a rowboat approaching two people on a raft for Georges G.-Toudouze's "Un détective de treize ans" [A Thirteen-year-old Detective]. 12 February 1938.

FS.25. One drawing, of an old woman with a book sitting by the fire, surrounded by farm animals, for Marie Colmont's "La bonne vieille" [The Good Old Woman]. 19 February 1938.

FS.26. Two drawings, of a pampered cat, and of a woman with the same cat in her lap, for Marie Colmont's "Le Roi Chat" [The King Cat]. 12 March 1938.

FS.27. One drawing, of a standing boy with a shovel facing a girl, for André Lichtenberger's "Histoires de Trott" [Stories of Trott]. 26 March 1938.

FS.28. One drawing, of a native African boy carrying Philippe over his shoulder, for "Comment Alabouri, le petit nègre, sauva Philippe dans le jungle" [How Alabouri, the little negro, saved Philippe in the jungle]. [Christian Schewaebel]. 2 April 1938.

FS.29. Two drawings, of four animals (cat, frog, snake and heron) and egg, and of a girl with hen and chicks at her feet, for Marie Colmont's "Histoire de Pauv' Coco" [Story of Poor Coco]. 16 April 1938.

FS.30. Two drawings, of the gold tiger, and of a sitting fakir, for Marie Colmont's "Le moineau de plomb et le tigre doré" [The Lead Sparrow and the Gilded Tiger]. 21 May 1938.

FS.31. One drawing of two mice in leaves, for Alexei Remizov's "Aventure de Rongetout trapue et de Trottinette moustachue" [The Adventure of Squat Rongetout and Moustached Trottinette]. 4 June 1938.

FS.32. Two drawings, of insects with twigs and leaves, and of a little girl on all fours with a collecting net, for Marie Zindel's "La guêpe et la mouche" [The Wasp and the Fly]. 2 July 1938.

FS.33. One drawing, of the boy Trott and an African boy, for André Lichtenberger's "Trott et le Roi Bango" [Trott and King Bango]. 9 July 1938.

FS.34. Two drawings, of a boy store clerk, and of several children with a dog, for Marie Colmont's "Chien Fou" [Mad Dog]. 23 July 1938.

FS.35. Two drawings, of the boy Trott and a crab fisherman, and of the boy looking at open sea, for André Lichtenberger's "Trott et le crabe géant" [Trott and the Giant Crab]. 27 August 1938.

FS.36. Two drawings, of a boy petting a goat, and of a woman and a jumping goat, for Marie Colmont's "Ma douce . . ." [My Sweet . . .]. 10 September 1938.

FS.37. One drawing, of a wood sprite, owl, crow, and mushroom, for Marie Colmont's "Poulet des Bois" [Poulet of the Woods]. 3 December 1938. Story continued, with a drawing of sprite, frog, and bird on lily pads. 10 December 1938.

FS.38. Large drawing for Marie Colmont's "L'arbre de Noël d'Anne-Lise" [Anne-Lise's Christmas Tree]. 24 December 1938. The first publication of FR's familiar Christmas design of young girl sitting in snow beside decorated tree and surrounded by small animals. Similar drawings were later published [B5, CP.2; B6, AP.4; and B8, CA.4, 25].

FS.39. One drawing, of a hare, a monkey and two humorous blazons, for André Demaison's "Le singe et le lièvre" [The Monkey and the Hare]. 18 March 1939.

FS.40. Two drawings, of an old woman, cat and chicken, and of a chicken with sprites in bean pod, for Simonne Ratel's "Verduret,

Mignonnet et la petite Velours" [Verduret, Mignonnet and Little Velvet]. 8 April 1939.

FS.41. Three drawings, of a hobby horse, of a girl on flying carpet, and of a boy on flying horse, for Françoise Estachy's "Zamou et le cheval" [Zamou and the Horse]. 29 April 1939.

FS.42. Two drawings, of a hare with sparrows, and of a hare with Buddha figure, for André Demaison's "Le lièvre et les moineaux" [The Hare and the Sparrows]. 3 June 1939.

FS.43. One drawing, of a mother and two children at tables writing letters, for Maxence Van der Meersch's "Pourra-t-il venir le soir de Noël?" [Will He Come Home for Christmas Eve?] 22 December 1939.

B4

British and American Children's Books

For 25 different English-language, mostly American publishers, Rojankovsky illustrated 45 full children's books—all in addition to the books for Golden Press listed in the last section and the many Golden Books for Simon & Schuster.

The first three titles were completed while the illustrator was still in France: Moncrieff's *The White Drake* (London: Methuen, 1936), Dunne's *An Experiment with St. George* (London: Faber & Faber, 1939), and Cothren's *The Adventures of Dudley and Gilderoy*. The last from this period was completed just before he left France in mid-1941 and was published almost simultaneously in 1941 in New York by Dutton and a few months later in London by Faber and Faber. The drawings for *Cortez* were done earlier, also in France, but not published until 1947 (Random House, New York).

The books published between 1942 and 1951, with a few granted exceptions, were governed by Rojankovsky's exclusive contracts with Georges Duplaix and Western Publishing. The books were designed and manufactured by the Artists and Writers Guild (Western Publishing), wholesaled to other publishers, and issued with the imprints of Harper,

Garden City, and Grosset & Dunlap. After the Guild contract expired in 1951, Rojankovsky was free to work independently, and he created books with Viking Press, Scribner's, Harcourt Brace, and other prominent houses.

Rojankovsky illustrated a few children's books that do not bear his name and, until now, have been unattributed—namely, the two panoramas published by Platt & Munk in the 1940s. The Russian-language book *Zaichata* (New York, 1955) was also illustrated anonymously. Eluding us, a few others possibly exist.

Many of the books have statements on the copyright pages that they were "published simultaneously" in Canada. That is, the American editions were distributed by Canadian subsidiaries or other publishers in Canada but none bear Canadian imprints. In the 1930s, a number of Rojankovsky's Père Castor picture books were translated into English and reissued in the United States and Britain, and these are listed under Père Castor. Domino Press also published the primary English-language version of *Tales of Poindi* (1938) in New York.

British Books (AB.1 - AB.2)

AB.1. Moncrieff, Ann Scott. *The White Drake and Other Tales.* London: Methuen, 1936. ix + 165 pp. 20.4 x 14.7 cm. Copyright page: design of small arch and "First published in 1936."

Fifteen line drawings, including those on half-title, frontis, and title page. "Illustrated by Rojan." White cloth covers, blocked in blue, with design of standing drake, repeating the small drawing on the title page. Dust jacket (in black and blue) repeats the frontis picture, with "5 s. net" on back panel.

AB.2. Dunne, John William. *An Experiment with St. George.* London: Faber & Faber, 1939. 230 pp. 22.2 x 16 cm. Copyright page: "First published in November MCMXXXIX."

Thirty-one line drawings, including the frontis and title page. Pinkish brown cloth, with the spine lettered in gold. Plain white end papers. Dust jacket decorated with a pastiche of several illustrations in the book.

J. W. Dunne was immensely pleased with the art work and closely attentive to the details and asked FR to make several changes to bring the pictures into complete harmony with the text.

In the past, St. George slew the dragon and won the princess. This sequel picks up when an earthquake has just released all the world's evil spirits, led by the witch Circe. St. George and his bride, Princess Cleodolinda, outwit Circe and her minions and trap them beneath a volcanic explosion.

American Books, Various Publishers (AB.3 - AB.45)

AB.3a. Cothren, Marion B[enedict]. *The Adventures of Dudley and Gilderoy. An Adaptation of Algernon Blackwood's Story*. New York: E. P. Dutton and Company, 1941. 32 pp. 24 x 16 cm. Copyright page: "First Edition."

Eighteen line drawings, including on the title page. Pictorial light blue cloth, black stamping, repeating the design on the title. Plain yellow end papers. The color pictorial dust jacket, with $1.00 on the flap, reproduces a watercolor of the parrot pulling the ear of the cat, an image that does not appear in the book. According to E.P. Dutton's successor, this book was on Dutton's 1941 spring list and was sold to Faber & Faber on October 31, 1941. See first British edition below.

Cothren's adaptation for children is faithfully extracted from Blackwood's much longer *Dudley & Gilderoy: A Nonsense* (London: Ernest Benn, 1929), an extended meditation on the relationship of two good but uneasy friends. The unlikely pair—

Dudley, a grey parrot, and Gilderoy, a scruffy street cat—leave their comfortable existence in a manor house in Kent and travel by train for a two-day adventure in London, before returning to the security of home.

AB.3b. Cothren, Marion B[enedict]. *The Adventures of Dudley and Gilderoy. Adapted from Algernon Blackwood's Story by Marion B. Cothren.* Preface by Algernon Blackwood (which the Dutton edition does not have). London: Faber and Faber, 1941. 35 pp. 25.5 x 16 cm. Copyright page: "First published in October MCMXLI by Faber and Faber Limited."

Pictorial yellow cloth, black stamping. Plain white end papers. Listed at 3s 6d. The white pictorial dust jacket reproduces in blue ink the drawing from page 12—the parrot riding on the back of the cat. Lettering in red. Same 18 line drawings and main text as the Dutton edition, though the size, pagination, layout and typography vary.

AB.4. *The Tall Book of Mother Goose.* New York: Harper & Brothers, 1942. 120 pp. 31 x 13.5 cm. Stated "First Edition."

In the first printing, on page 31, the last line reads "Oh! they are sluts indeed." The word *sluts* is altered to *bad* in the next four printings, though all indicate "First Edition."

Full-color illustrations alternating with halftones. Pictorial paper-covered boards. Pictorial end papers. Dust jacket (same design as covers), with picture continuous from back to front. $1.00 on front jacket flap.

The first book Rojankovsky illustrated after coming to the United States in late 1941. Uniform with *The Tall Book of Nursery Tales*, below.

AB.5. *The Tall Book of Nursery Tales.* New York: Harper & Brothers, 1944. 120 pp. 31 x 13 cm.

Full-color and halftone pictures. First or early printing examined is in paper-covered boards, with a wraparound illustration, continuous front to back. Pictorial end papers include a small picture of the earlier *The Tall Book of Mother Goose*. Dust jacket has an expansion of the picture on page 6, continuous front to back. The front jacket flap has an ad (but no blurbs) for only this book, $1.00 at top, and "No. 5434" at bottom. Back flap has three blurbs for the earlier *The Tall Book of Mother Goose* and "30 up/No. 5102" at bottom.

Just So Stories Series (AB.6 - AB.12)

The six books in the *Just So Stories Series* were issued in identical formats and materials. All have 28 pages and are 24 x 17.5 cm. All have a mix of multicolor and halftone pictures. All are in paper-covered boards, each with a different cover picture that is repeated on the dust jacket. The end papers in all six books have the same design. The first four were published simultaneously at 50 cents each. The last two were published five years later in 1947, also at 50 cents each.

AB.6. Kipling, Rudyard. *The Elephant's Child.* Garden City, NY: Garden City Publishing, 1942.

AB.7. Kipling, Rudyard. *How the Camel Got His Hump.* Garden City, NY: Garden City Publishing, 1942.

AB.8. Kipling, Rudyard. *How the Leopard Got His Spots.* Garden City, NY: Garden City Publishing, 1942.

AB.9. Kipling, Rudyard. *How the Rhinoceros Got His Skin.* Garden City, NY: Garden City Publishing, 1942.

AB.10a. Kipling, Rudyard. *Four Famous Just So Stories.* Garden City, NY: Garden City Publishing, nd [1942]. 25 x 37 cm.

A pictorial pop-up box designed by FR to contain the four

books of *Just So Stories*. For an early promotion, the first editions of 1942, stacked two high and two wide, came thus packaged and were collectively titled *Four Famous Just So Stories*. The pop-up design incorporates the chief story characters and is a composite scene from the four books. The folded yellow cardboard box is also decorated top and bottom and is marked "licensed under Ben Klein." Photo in Alderson (1992).

A one-volume edition incorporating the first four books in Garden City's *Just So Stories* series (1942) was issued as:

AB.10b. Kipling, Rudyard. *The Elephant's Child and Other Just-So Stories*. Garden City, NY: Junior Literary Guild and Garden City Publishing Company, nd [1942]. 112 pp. 23.5 x 17 cm.

This combined edition was chosen by the Editorial Board [including Eleanor Roosevelt] of the Junior Literary Guild "as an outstanding publication of the month for youngest readers (P Group)." Full-color and halftone illustrations, as in the originals. Dust jacket has the same illustration as the jacket and cover of *The Elephant's Child*.

AB.11. Kipling, Rudyard. *The Butterfly That Stamped*. Garden City, NY: Garden City Publishing, 1947.

AB.12. Kipling, Rudyard. *The Cat That Walked by Himself*. Garden City, NY: Garden City Publishing, 1947.

* * *

AB.13. *Grandfather's Farm Panorama: Ten Feet Long*. New York: Platt & Munk Co., 1943. No. 890. Folded cover 22 x 25.50 cm, unfolded 22 x 300 cm.

A folding, panoramic shape book without a text. Full-color pictures are of different farm animals and their babies. Pictorial paper-covered boards. The cloth spine is one inch wide to accommodate the ten heavy folding panels, which are hinged with the same cloth tape. The two covers and each of the ten panels have pictures printed as mirror images, front and back, so the panorama can be viewed on either side. All the interior panels are shaped (die cut) along the top profile of each animal. Published at $2.00. Publisher announced first printing of 50,000 copies.

This book is unusual because FR's name does not appear on it and the illustrations are not signed in the plate. Yet the publisher identified FR on the review slips; the review in the *New York Times Book Review* (26 March 1944: 7) names FR as the illustrator; the publisher's records and other accounts confirm this. Cf. *Choo-choo Panorama* (1945) below.

AB.14. *Choo-choo Panorama: Ten Feet Long.* New York: Platt & Munk Co., 1945. No. 891. Folded cover 22 x 25.50 cm, unfolded 22 x 300 cm.

A folding, panoramic shape book without a text. Full-color pictures. Pictorial paper-covered boards. The cloth spine is one inch wide to accommodate the ten heavy folding panels, which are hinged with the same cloth tape. The back cover and each of the ten panels have pictures printed as mirror images, front and back, so the panorama can be viewed on either side. The front cover has a picture of a modern streamlined diesel train, with the first, station scene on the verso. The panorama pictures the boarding of passengers, the engine, and each car of a toy-like steam train, one car to a panel, as it moves through the countryside. Most cars are loaded with circus and farm animals, children, or families. All the interior panels are shaped (die cut) along the top profile of each picture. Published at $2.00. Publisher announced first printing of 50,000 copies. In certain later issues, the tops of the panels are not die cut to shapes but are straight edged.

This book is unusual because FR's name does not appear on it and the illustrations are not signed in the plate. Yet the publisher identified FR on the review slips; the review in the *New York Times Book Review* (18 November 1945: II-2) names FR as the illustrator; the publisher's records and other accounts confirm this.

AB.15a. Andersen, Hans Christian. *The Ugly Duckling*. New York: Grosset & Dunlap, 1945. [ii] + [30] pp. 24 x 21 cm.

Nine full-page, full-color lithographs from watercolors, alternating with seven black halftones, plus a small drawing of the hatchling swan on the title page and illustrated end papers. Signed in plate of title page as "F. Rojankovsky."

Pink paper-covered boards, with color picture of young "duckling" on front cover and a smaller halftone of a mature swan on the back. End papers have color picture of young "duckling" calling to swans flying overhead. The pink dust jacket repeats the designs on the front and back boards. Front flap has an ad for this book and "5050" at top right, indicating 50 cents, the announced price. Back flap has ad for *Peter Pan* for this first or early printing.

AB.15b. Andersen, Hans Christian. *Das hässliche junge Entlein.* Saarbrücken: Saar Verlag, nd [c. 1950?]. [ii] + 38 pp. 23 x 21 cm.

Eighteen full-page, full-color lithographs from watercolors. Covers of blue paper-covered boards. Front cover has picture of seated old woman, animals and tall clock, a revised version of that on page [18] of the Grosset and Dunlap/Artists and Writers Guild edition of 1945 [AB.15a].

This German-language edition has all revised artwork and three entirely different color pictures of (page 9) various fowl in a chicken yard, (page 15) a peasant woman and child with dog chasing the duckling, and (page 29) a peasant man and the duckling in a snowy meadow. The artwork was apparently revised and supplemented by FR, possibly for the publisher to avoid copyright infringement; this German edition bears no copyright data or reference to the earlier edition. Compared to the original Grosset and Dunlap edition, the artwork in this German edition is redrawn with minor rearrangements of figures and objects and with color variations; some scenes are truncated, others have new and different details; all the images are reversed as if loosely copied from printed impressions; some text pages have added in-text sepia halftones of details extracted from the color illustrations on the facing pages; the two pictures of the duckling on Grosset and Dunlap's cover and title page are omitted.

AB.16. Averill, Esther. *Daniel Boone.* New York: Harper & Brothers, 1945. 60 pp. 28.5 x 21.5 cm. Stated "First edition," i.e., first thus by Harper.

A new but pictorially rearranged edition, with an expanded text by Averill. See full descriptive entry under Domino Press [B2, DP.1f].

AB.17. Newcomb, Covelle. *Cortez the Conqueror.* New York: Random House, 1947. 106 + [5] pp. 33.5 x 26 cm.

Large line drawings throughout (double-page, full-page, half-page), some embellished in dull gold ink, with smaller head and tail pieces and other decorations, plus pictorial half title, title, copyright, and contents pages.

Orange cloth covers with Aztec design above the title on front. Gold end papers with various Aztec designs in black and white. Dust jacket illustrated front and back (gold and black on maroon).

Dust jacket has ad for this book and age code "(100-140)" on the front flap. Rear flap has ad for White's *Lost Worlds*. Announced at $3.

The illustrations for *Cortez* were made in Paris in the late 1930s, before FR left in 1941. He originally intended this project as a more highly designed production for Domino Press.

AB.18. Abbott, Moreton. *The Puss 'n Boots Book*. Wilmington, CA: Coast Fishing Company, 1949. [21] pp. 23.5 x 14.3 cm.

Twelve illustrated pages, 11 in color, with two drawings each. Pictorial paper covers, center stapled.

On verso of front cover: "The drawings in this book, reproduced from [*Saturday Evening Post*] advertisements prepared for Coast Fishing Company, are by Feodor Rojankovsky, whose talent, imagination, and humor have made him one of the country's foremost illustrators of children's book." The booklet is an advertisement for the company's "Puss 'n Boots" brand of canned cat food and was distributed as a product promotion. [See B8, AA.12. for description of corresponding ads].

A series of double-page spreads makes a partial ABC book of nine selected letters of the alphabet, A for Aardvark to W for Walrus. Each verse-like description of the favorite food of a different animal is followed by "C is for CAT" and the illustrated ruminations of a cat on her favorite food—always fish. The book concludes with a pitch for "Puss 'n Boots" cat food and a picture of a can of the company's cat food, with some of FR's animal drawings around it.

AB.19. Prishvin, M[ikhail Mikhailovich]. *The Treasure Trove of the Sun*. Translated from the Russian by Tatiana Balkoff-Drowne. New York: The Viking Press, 1952. 80 pp. 27.25 x 19.50 cm. "Published by the Viking Press, Inc., September 1952."

Fifty full-color lithographs, including several full-page pictures and numerous small drawings. Beige cloth with orange design (sun over trees) on front cover, with spine lettered in orange. Pictorial end papers. Dust jacket, with illustrations from the book on front and back panels. $2.75 on front flap.

Reissued from new plates in August 1967; the new overall size is slightly smaller at: 26.5 x 19 cm.

A modern story by the Russian nature writer about an orphaned brother and sister, Russian peasant children, who wander into a forest to pick cranberries. They become lost in a rich peat bog called "the treasure trove of the sun," encounter many animals, and have frightening adventures, all in a single day.

FR clearly deferred to the Soviet illustrator Evgenii Rachev's conception of the two children in the first illustrated edition of the book five years earlier (Moscow, 1947). In FR's rendition, the girl's shawl, short jacket with puffed sleeves (dress showing below), and too-big, over-the-ankle boots and the boy's cap, long overcoat, sling-carried rifle, and hatchet in belt are all strikingly similar to Rachev's version of 1947.

AB.20. Bishop, Claire Huchet. *All Alone*. New York: The Viking Press, 1953. 95 pp. 25.25 x 17.5 cm. "First published by The Viking Press in March 1953."

Forty line drawings, many of them across two pages and in the text. Beige pictorial cloth. Green pictorial end papers. Dust jacket has picture on page 67 reproduced on the back panel. $2.50 on jacket flap.

A Newbery Honor Book in 1954 for the author, Claire Bishop.

The story of two friends, young boys who herd their families' cows in the French Alps of Savoie. Ten-year-old Marcel must choose between obeying his grandfather's peasant rule of minding his own business and always putting himself first—or helping a friend in need. His moral choice leads his village into a new era of cooperation. In the late 1930s, FR lived in this region and knew the local scene.

AB.21a. Kalashnikoff, Nicholas. *My Friend Yakub*. New York: Charles Scribner's Sons, 1953. [vi] + 249 pp. 21 x 14.5 cm. First edition: "A" on copyright page.

Large double-page black ink drawing for the title page, plus three large double-page black ink drawings in the text. Rose cloth covers, with black lettering on the spine and front cover. Plain white end papers. Color pictorial dust jacket, with $2.75 on flap.

The author's autobiographical story of his boyhood friend, a Tartar farm hand named Yakub, their good relationship, and life in the village of Nikolsk in pre-Revolutionary Siberia.

AB.21b. Kalashnikoff, Nicholas. *My Friend Yakub*. London: Oxford University Press, 1961. vi + 212 pp. 22 x 14.5 cm. "First published in U.S.A. by Charles Scribner's Sons in 1953. First published in this edition 1961."

Black cloth cover, silver lettering on spine only. Pictorial color dust jacket, with 12s 6d on flap.

The Oxford edition has new and revised art work. New color jacket art, similar scene but entirely repainted for the 1961 Oxford edition. End papers decorated with ink drawing of a Russian village scene, redrawn version of the title-page drawing in Scribner's edition with many small changes in human figures, etc. Small but elaborate black ink drawing on title page is new art for this British edition. The three double-page ink drawings in the text are closely similar to the New York edition, but are redrawn with many small changes in the details.

AB.22. Tchaika, Florence [Esther] Matthews. *Trouble at Beaver Dam.*

Everyday Science Stories [series]. New York: Julian Messner, 1953. 63 pp. 21.5 x 14 cm.

Twenty-eight line drawings printed in brown ink. Brown pictorial cloth. Pictorial end papers (similar to cover design and probably generic for the Everyday Science series).

Examined three pristine copies of first or early issues; these had no dust jackets, and the book was probably so issued. Announced at $1.60. No later printing is shown on copyright page and, following this publisher's usual practice, would so indicate a first edition.

A twelve-year-old farm boy finds a beaver colony. He prevents a train wreck nearly caused by the beaver dam, helps remove the beaver colony to a new location, tames an injured beaver, and reunites the animal with his mate.

The author, Florence Tchaika, was the American wife of the Russian artist Grisha Tchaika. Residents of the Russian Village in Southbury, Connecticut, the Tchaikas were among Rojankovsky's and his wife's several friends in the wooded, hilly enclave of Russian émigrés and their families.

AB.23. Koch, Dorothy [Clarke]. *I Play at the Beach*. n.p. [New York]: Holiday House, 1955. [28] pp. 23.5 x 19.5 cm.

Full-color drawings in lithographic crayon on every page. Pictorial blue cloth. Pictorial end papers. Pictorial dust jacket, with $2.50 on front flap. Another state of the jacket has $3.50, and we presume the higher price is later. Library edition by E. M. Hale, Eau Claire, WI, 1961.

A summer idyll through the eyes of a little girl exploring nature and playing on a beach by the sea.

AB.24. Langstaff, John. *Frog Went A-Courtin'*. New York: Harcourt,

Brace and Company, 1955. [32] pp. 27.50 x 22.25 cm. Stated "First Edition."

Four-color and two-color lithographs alternate on every page, made with brush, ink, and crayon on acetate color separations for line reproduction. Pictorial end papers. Pictorial dust jacket. $2.50.

The Caldecott Medal winner in 1956 for FR's illustrations. In 1991, one picture from the book was made into a "Caldecott Award Puzzle," a tray puzzle issued by JTG of Nashville. Some of FR's illustrations were also used later in teaching materials from Weston Woods Studios [B5, CR.7].

Langstaff's comical story of a courting frog and his many friends who come to the wedding feast. Retold from various old Scottish ballads, with a traditional tune of the Southern Appalachians.

AB.25. Averill, Esther. *Cartier Sails the St. Lawrence.* New York: Harper and Brothers, 1956. x + 109 pp. 26 x 19 cm.

A new and truncated edition of *The Voyages of Jacques Cartier* (Domino Press, 1937). See full description under Domino Press. [B2, DP.4b]

AB.26. Riesenberg, Jr., Felix. *Balboa, Swordsman and Conquistador.* World Landmark Books [W-25 in series]. New York: Random House, 1956. x + 178 pp. 21.5 x 14.5 cm. Indexed.

Full-page illustrations in green monochrome, with smaller line drawings. First or early issue examined has green cloth covers, with a ship's compass (book title in the middle) and a ship beneath. End papers (repeated) have a map of world with small figures of people and ships. Dust jacket with $1.50 on flap.

On this book FR spells his name "Fedor," not "Feodor."

Reissued as a Book-of-the-Month Club, Young Readers of America Selection, and with different end papers. Library edition by E. M. Hale, Eau Claire, WI.

The Spanish conquistador and explorer Balboa sails to the New World and marches across the Isthmus of Panama and discovers the Pacific Ocean in 1513, before he comes to a bad end.

Music for Living Series (AB.27 - AB.31)

Mursell, James L., *et al. Music for Living Series.* Morristown, NJ: Silver Burdett Co., 1956.

The *Music for Living Series* was a music education system for elementary schools comprising 13 volumes of song scores and lyrics for teachers and students. Morristown, NJ: Silver Burdett Co., 1956. First editions, all volumes: Numeral "1" and date "56" present in series, 1-15, "-JCP-" and "64 . . . 56," vertically in gutter of last page.

The 13 physical volumes comprise six nominal Books, each with a Teacher's Book and a Companion Book for students. Book One, however, has two Companion Books: Part 1, *I like the Country* and Part 2, *I Like the City*, and the Teacher's Book One is titled *Music Through the Day.* Books 2-6 each have only one Companion Book, and both volumes are titled the same: 2, *In Our Town*; 3, *Now and Long Ago*; 4, *Near and Far*; 5, *In Our Country*; 6, *Around the World.* All issued without dust jackets.

FR illustrated four of the six students' Companion Books, Books 1-4. Jean Mursell illustrated the other two, Books 5-6. Most of FR's illustrations in the two students' Companion Books for Book One also appear, but often cropped, in the quarto cloth-bound Teacher's Book One. The illustrations in Companion Books 2-4, however, do not appear in the corresponding oblong, soft-cover, spiral-bound Teacher's Books 2-6. FR's illustrations of active children profusely decorate the wide margins of music scores in four students' Companion Books (five physical volumes):

AB.27. [Book 1, part 1], *I Like the Country*, iv + 37 pp. 20.75 x 23.5 cm.

Paper-covered boards, with continuous wraparound picture. Pictorial end papers. Oblong. Color illustrations throughout.

AB.28. [Book 1, part 2], *I Like the City*, iv + 37 pp. 20.75 x 23.5 cm.

Uniform with *I Like the Country* above.

Books 2-4 are in pictorial cloth bindings, each with a different cover picture, all with plain white end papers, each 23.5 x 19.25 cm, and are illustrated throughout.

AB.29. Book 2, *In Our Town*. [iv] + 156 pp.

AB.30. Book 3, *Now and Long Ago*. [iv] + 172 pp.

AB.31. Book 4, *Near and Far*. [iv] + 188 pp.

* * *

AB.32. Langstaff, John. *Over in the Meadow*. New York: Harcourt, Brace and Company, 1957. [32] pp. 28 x 21.5 cm. Stated "First Edition."

Half of illustrations are in full color, half in two colors. Pictorial paper-covered boards. Pictorial end papers. Pictorial dust jacket. $2.75.

Reissued by Harcourt, Brace & World, Inc., New York, nd [1967], with a 33-1/3 rpm phonograph record: "Special Scott, Foresman and Company Edition for *Scott, Foresman First Talking Storybook Box*." The date of 1967 appears only on the label of the record. Some of FR's illustrations were also used later in teaching materials from Weston Woods Studios [B5, CR.7].

Langstaff's version of an old counting rhyme with ten animals of the meadow. Their mothers tell them to dig, run, sing, play, hum, build, swim, wink, spin, and hop. A simple arrangement of the tune is on the last page.

AB.33. Thayer, Jane (pseudonym of Catherine Woolley). *The Outside Cat.* New York: William Morrow, 1957. [32] pp. 26 x 19 cm.

Twenty-seven full-color lithographs, with several two-page spreads. First or early issue examined has "New York 1957" under imprint on title page. Pea green cloth covers, with design of cat looking through picket fence. End papers repeat picture of cat in snowy alley. Dust jacket has picture of cat on roof; back panel has seven ads for "Other Books by Jane Thayer." Front jacket flap has $2.95 and ad for this book , and at bottom "Morrow Junior Books" and age code "004-008."

Also issued in a Morrow Eagle Library binding. British edition by Brockhampton Press, Leicester, 1958. 10s 6d.

Samuel, an outside cat, longs to live in the house like a regular house cat. The family of the house moves away and leaves him behind. But a new family soon moves in. Samuel wins their acceptance, and he finally becomes an inside cat, snug beside the fire. The house depicted in the illustrations was, in fact, the Rojankovsky's family home on McIntyre Street in Bronxville, NY.

AB.34. Fritz, Jean. *The Cabin Faced West.* New York: Coward-McCann, 1958. 124 pp. 21 x 14.5 cm.

Eighteen line drawings from lithographic crayon, including frontis. Blue cloth cover with black design on front. Plain white end papers. Pictorial dust jacket, "CFW $3.00" on flap.

First or early issue examined does not indicate a first edition or printing, but neither did it indicate a later printing, as did another copy that stated "Ninth Impression."

A fictionalized biography of the author's great-great-grandmother, Ann Hamilton. As a ten-year-old girl, Ann copes with and learns to understand the rough demands of everyday life upon wilderness settlers in Western Pennsylvania.

AB.35. Rand, Ann. *The Little River.* New York: Harcourt, Brace and Company, 1959. [35] pp. 21.5 x 25.5 cm. Stated "First edition."

Full-color pictures in a variety of layouts on every page. Blue cloth covers with small design of grass, water, fish, and insect, bottom right. Dust jacket with wraparound pastoral scene; $2.95 on front flap. Ad for Rand's *Sparkle and Spin* on rear flap. Pictorial end papers with river scenes. Also issued in a library binding.

Dedicated "To Catherine and Tania [FR's daughter] and to all children who want to know where and how rivers go." Accompanying Rand's verses, the panoramic sequence of pictures follows the course of a little river from its source through different natural and human habitats until it flows into the sea. The concept was perhaps influenced by Alexandra Exter's *Panorama du Fleuve* for the Père Castor series. Ann Rand was the wife of Paul Rand, the famous graphic designer, with whom she also published several children's books.

AB.36. Varley, Dimitry. *The Whirly Bird.* New York: Alfred A. Knopf, 1961. [32] pp. 26 x 20.5 cm.

Two- and three-color lithographs on every page. First or early issue examined has tan cloth covers, with red and green design of bird in box. End papers have design of bird and girl in backyard. Dust jacket has picture of cat watching robin on front panel and baby bird on back, with $3.00 on front flap. "Reinforced Binding" is vertically printed on the front jacket panel of the trade edition. Also issued in a library binding.

The true story of a baby robin who fell from the nest and is menaced by a cat. The baby bird is rescued by a little girl, kept in a box, raised, and finally sent off on its first flight. The author was a neighbor of the Rojankovskys in Bronxville, N.Y. and both families were engaged in the incident. The details of the house depicted was the Rojankovsky's family home on McIntyre Street in Bronxville.

AB.37. Kalashnikoff, Nicholas. *The Defender.* London: Oxford University Press, 1962. x + 118 pp. 22 x 14.5 cm. "First published in this edition 1962."

Four double-page line drawings, including the frontis, plus a small drawing on the title page. Orange cloth cover, with lettering only on the spine. Plain white end papers. The color pictorial dust jacket, with 10s 6d on flap, has an additional illustration of the Defender carrying a lamb down the mountain to safety.

The text was first published in 1951 by Charles Scribner's Sons, making this illustrated edition the "first thus."

Turgen, a Siberian tribesman called the "Defender," protects the mountain rams against starvation and hunters and is ostracized by the peasants because of his strange concern for wild beasts. But the villagers finally learn he is not "possessed" and come to appreciate his goodness.

AB.38. Rand, Ann. *So Small.* New York: Harcourt, Brace & World, Inc., 1962. [48] pp. 18.25 x 15.50 cm. Stated "First Edition."

Full-color and yellow-and-black lithographic crayon drawings alternate throughout, with 14 two-page spreads. Yellow cloth with black design of two mice on front cover. Plain white end papers. Dust jacket, blue, with wraparound picture of a cat stalking a mouse. $2.95. Also issued in library binding.

A story in verse about Little Bit, the smallest mouse of his litter, who shows his larger siblings that "It's better to be brave than never misbehave."

AB.39. Rojankovsky, Feodor. *Animals in the Zoo*. New York: Alfred A. Knopf, 1962. [40] pp. 27.25 x 21 cm.

Every page has lithographs in rich browns and blacks, including the front matter. First or early issue examined is in yellow cloth covers, with red giraffe at lower right. Pictorial end papers. Dust jacket repeats cover design, front and back, with $2.95 on front flap; ad for *Whirly Bird* on back flap. Also issued in library binding. This book parallels Knopf's *Animals on the Farm* (1967) [AB.41].

An ABC picture book, with a capital and lower case letter on each page accompanied by the name and picture of an animal, A for Alligator to Z for Zebra.

AB.40. Fisher, Aileen Lucia. *Cricket in a Thicket*. New York: Charles Scribner's Sons, 1963. 63 pp. 21 x 16 cm. ("A-8.63 [AJ]" on copyright page, "A" indicating first printing, in "-8.63," or August 1963, with "[AJ]" denoting the manufacturer).

Lithographic line drawings throughout; seven are full-page, but most are smaller and in the text. Pictorial cloth, with color design that is a version of the illustration on page 14. Plain end papers. Pictorial dust jacket, plain back panel, with $2.95 on front flap. Also issued in "Scribner's Library Binding," with a different cover design, specifically that on the dust jackets of both the trade and library editions.

A book of Fisher's light verse about nature, metered and rhymed for children.

AB.41. Rojankovsky, Feodor. *Animals on the Farm*. New York: Alfred A. Knopf, 1967. [40] pp. 28.5 x 20.5 cm.

Full-color lithographs on every page; about half are two-page spreads, the rest full-page. The only text in this picture book is the printed names of the animals.

First or early issue examined is in yellow cloth covers, with a small black picture of barn at lower right; back cover is plain. Pictorial end papers (repeated) of a single wide scene. Dust jacket has a different color picture of barn with farm animals in foreground; back panel has picture of farm in winter. Front flap shows price of $3.95, a blurb for this book, and a pair of crouching rabbits; back flap has ad for *Animals in the Zoo.* This book parallels Knopf's *Animals in the Zoo* (1962) [AB.39].

AB.42. Graham, John. *A Crowd of Cows.* New York: Harcourt, Brace & World, Inc., 1968. [32] pp. 26.5 x 21.75 cm. Stated "First edition."

Every page illustrated in full-color. Plain yellow paper-covered boards, lettered spine. Plain white end papers. Pictorial dust jacket. $3.50. Also issued in library binding.

Introduces collective nouns for groups of animals. "A crowd of cows is a herd. The *Herd* goes mooooo and gives milk for lunch." And so for sheep, bees, pigs, hens, doves, fish, lions, kittens, goats, and whales, each with a double-page spread. Finally, a *passel* of children gets the lion's share with five pages of illustrations.

AB.43. Daniels, Guy, editor and translator. *The Falcon Under the Hat: Russian Merry Tales and Fairy Tales.* New York: Funk & Wagnalls, 1969. 112 pp. 26 x 20 cm. "First published, 1969, by Funk & Wagnalls" and numeral "1," indicating first printing.

Mostly full-page, full-color illustrations, with black initials heading each chapter. Red cloth cover stamped with white letters and black devices. Green pictorial end papers. Pictorial dust jacket, with $5.95 on flap.

Translation of 16 old Russian folk or "merry" tales, beginning with the title story.

AB.44. Wahl, Jan. *The Mulberry Tree.* New York: Grosset & Dunlap, Inc. "A W. W. Norton Book," 1970. [32] pp. 26 x 21 cm.

Every page has soft-crayon, three-color (blue, yellow, black) lithographs, with many two-page spreads. First or early issue examined is in paper-covered boards, with a wraparound forest scene in same three colors. End papers with single wide scene of small perching birds. Dust jacket has same wraparound design as the covers. Front jacket flap has $4.50 and the numeral "58." The numeral "2138" is on the spines of the cover and jacket. The front jacket flap has a description of this book; the rear flap has bios for the author and the illustrator; the rear panel has an ad for Wahl's *The Fishermen*, with three review blurbs. Also issued in a library binding.

The story of a mulberry tree through the natural cycle of a year and of the animals and insects that visit and eat its fruit.

AB.45. Hall, Bill. *A Year in the Forest.* New York: McGraw-Hill Book Company, 1973. 68 pp. 28.75 x 26.00 cm.

Color illustrations throughout. The first or early issue examined is in paper-covered boards, with a wraparound forest scene. End papers with scene of sky and birds in flight. Dust jacket repeats the design on the covers, with $6.75 on front flap. The flaps have a description of this book and bios of the author and artist, continuing onto the back flap. Also issued in a library binding.

The illustrations for this posthumously published book were unfinished at the time of Rojankovsky's death in 1970. The book was filled out for publication with pictures that previously appeared in *I Am a Fox* (1967), *Animal Tales [Stories]* (1944), *Wild Animals* (1960, 1951), and *The Golden Book of Birds* (1943). The front matter contains an essay, "A Tribute to Feodor Rojankovsky 1891-1970," by Lucille E. Ogle, "New Hope, PA, January 30, 1973." Ogle was FR's long-time editor at Golden Press.

The text and pictures describe the lives of nine forest animals through the seasons of the year.

B5

The Golden Books and Other Children's Art

The first of thirty-seven original Golden Books illustrated by Rojankovsky was published in 1943, the last in 1970, the year of his death. He produced steadily for the imprint over three decades. In most years at least one Golden Book by Rojankovsky was released and in peak years several.

In the 1950s and 1960s, he also illustrated over thirty children's stories and seven original covers in the serials *Story Parade*, *Best in Children's Books*, and others. The children's magazine *Story Parade* was a property of Artists and Writers Guild and closely tied to Golden Books. During this period, Rojankovsky also painted pictures that were used to decorate toys and other playthings and for reproduction as children's prints and posters. Many are spinoffs of Golden Books or are of this style.

We list only the first American trade editions of the Golden Books and a few notable special issues. Most of FR's Golden Books went through multiple reissues and often bewildering transmutations—many before his death in 1970 and even more afterwards. Titles were reissued in different sizes and layouts, some with fewer or more pages and pictures. Some were reissued in different Golden series, with new numbers, even new titles. Books of similar themes were sometimes combined into larger, redesigned books with new titles. Parts of some books were reissued in magazines. Such derivative editions are omitted, unless in a few cases we know they contain new art work, cover designs, or other decorations by the artist.

We also omit the many foreign and translated editions. Golden Books were translated and issued in a dozen languages, and some of these otherwise vary from their American editions. French subsidiaries and licensees of Golden Books have reissued the greatest number of FR's titles. The licensees in the United Kingdom issued several variant English-language editions in the Golden Pleasure series and other imprints, some cobbled from various Golden books and given new titles. But we have not seen foreign editions with new art work.

Between the late 1940s and the early 1960s, Golden Books indicated on the copyright page: "Published simultaneously by the Musson Book Company, Ltd., Toronto." Musson was the nominal publisher and distributor of record to satisfy the Canadian import laws and none were issued under a Musson imprint. FR's other American publishers also had similar import arrangements with Canadian firms, including Musson.

By 1950 most U.S. editions of Golden Books were simultaneously issued in Goldencraft processed-cloth library bindings and indicated that they, too, were first editions. In the library versions of the large-format books, the end papers are plain. But the illustrated end papers from the corresponding trade editions are preserved as two sets of bound-in loose leaves, with the illustrated sides facing each other, in both the front and back.

In 1966 the Golden Press reissued five of Flammarion's Père Castor titles: four of the eight titles (*Ploof, Bruin, Scuff*, and *Spiky*) from *Le roman des bêtes*, which were published in translation by Harper and Brothers in the 1930s, and *Christmas Bear*, a new translation of *Michka*. These are not original Golden Books and are listed as variant but important English-language editions of Père Castor books.

All Golden Books have certain common descriptive traits in their trade editions. All are profusely illustrated throughout, typically on every page, and often the front matter is illustrated as well. The pictures are reproduced by the screened, four-color process, printed by offset lithography, and are often mixed in with black halftones. All the trade editions were issued in full-color, pictorial, laminated, paper-covered boards, though with variations of construction in different subseries.

The Little Golden Books, the first series in the line, went through several changes of appearance over the years. The early books were backed with dark blue cloth spines, later changed to decorated gold paper, and then to the gold foil spine. The earliest books with cloth spines were issued in dust jackets whose designs duplicated the front and back covers of the book, such as FR's *The Golden Book of Birds* (1943), but jackets were dropped before FR's second book in the series, *The Three Bears* (1948).

All the Little Golden Books are about 20 x 17 cm. The edges of the boards are cut flush with the text block and stained (usually blue, red, or yellow) and are bound by side stapling. None have free end papers but open directly to the title page. The covers usually have ads or blurbs on both sides of the rear boards. The insides of the front boards usually have a blank child's *ex libris* printed on the paper.

The Big and Giant Golden Books, in their trade editions, have boards covered with single sheets of printed paper wrapped around the edges of the boards and its margins glued under the end papers—in the more usual practice of book binding. The lettered spine is usually part of the single sheet. Sometimes the covers are adhered to thin sheets of clear plastic, giving them a high gloss. The end papers have original color designs, and in some the front and rear end papers are different.

Identifying First Editions of Golden Books

First issues over the years were indicated by several systems. Some of the early small and large books of the 1940s indicate "First Printing" (with month and year) on the copyright pages, and these are noted case by case.

The later Little Golden Books have alphabetic codes, namely a capital letter "A" in the lower right corner of the last page of the text block to indicate a first printing, "B" a second printing, and so on. The books in large formats, on a front end paper, have a capital letter "A", "B", "C", etc., followed by six numerals, which are the list price repeated twice. For example, "A150150" indicates a first printing, "A", published at $1.50 retail. The last large books of the 1970s have on an end paper the series "ABCDEFGHIJ", where the presence of the letter "A" indicates a first printing. Codes for the first trade editions are indicated in each entry.

Simon & Schuster, 1943 - 1958 (GB.1 - GB.26)

GB.1. Lockwood, Hazel. *The Golden Book of Birds.* A Little Golden Book, No. 13. New York: Simon & Schuster, 1943. [42] pp. 20 x 17 cm. Stated: "First Printing, April, 1943."

Dark blue cloth spine. Issued in a dust jacket duplicating the covers. This is the only one of FR's Little Golden Books issued in a jacket, which were shortly thereafter discontinued for all books in the "Little" series.

How ten species of birds live with their young—with their imagined dialogue. FR's first Little Golden Book, the 13th in the first series, and the first after the initial 12 books of the new imprint published simultaneously in 1942.

GB.2a. Duplaix, Georges. *Animal Stories.* A Giant Golden Book, No. 550. New York: Simon & Schuster, 1944. 92 pp. 33 x 26 cm. Stated: "First Printing, July, 1944."

The front cover is lettered with the title, author, and illustrator in a white circle imposed on the torso of an elephant, with other animals around it. The dust jacket has a different design, a garland of animals, with $1.50 on front flap. First printing was

125,000 copies. Another binding, also a stated first edition, is non-pictorial in plain, grey-green paper-covered boards, lettered spine, with only the lettered white circle on the front. The primacy of the two states was not determined.

End papers have 2 full-page color pictures, each of various animals sitting around a table enjoying refreshments.

The 1944 edition was later heavily abridged as *Animal Tales* in a variety of versions and formats.

Images and texts from *Animal Stories* were used in a Little Golden Record set (1948) [CR.1], and broadcast on early children's television, 1948-49. The animal alphabet (pp. 21-26) and other pictures were later used in sets of children's nesting blocks [TO.5]; some of the pictures were used in jigsaw puzzles [TO.7]; and seventeen small watercolors of animals were reproduced as a combination jigsaw tray puzzle and clock counting-game [TO.8].

GB.2b. **Deluxe limited edition in cloth binding**. Same as trade edition, except bound in light-grey cloth and with a full-size color panel of the trade dust jacket mounted on the front cover. Of this binding, 300 copies were issued with a mounted printed slip: "This first, specially printed edition of *Animal Stories* is limited to 300 copies of which this is number [000]." Signed by George Duplaix, some also by FR. Other copies are without the pasted-in slip, however, and are out of series.

GB.3. *Pictures from Mother Goose*. "A Golden Portfolio containing Jack and Jill * Mary Had a Little Lamb * Little Boy Blue * The Old Woman in the Shoe * Little Tommy Tittlemouse * Rain, Rain, Go Away * Little Miss Muffett * Pussy Cat, Pussy Cat." New York: Simon & Schuster, 1945. Portfolio size: 48 x 36.5 cm. No discernible edition code.

Eight loose leaves of titled, color offsets (from watercolors) printed on one side; each leaf is 47.75 x 36 cm. All are signed "F. Rojankovsky" in the plate. Grey-brown stiff paper portfolio with 45.5 x 34 cm full-color paper sheet mounted on front. Inside of front cover has a large green pen drawing of Mother Goose pushing a baby carriage and repeats lettered information from the cover label. $2.50 on front flap, beneath a sketch of FR in profile, a bio, and a blurb for The Golden Library. Portfolio flap sealed with 12.5 x 9.5 cm. label which must be broken or lifted to open. The label has a full-color picture of a goose dressed as an artist carrying an easel and a portfolio and labeled "My Portfolio."

GB.4. Werner, Elsa Jane, ed. [Jane Werner Watson]. *The Golden Bible: From the King James Version of the Old Testament.* A Giant Golden Book, No. 704. New York: Simon & Schuster, 1946. 124 pp. 33 x 26 cm. Stated: "First printing."

Front cover has a picture of the Creation and, on the back cover, a dove of peace. Brown cloth spine, lettered. Pictorial end papers. Dust jacket, on front panel, has a picture of Noah's Ark under construction and a parade of animals beneath; ads on back panel. On front jacket panel: "A Giant Golden Book. De Luxe Edition." Front flap has $2.50 at bottom, and a blurb for the book, continued to the back flap, which also has a bio and sketch of FR in profile.

The Catholic Child's Bible [GB.24] was made from the illustrations in *The Golden Bible*, but with new cover designs. A booklet using illustrations from *The Golden Bible* was issued to accompany *The Golden Record Bible Library* [CR.4].

GB.5. *The Three Bears.* A Little Golden Book, No. 47. New York: Simon & Schuster, 1948. [42] pp. 20 x 17 cm. Last page: "A".

The cover of the first printing (A) has a picture (with black border) of the bear family walking in the woods, specifically a variant of the picture on page 3 of all printings. The second and later printings have a cover with Goldilocks discovered in Baby Bear's bed. The larger Big Golden Book version (c. 1966) rearranges the color pictures and omits all fourteen of the black-and-white illustrations. Golden also reissued this book with an accompanying record [CR.2]. Recently, a Russian publisher issued a Russian version with FR's illustrations, a first in Russia for FR's non-Russian children's books.

This is the traditional nursery telling of the tale, with emphasis on big, middle-sized, and small everything. See B5, GB.36 for the redrawn and rewritten edition (1967). Some of the pictures were used for eight Playskool jigsaw puzzles about 1961 [TO.7].

GB.6. Jackson, Kathryn and Byron. *Big Farmer Big* [and] *Little Farmer Little*. A Big-and-Little Golden Book. New York: Simon & Schuster, 1948. [60] pp. 32.5 x 14 cm; [32] pp. 13 x 6.5 cm. End paper: "A100100".

This book is complete only with the publisher's enclosure of the miniature book, *Little Farmer Little*, in the notched red paper pocket mounted on the front cover. The pocket bears the titles of both books and the names of the authors, the artist, and the publisher. Publicity for the book in *Story Parade* magazine: "Like a kangaroo—this BIG book has a little book tucked inside."

The giant named Big Farmer Big found his animals too small in proportion to his own size and fed them up to giant sizes, much larger than himself. But the neighbors complained of the giants and he fed them back down proportionate to his own size. Little Farmer Little, who has the opposite problem, raises a miniature crop and trades it for a new bed crafted from a match box.

GB.7. McGinley, Phyllis. *A Name for Kitty*. A Little Golden Book, No.

55. New York: Simon & Schuster, 1948. [28] pp. 20 x 17 cm. Last page: "A".

A young farm boy with a new kitten to name rejects the facetious names suggested by his parents, grandparents, and (seemingly) by the farm animals—before deciding on "Kitty," the most obvious name of all. Reissued as *Kitty on the Farm*.

GB.8. Nast, Elsa Ruth [pseudonym of Jane Werner (Watson)]. *Our Puppy*. A Little Golden Book, No. 56. New York: Simon & Schuster, 1948. [28] pp. 20 x 17 cm. Last page: "A".

All the things "Our Puppy" does one morning before having lunch with the children and settling down for a nap. Only a few words on each page. Some of the pictures were used for eight Playskool jigsaw puzzles about 1961 [TO.7].

GB.9. Duplaix, Georges. *Gaston and Josephine*. A Little Golden Book, No. 65. New York: Simon & Schuster, 1948. [42] pp. 20 x 17 cm. Last page: "A".

An abridged version of Duplaix's *Gaston and Josephine* (London: Oxford, 1933; New York: Harper, 1936), originally also illustrated by Duplaix, but here newly illustrated by FR.

Two French pigs from a provincial farm set off to visit their American cousins, having adventures making their way through Paris and the countryside to Le Havre. Sailing away, they soon save the ship from disaster, dine at the captain's table, and arrive in New York as celebrities—all before they set out for the American West, the subject of Duplaix's sequel, *Gaston and Josephine in America* (Oxford, 1934). The sequel was not re-illustrated by FR.

GB.10. *Favorite Fairy Tales*. A Big Golden Book. New York: Simon & Schuster, 1949. [26] pp. 33.5 x 20.5 cm. End paper: "A100100".

The 12 pictures were first published as 12 leaves of an advertising calendar (1948), made for John Morrell and Company, a meat-packing firm, and also issued as sets of 12 loose prints [listed both as B5, CP.4 and B8, AA.14]. The real-life model for the blond prince in "Rapunzel" was FR's wife, Nina.

Twelve traditional European fairy tales are presented as 12 double-page spreads with a short text for each. Each picture (unlike the calendar prints) is marred by the gutters of the text block. Four of the most popular pictures are reproduced on single pages in *Rojankovsky's Wonderful Picture Book* (1972) [GB.38].

GB.11. Jackson, Kathryn & Byron. *The Big Elephant.* A Big Golden Book. New York: Simon & Schuster, 1949. [30] pp. 33.5 x 21 cm. End paper: "A100100".

The end papers are illustrated with a version of the Aesopian fable of the city mouse and the country mouse, with its own text and 21 pictorial panels. Reissued as Little Golden Books, in one instance retitled *What's Next, Elephant?*

A big elephant leaves the circus, goes into town, builds a house, makes many friends, and joins the town band.

GB.12. Rojankovsky, Feodor. *The Great Big Animal Book.* A Big Golden Book, No. 468. New York: Simon & Schuster, 1950. [25] pp. 33.5 x 27 cm. End paper: "A100100".

Full-page pictures of familiar farm and domestic animals, each accompanied by a single line of text. Wraparound cover with six farm animals looking over a fence. Some of the pictures were used for eight Playskool jigsaw puzzles about 1961 [TO.7].

GB.13. Nina [Nina Rojankovsky]. *The Kitten's Surprise.* A Little Golden Book, No. 107. New York: Simon & Schuster, 1951. [28] pp. 20 x 17 cm. Last page: "A".

Joan gets a kitten for her third birthday, treats it roughly like a lifeless doll until it runs away. In the nearby woods the kitten learns it is not a rabbit or a squirrel and returns home to the little girl, who has now learned to treat it like a kitten, not a doll. Joan was modeled on FR's daughter, Tanya, who was three in 1951. Also issued as a Young America filmstrip, about 1955. Book reissued as *Little Lost Kitten.*

GB.14. Rojankovsky, Feodor. *The Great Big Wild Animal Book.* A Big Golden Book, No. 563. New York: Simon & Schuster, 1951. [35] pp. 33.5 x 26.5 cm. End paper: "A150150".

Full-page pictures of wild animals, each with one line of text. Wraparound cover picture shows three heads of lion family with elephants, zebras, and giraffes behind. A truncated LGB edition is *Wild Animals* (1960) [GB.30]. Some of the pictures were used for eight Playskool jigsaw puzzles about 1961 [TO.7].

GB.15. Coatsworth, Elizabeth. *The Giant Golden Book of Cat Stories.* A Giant Golden Book, No. 572. New York: Simon & Schuster, 1953. 66 pp. 33 x 25 cm. End paper: "A195195".

Anthology of 35 cat stories and poems, the narrative texts previously published in the 1930s and 1940s.

GB.16. Coatsworth, Elizabeth. *The Giant Golden Book of Dog Stories: 31 Original Stories and Poems.* A Giant Golden Book, No. 578. New York: Simon & Schuster, 1953. 66 pp. 33 x 25 cm. End paper: "A195195".

Anthology of 31 dog stories and poems, previously published in the 1930s and 1940s. A companion to *Cat Stories* in same format.

GB.17. Coatsworth, Elizabeth Jane, and Kate Barnes. *Horse Stories.* A Big Golden Book, No. 486. New York: Simon & Schuster, 1954. 30 pp. 32.5 x 24 cm. End paper: "A100100".

Anthology of horse stories and poems. Front and rear

pastedowns are a continuous scene of a paddock; the recto of the front end paper is third panel (thus a third dimension) of the scene. A companion to *Cat Stories* and *Dog Stories* in same format.

GB.18. Coatsworth, Elizabeth. With Three Stories by Kate Barnes. *The Giant Golden Book of Dogs, Cats, and Horses: 61 Stories and Poems.* New York: Simon & Schuster, 1957. 124 pp. 32.5 x 23.5 cm. End paper: "A295295".

Anthology of stories and pictures made up from the three Golden Books of dogs, cats, and horses. New cover art.

GB.19. Watson, Jane Werner. *The True Story of Smokey the Bear.* A Big Golden Book, No. 429. New York: Simon & Schuster, 1955. [26] pp. 32.5 x 24 cm. End paper: "A100100".

The orphaned bear cub survives a forest fire, is rescued, grows up in a zoo, gets job as a forest ranger, and makes a career protecting the wilderness from fire. "Authorized and Approved by the State Foresters and by the Forest Service, United States Department of Agriculture, in cooperation with the Advertising Council, Inc." Two pages of "Smokey Rules" are at the end.

GB.20. Duplaix, Lily. *The White Bunny and His Magic Nose.* A Little Golden Book, No. 305. New York: Simon & Schuster, 1957. [24] pp. 20 x 17 cm. Last page: "A".

"Wiggle-diggle-dee!/Oh, it's fun to be a rabbit/ With a magic habit/ Of turning pink or blue/ Anyone who annoys you!/ Wiggle-diggle-doo!"—so sings the bunny as he strums a Russian balalaika in the frontis. The rabbit exercises his powers on several animals until he accidentally turns himself pink as well. Now all must take a bath, but white bunny did not wash his ears, and they remain pink inside to this day. Also made into a Columbia record set about 1967 [CR.6].

GB.21. *The Little Golden Mother Goose: 75 Favorite Rhymes.* A Little Golden

Book, No. 283. New York: Simon & Schuster, 1957. [24] pp. 20 x 17 cm. Last page: "A".

Each of 75 rhymes has one or more color illustrations.

Pictures and rhymes from this and the two Mother Goose books below also decorate a set of children's stacking blocks by Playskool about 1961 [TO.6].

GB.22. *More Mother Goose Rhymes: 57 Favorite Rhymes.* A Little Golden Book, No. 317. New York: Simon & Schuster, 1958. [24] pp. c20 x 17 cm. Last page: "A".

Preface: "This is the second Little Golden Book of Mother Goose rhymes containing Feodor Rojankovsky's delightful pictures. His first one was #283 THE LITTLE GOLDEN MOTHER GOOSE. It contains a wonderful selection of all the best-known rhymes."

GB.23. *Mother Goose Rhymes: 154 Childhood Favorites.* A Giant Little Golden Book, No. 5016. New York: Simon & Schuster, 1958. 56 pp. 20 x 17 cm. Last page: "A".

Compiled from *The Little Golden Mother Goose: 75 Favorite Rhymes* (1957) and *More Mother Goose Rhymes: 57 Favorite Rhymes* (1958). New cover art (picture of Old Woman Who Lived in a Shoe) and ten pages of additional rhymes and illustrations. Indexed.

GB.24. Werner, Elsa Jane [Jane Werner Watson] and Charles Hartman. *A Catholic Child's Bible. Stories from the Old Testament.* A Giant Golden Book, No. 665. New York: Simon & Schuster, 1958. 132 pp. 32.5 x 25.75 cm. End paper: "A395395".

For this revised Catholic edition of the 1946 *The Golden Bible* [GB.4], FR designed new front and back covers. The interior art is identical through page 105. Pages 106-114 add new stories and new color and halftone pictures. Between pages 116-132, certain color pictures in the original edition become halftones, and vice versa, and some images are reversed. The large halftone on page 121 of the 1946 edition is omitted.

GB.25. Purcell, John Wallace. *Baby Wild Animals*. A Golden Stamp Book, No. P-54. New York: Simon & Schuster, 1958. 48 pp., plus four sheets of stamps. 28 x 21 cm. Back cover: "A".

Pictorial paper covers and end papers. Forty-eight color pictures of animals on four perforated sheets (12 stamps each) and line drawings throughout. A later edition retains FR's color stamps but has cartoonish drawings by another artist.

The project is to tear out each stamp and match it with the correct square on the 48 coloring pages. "With 48 stamps in color, showing young wild animals from all over the world—baby hippos, chipmunks, crocodiles, giraffes, leopards, porcupines, spider monkeys, and walruses, and many others, plus a story, and black-and-white drawings on every page."

GB.26. Daly, Kathleen N. *Wild Animal Babies*. A Little Golden Book, No. 332. New York: Simon & Schuster, 1958. [24] pp. 20.25 x 16.50 cm. Last page: "A".

Twenty-one color pictures selected from the Golden Stamp Book above, plus new cover art, new picture on copyright page, and a redrawn koala. Cf. copyright date of 19 February 1958 on the stamp book with 23 September 1958 on the Little Golden Book.

Golden Press, 1960 - 1972 (GB.27 - GB.38)

GB.27. Buell, Ellen Lewis, ed. *A Treasury of Little Golden Books: 48 of the Best-Loved Stories for the Very Young*. Forward by Ellen Lewis Buell. A Giant Golden Book, No. 766. New York: Golden Press, 1960. 31 x 27 cm. 156 pp. End paper: "A395395".

This edition has new decorations: "The cover and end paper designs are by Feodor Rojankovsky." But the new art also includes the letter forms on the title page and the parade of fowl across the copyright and contents pages. The end papers show 21 different redrawn covers of LGBs in which FR represents other artists'—and his own—covers.

A collection of 48 attenuated versions of stories, poems, and art originally published in separate editions of Little Golden Books, including *A Name for Kitty* and *Gaston and Josephine.*

GB.28. Defoe, Daniel. *Robinson Crusoe.* A Giant Golden Book, No. 698. Adapted by Anne Terry White. New York: Golden Press, 1960. 96 pp. 26 x 23 cm. End paper: "A395395".

The juvenile classic was FR's life-long favorite. At the age of nine in St. Petersburg, he first drew pictures for it. In January 1939, FR wrote E. Averill that he had just met with his Polish publisher, R. Wegner, in Nice and discussed projects. "I shall do Robinson Crusoe for him, but unfortunately not in the style that I had imagined for this work." (Averill, 1985). The Polish National Library records no such edition. It may have been drafted, all or in part, but never published; the Germans invaded Poland in September 1939. This eventual illustration of *Robinson Crusoe* for Golden Books may have been more in the style he imagined.

GB.29. Watson, Jane Werner. *Animal Dictionary.* A Little Golden Book, No. 379. New York: Golden Press, 1960. [24] pp. 20 x 17 cm. Last page: "A".

ABC book with animals or insects whose names begin with each letter of the alphabet. FR drew several different creatures for most letters, concluding with Z for *Zoo.*

GB.30. *Wild Animals.* A Little Golden Book, No. 394. New York: Golden Press, 1960. [24] pp. 20 x 17 cm. Last page: "A".

A diminished edition of *The Great Big Wild Animal Book* [GB.14], with a revised text and a dozen pictures from the original edition, omitting about six images.

In 1984 a landscape designer, Edwina van Gal, used her daughter's copy of *Wild Animals* to create the topiary figures of animals installed in Rockefeller Center's Channel Gardens, one of New York's major tourist sites. The *New York Times* commented "this scene could easily be in an African game preserve with a 14-foot giraffe, an elephant with a 6-foot ear span, a lion, camel, rhinoceros and flamingo wandering amid clumps of dwarf fountain grass and African daisies."

GB.31. Memling, Carl. *10 Little Animals.* A Little Golden Book, No. 451. New York: Golden Press, 1961. [24] pp. 20 x 17 cm. Last page: "A".

A classic counting book in the tradition of Ten Little Indians. At the onset of winter ten (different) little forest animals, one by one, are gathered in by their parents and put to bed.

GB.32. Memling, Carl. *I Can Count.* A Big Golden Book, No. 10833. New York: Golden Press, 1963. [28] pp. 32 x 24 cm. End paper: "A100100".

The covers have a wraparound zoo scene, continuous from front to back. The 19th century bestiary architecture, onion-domed Russian church, women in turn-of-the century costumes, and children in middy blouses and knickers signify the artist's boyhood love of zoos in old Russia.

A classic counting book. The end papers announce the book's counting scheme of one hippo, two alligators, three giraffes, four lions, five monkeys, six kangaroos, seven elephants, eight bison, nine seals, and ten tigers.

GB.33. Krinsley, Jeanette. *The Cow Went Over the Mountain.* A Little

Golden Book, No. 516. New York: Golden Press, 1963. [24] pp. 20 x 17 cm. Last page: "A".

A young cow goes over the mountain where the grass is greener or "munchier," on the way gathering an entourage of a frog, a duck, a pig, and a bear. Finally, they all return home to learn that what they sought elsewhere was in fact tastier at home.

GB.34. Scarry, Patricia M. *Hop, Little Kangaroo.* A Little Golden Book, No. 558. New York: Golden Press, 1965. [24] pp. 20 x 17 cm. Last page: "A".

Little Kangaroo's mother puts him out of her pouch to learn to hop on his own. Mother goes over the hill, leaving him to hop home. But he is reluctant to try his young legs. Various Australian bush animals encourage him just to hop home, which he does very well, to his mother who waits with a treat.

GB.35. Risom, Ole. *I Am a Fox.* A Golden Sturdy Happy Book, No. 12128. New York: Golden Press, 1967. [24] pp. 30.5 x 16.75 cm. End paper: "A195195".

The leaves are stiff laminated boards. Single sentences of text on alternate pages describe the life of Billy, a young fox, who lives in the woods with his family and other animals.

GB.36. Daly, Kathleen N., Adapted by. *The Three Bears.* A Golden Square Book, No. 10671. New York: Golden Press, 1967. [24] pp. 25.5 x 25.5 cm. Last page: "A".

A completely redrawn edition, with a new text, notable for the concentration on the quandary of the three bears at the intrusion. Goldilocks appears only as a tiny figure approaching the bears' house and in flight from it. Also made into a Columbia record set about 1967 [CR.6].

GB.37. Rojankovsky, Feodor. *F. Rojankovsky's ABC: An Alphabet of*

Many Things. A Big Golden Book, No. 13529. New York: Golden Press, 1970. [56] pp. 32.5 x 23.5 cm. End paper: "ABCDEFGHIJ".

Each double-page spread displays the upper and lower cases of each letter of the English alphabet. About a dozen color, free-floating animals, plants, people, and common objects illustrate the initials of key words. The covers and end papers have strikingly original letter forms in the display alphabets. The cover design originally appeared as one of FR's privately printed Christmas cards [B8, CA.4, 28]. Rojankovsky's last book for children.

GB.38. Rojankovsky, Nina, ed. *Rojankovsky's Wonderful Picture Book: An Anthology Illustrated by Feodor Rojankovsky*. A Golden Book, No. 16836. New York: Golden Press, 1972. 117 pp. 30.5 x 26.5 cm. End paper: "ABCDEFGHIJ".

A posthumous book with pictures selected from earlier Golden Books. Introduction by Lucille Ogle, his editor at Golden Press. Though not stated, the pictures are all from *Animal Stories*, the two *Tall Books*, *Fairy Tales*, the three books of *Cat, Dog,* and *Horse Stories*, *Gaston and Josephine*, *The Kitten's Surprise*, *Robinson Crusoe*, and *The Bible*. Only the atypical end papers are new to this edition.

American Stories and Covers (AS.1 - AS.40)

AS.1. Cover design. *The American Girl*. Published by the Girl Scouts. June 1943. Watercolor of two rabbits in a hutch.

AS.2. Evelyn Ray Sickels. "Toppy the Little Circus Elephant." *Child Life*, Vol. XXII, No. X (October 1943). pp. 4-6, 39.

AS.3. *The Christmas Treasure Book: Stories, Songs, and Poems*. A collection. New York: Simon & Schuster and Phillips Publishers, 1950. "Arranged by" Hilda Marx. Fourteen illustrators are listed on the title page, but none are credited for individual story illustrations. FR illustrated "The Birds' Christmas" (pp. 22-23). The picture on page 22 is reused from

The Golden Book of Birds (1943) [GB.1]; the five bird watercolors on page 23 are, we assume, also by FR and first appear here.

Story Parade (AS.4 - AS.21)

Story Parade [magazine]. Story Parade, Inc: Poughkeepsie, NY, published from 1936 to 1954. 25 x 17 cm.

FR illustrated eleven stories and poems and seven color covers for the magazine. The Artists and Writers Guild became associated with the magazine in 1950 and the production offices were moved to Poughkeepsie. FR illustrated for *Story Parade* from the merger in 1950 until the magazine closed in 1954.

FR's stories, often placed prominently at the front of the issues, usually have a mix of color and halftone pictures. Several were reprinted in other children's magazines and readers.

AS.4. R. Palmer. "The Enchanted Rabbit." March 1951, pp. 5-9.

AS.5. A. Fisher. "Halloween Concert." October 1951, pp. 26-27.

AS.6. A. Fisher. "The Outdoor Christmas Tree." December 1952, p. 5. Also cover by FR [AS.18] on this issue.

AS.7. W. R. Brooks. "Ambrose." January 1953, pp. 6-12.

AS.8. E. Coatsworth. "A Cargo of Cats." March 1953, pp. 29-32.

AS.9. E. Weiss. "The Missing Bone Mystery." April 1953, pp. 6-10.

AS.10. M. Hager. "Muggins." November 1953, pp. 5-9.

AS.11. M. Springer. "Nicky, the Neighborhood Dog." March 1954, pp. 7-10.

AS.12. M. L. Fisher. "The Hitch-Hiking Cat." May 1954, pp. 34-35. Also cover by FR [AS.20] on this issue.

AS.13. W. R. Brooks. "Henry's Dog Henry." June 1954, pp. 3-8.

AS.14. E. Coatsworth. "Lullaby" and "The Old Mouse." September 1954, p. 3. Also cover by FR [AS.21] on this issue.

Unrelated to the above story illustrations and most in other issues, the seven titled seasonal color covers on *Story Parade* are:

AS.15. "The First Day of School." September 1950. Animals at school desks raise their hands.

AS.16. "Reindeer Roundup." January 1951. Children lassoing two reindeer in snow.

AS.17. "Woodland Symphony." April 1951. Orchestra of small animal musicians.

AS.18. "Christmas in the Forest." December 1952. Animals dancing in circle around Christmas tree. Reprinted in *Childcraft*, Vol. 1 (1974), pp. 72-73. Also story illustration by FR [AS.6] in this issue.

AS.19. "The Race." January 1954. Teenage boy and girl skiing downhill.

The last page of this issue contains an ad for subscribing to *Story Parade* with an unattributed illustration by FR of rabbits and snow-covered Christmas tree branches.

AS.20. "Circus Time." May 1954. Large faces of a clown and lion. Also story illustration by FR [AS.12] in this issue.

AS.21. "Barnyard Antics." September 1954. Dog and horse doing a trick for an animal audience. Also story illustration by FR [AS.14] in this issue.

* * *

AS.22. Esther Averill. "The Life of Daniel Boone." *Children's Digest.*

Part One, Vol. II, No. 18 (May 1952): pp. 57-60; Part Two, Vol. II, No. 19 (July 1952): pp. 73-82.

This illustrated story is, in effect, a third textual and illustrative edition of *Daniel Boone*, here called a "book condensation." The new art and text are a short version of Averill's *Daniel Boone* (Harper & Brothers, 1945) [AB.16], which was adapted from Averill's *Daniel Boone* (Domino Press, 1931) [DP.1]. FR drew all new but fewer pictures for this magazine edition, though they are similar to those in the book versions.

AS.23. Elizabeth Coatsworth. "A School for Bears." *The Golden Digest for Boys and Girls*, No. 1, 1954. pp. 7-12.

Best in Children's Books (AS.24 - AS.38)

Best in Children's Books (series). Garden City, NY: Nelson Doubleday, Inc., 1957-1961.

A monthly anthology series issued as hard-bound, jacketed volumes, nos. 1-42, 1957-1961. Each volume has about 160 pages and is 21.75 x 14.5 cm.

FR, among a number of other prominent artists, illustrated stories in the series. The illustrations are variously color offsets and halftones, and appear here for the first time. Each volume is bound in pictorial boards covered with processed paper of various colors. All have pictorial end papers. All were issued in pictorial dust jackets. Most issues contain seven stories and a few non-fiction articles.

The volume numbers (except on volume 1) are in the lower right corner of the table of contents on the front free end paper, on the (duplicate) rear paste-down, and at the bottom of the rear dust jacket flap. On volume 1, the number appears only on the bottom of the rear jacket flap. Reissues are indicated by a letter "A" after the volume number. FR's story illustrations appear in the following 15 issues:

AS.24. "Goldilocks and the Three Bears." No. 2, 1957, pp. 77-84.

AS.25. D. Peattie. "The Story of the First Man." No. 7, 1958, pp. 85-108.

AS.26. Hamilton Williamson. "Baby Bear." No. 9, 1958, pp. 37-44.

AS.27. "The Gingerbread Boy." No. 11, 1958, pp. 37-44.

AS.28. "The Old Woman and Her Pig." No. 14, 1958, pp. 77-84.

AS.29. "Five Favorite Fables, adapted from Aesop." No. 18, 1959, pp. 77-84.

AS.30. Hamilton Williamson. "Lion Cub." No. 21, 1959, pp. 38-44.

AS.31. "Ali Baba and the Forty Thieves." No. 23, 1959, pp. 1-37.

AS.32. T. Burgess. "Unc' Billy Possum." No. 26, 1959, pp. 117-123.

AS.33. Miriam Schlein. "Elephant Herd." No. 28, 1959, pp. 85-99.

AS.34. "Three Billy Goats Gruff." No. 29, 1960, pp. 77-84.

AS.35. S. Burnham. "Alfred, The Saxon King." No. 32, 1960, pp. 74-83.

AS.36. "Obedient Jack." No. 38, 1960, pp. 117-124.

AS.37. "A Farmyard Song." No. 40, 1960, pp. 136-142.

AS.38. R. Kipling. "How the Camel Got His Hump." No. 41, 1961, pp. 77-84.

* * *

AS.39. T.S. Eliot. "Growltiger's Last Stand," in Beust, Nora, ed., *Adventures Here and There: Heroes on Land and Sea*, 1958. E. M. Hale and Company, Eau Claire, WI.

Two illustrations of cats. The book was issued the same year also by Grolier: New York and by Lothrop, Lee and Shepard Co.: New York, with Hale as the original publisher.

The fourth volume in a series *Through Golden Windows*, Jeanne Hale, editor in chief, issued by all three publishers.

AS.40. Mary Cober. "How It Snowed Fur and Rained Fry Cakes in Western Virginia." Vol. 2, *Stories and Fables*, 1966 edition, pp. 266-69. Reprinted in 1971 and 1981 editions.

The second volume in *Childcraft: The How and Why Library*. Chicago: Field Enterprises Educational Corporation. A set of about 15 volumes, each on a different subject of children's interests.

Children's Prints and Posters (CP.1 - CP.7)

FR painted watercolors for lithographed children's prints and posters intended for framing, wall mounting, or school use. Two children's-book event posters are included. Also see *Pictures from Mother Goose* (1945) [GB.3], a portfolio of eight loose, frameable prints.

CP.1. Children's Spring Book Festival. Sponsored by the *New York Herald Tribune*, May 1943 [listed also as B8, TP.10]. Watercolor of little girl, viewed from the back, seated at a wooden picnic table and reading a picture book spread on the table before her; she sits on two other books for elevation. Reproduced on cover of *New York Herald Tribune Weekly Book Review*. Sunday, May 23, 1943. Derived from a sketch made in Paris, 1930s, of a young friend of the artist. An early variant is in *Calendrier des enfants* (1936) [B3, PC.12a].

CP.2. Children's poster. Undetermined American publisher, about 1943. Exact size not known (but roughly 2 x 3 feet); existence was determined from a photograph. This full-color wall poster was made by enlarging an earlier drawing of a young girl seated in a forest and surrounded by small woods animals. The image had been previously published in *Paris-Soir*, December 24, 1938 [B3, FS.38], and a variant on the cover of the *New York Times Book Review*, November 14, 1943 [B6, AP.4]. FR also used the image for personal Christmas cards in the 1940s [B8, CA.4, 25].

CP.3. U. S. Government School Savings Program, War Finance Program. Tabloid-sized publication on newsprint titled *Schools at War: Quarterly War Savings News Bulletin for Teachers.* February 1945. Contains three posters:

(a) A large (55 x 71 cm) fold-out map of the U.S. showing productive activities in various regions. Bordered with vignettes of different war matériel and the dollar costs, so children will realize the financial costs of war and be encouraged to invest in U. S. Saving Bonds.

(b) A smaller (37.5 x 55 cm) color poster with a dramatic sequence of a downed aviator who bails out at sea, survives in a life raft, and finds rescue at an American island base. Captioned "Let Your War Savings Help a Flyer to Fly and Fight Again," the poster enumerates the equipment that makes possible the flyer's survival, along with the cost of each item.

(c) A still smaller cut-out poster (35.5 x 27.5 cm), captioned "Safe Landing When Everybody Saves," shows the burning plane and the sea below and marks the path of the parachuting flyer as he descends to safety in the life raft. The stages of his descent chart the class's progress toward full participation in the school savings program.

After the war, FR received a citation (December 31, 1945) from the U.S. Treasury Department for "Distinguished services rendered in behalf of the War Finance Program." He also received another citation (March 12, 1946) from the U.S. Treasury Department for other services rendered.

CP.4. John Morrell & Co. 1948 advertising calendar, titled "Fairy

Tales," and children's prints of twelve traditional fairy tale scenes. Copyright 1947. [Also listed as B8, AA.14].

FR painted 12 watercolors illustrating famous fairy tales, one for each month, which were made into a 12-leaf, full-color advertising calendar for the meat-packing firm. Issued in two calendar sizes: the large version is 70 x 35 cm overall; the small version is 46.5 x 21 cm overall.

The 12 images were also issued as loose, frameable children's prints and in two sizes. The larger (on heavier paper, sheet size 50.5 x 37.5 cm) were sold for 50 cents each. The somewhat smaller prints, on lighter paper, are 42.5 x 34.5 cm. All prints marked "Painted for John Morrell & Co. by F. Rojankovsky, 1947" and Morrell's copyright line.

The calendar prints include "Snow White," for which FR was awarded the Art Directors Club Medal in 1948 for color work in advertising (Carrick, 1949). "Snow White," sitting in a glade and surrounded by animal companions, is reproduced in the *Twenty Seventh Annual of Advertising Art* (1948), pp. 74-75. Reproductions from the Annual National Exhibition of Advertising and Editorial Art shown at the Grand Central Galleries, June 1-19, 1948. Also reproduced in Pitz (1948).

In addition, the pictures appear as 12 double-page spreads in *Favorite Fairy Tales* (1948) [B5, GB.10]. Four of the most popular paintings are also reproduced in *F. Rojankovsky's Wonderful Picture Book* (1972) [B5, GB.38].

CP.5. John Morrell & Co. Calendar for the year 1950. Copyright 1949. Titled "The Greatest Calendar Show on Earth." Features 12 full-color circus scenes by FR, plus a pictorial advertising cover sheet decorated by another artist. Overall size: 49.5 (full calendar length) x 21 cm. Any variant calendar sizes or loose prints, as for the 1948 Morrell calendar above, not found [also listed as B8, AA.15].

In December 2000 the Ottumwa Regional Health Center, in the Morrell company's home city, donated five of the 12 original circus scenes, which they owned, to the Children' Care Hospital in Sioux Falls, SD., which already owned the other seven. All twelve original paintings are now on display for the children at the hospital.

CP.6. Encyclopedia Brittanica, Inc., Chicago, Illinois, [1955]. A children's portfolio of four prints titled *A Portfolio of Pictures*. Printed on heavy paper and contained in a pictorial envelope. Frameable, full-color lithographs from paintings, one each by four different children's artists: Busoni, Fox, Rojankovsky, and Watson. A laid-in strip of labels (intended for attachment to backs of framed prints) has bios of the artists. Each print is marked with its title, artist's name, and "COPYRIGHT 1954 BY E.B. INC." Paper size of all prints is 45.5 x 35.5 cm, and is slightly smaller than the portfolio envelope. Issued in 1955 and mailed to subscribing "Britannica Junior Homes" in a stiff outer carton. FR's print from a watercolor is titled "The Bear Family" and pictures a standing mother bear and three cubs in the woods (image size: 35 x 29.5 cm).

CP.7. Children's Book Week 1959. (a) Poster made from a painting of the artist's daughter, Tanya, at age two and one half. She sits on a box and looks at a picture book, a stack of books at her feet. Captioned: "Go Exploring in Books. Book Week Nov. 1-7." 61 x 43 cm. The portrait is one of three versions, others on cover of the *AIGA Journal* (c. 1951) [B6, AP.11] and in *Dog Stories* (1953) [GB.16]. Reproduced in *75 Years of Children's Book Week Posters* (New York: A. A. Knopf, 1994), p. 37. The poster design was simultaneously issued as (b) sheets of stamps and (c) a bookmark, both with tiny images of the poster. The design later appeared on a 1969 calendar (leaf for October) commemorating the "Fiftieth Anniversary of Children's Book Week, 1919-1969."

Toys and Playthings (TO.1 - TO.8)

FR's artwork from his Golden Books, chiefly, was used to decorate a number of spin-off children's toys and playthings. In the language of bibliography, these objects are "first thus" publications of artwork that originally appeared in books. Only the Fisher-Price toy dog and the French puzzles used wholly original artwork. We include these objects because of their novelty formats and popularity as collectibles. The list is restricted to materials first issued before FR's death in 1970.

TO.1. Fisher-Price toy dog**.** Catalog No. 447. Fisher-Price Toys issued "Woofy Wagger" as one of five new toys in 1947. This pull-string toy on wheels is a two-sided image of a black-and-white spotted puppy that wags its tail and "woofs" when pulled. The puppy image is original here and is signed. Lithographed paper mounted on wood, with a painted red base and green wheels. 24 x 18 x 10 cm. Manufactured for two years, until 1949. Mention and color photo in Murray and Fox, pp. 103-04.

TO.2. Decorated tin candy box**.** Oblong octagonal, with hinged lid. 11 x 14 x 5.5 cm. Issued by firm of Côte d'Or, Le Bon Chocolat Belge, to package and promote their retail candy product. Probably late 1940s, but no later than 1958.

Marked on rear lip of cover: "THE METAL BOX COMPANY LTD (B.W. & M Branch) MANSFIELD / CONTAINER MADE IN ENGLAND." Marked on lower left of rear panel: "FROM THE LITTLE GOLDEN BOOK NO. 47 THE THREE BEARS, PICTURES BY FEODOR ROJANKOVSKY C. [copyright] 1948 BY S & S INC. AND A & W GUILD INC. ALL RIGHTS RESERVED."

Lid features a version of the best known cover design from *The Three Bears* (2nd issue cover, 1948), with the Three Bears discovering the startled Goldilocks in the smallest bed. The artwork for the lid is a wider, horizontal version of the narrower, vertical 1948 book cover, wherein (among other minor details) Mother Bear is standing more to the left and clear of the foot of the bed. Sides of box also have variant scenes and words from book. FR may have prepared these versions of the drawings specially for this box project, or they may be from existing, but unused illustrations for the book.

TO.3. French jigsaw puzzles. "Animaux sauvages - animaux domestiques / Dessins de Rojan / Boîte de 6 jeux de patience" [Wild animals - domestic animals / Pictures by Rojan / Box of 6 jigsaw puzzles]. Jouets Vera, Paris [nd].

Six wooden puzzles, three depicting groups of wild animals (hippo, rhino, tiger, elephant, lion, giraffe, zebra, monkeys and water birds) and three depicting groups of farm animals (cow, horses, donkey, sheep, goat, pigs, geese, chickens, rabbits, etc.). Dimensions not known. Each puzzle signed F. Rojankovsky. We do not know if these were ever issued in the U.S. Jouets Vera also issued the puzzles in boxes of 3, one with wild animals and one with farm animals. And Jouets Vera issued a *Jeu de Cubes* [Block Puzzle] of 30 blocks with these pictures, so that each of the 6 pictures could be assembled by combining the 6-sided blocks.

TO.4. Platt and Munk jigsaw puzzles. Platt and Munk, Inc., New York, reissued all twelve pictures of farm animals and farm scenes in their *Grandfather's Farm Panorama* (1943) [B4, AB.13] as jigsaw puzzles for very young children. The artwork is not signed or credited to FR, as was the case for the 1943 panorama. Issued as three different boxes of puzzles, with four picture-puzzles per box. We have seen one boxed set titled "Baby Animal Puzzles: Four Die-Cut Puzzles in This Box." Catalog No. 142B. Copyright 1949. Picture of cow and calf on box cover, repeating one of the puzzles inside. 23x 27 cm. All reissued in 1969 as "Animal Friends Puzzles."

TO.5. Playskool Golden Book Nested Blocks. Golden Press, Inc. Licensed by Playskool, Inc. Animal pictures and decorated letter forms from the ABC in *Animal Stories* (1944), pp. 21-26 [GB.2a], were used on a set of eight hollow nested blocks. Paper mounted on board. Issued in at least two different-sized sets; no primacy is known to us. Nd. First issued in, or in the years after, 1958, the formation date of Golden Press, Inc.

TO.6. Golden Press stacking blocks. Pictures from the three Little Golden Books of Mother Goose rhymes [GB.21-23] used on a set of nine hollow blocks, each 7.5 cubic cm. Paper mounted on cardboard. Nd. First issued in, or in the years after, 1958, the formation date of Golden Press, Inc.

TO.7. Playskool jigsaw puzzles. Golden Press, Inc. Licensed by Playskool, Inc. A number of FR's pictures from various Golden Books were reused as pictures for jigsaw puzzles. Nd. First issued in, or in the years after, 1958, the formation date of Golden Press, Inc. Issued in at least two sizes: about 25.5 x 20.5 cm and 38 x 28 cm. Some are credited to FR and the book source, others are not. Some were issued alone, some in boxed sets of two, some in mixed sets with other Golden Book artists. We have seen jigsaw puzzles made from FR's artwork in these books: *Animal* Stories (1944) [GB.2A]; The *Three Bears* (1948) [GB.5]; *Our Puppy* (1948) [GB.8]; *The Great Big Animal Book* (1950) [GB.12]; *The Great Big Wild Animal Book* (1950) [GB.14].

TO.8. *Playskool Golden Book Animal Count Clock Puzzle*. Golden Press, Inc., [1960s]. Twenty-four-piece combination jigsaw tray puzzle and clock counting-game toy. 31.5 x 30.5 cm. Paper-covered heavy cardboard, with moveable red plastic clock hands. Decorated with seventeen small watercolors of animals from *Animal Stories* (1944) [GB.2a], ten of which are from pages 70-71. Twelve small pictures of animals decorate the hour positions on the clock face (the number of animals in each picture corresponds to the number of the hour, "Ten mice o'clock," etc.). One picture (a baby bear) is at the center of the clock face; four pictures (chickens and owls, awake and sleeping, symbolizing day and night) are in the four corners outside the clock circle. Credited "Illustrations by Feodor Rojankovsky, from Animal Stories."

Children's Phonograph Records (CR.1 - CR.7)

Golden Books and a few other publishers issued as book-record sets some of FR's (and other illustrators') picture books, newly accompanied by phonograph records of narration, song and music. None have significant new artwork by FR.

CR.1. Little Golden Records. Simon & Schuster, New York. Set of 12 records. Three of the 12 records reproduce a selection of FR's illustrations from Duplaix's *Animal Stories* (1944) [GB.2a], though FR did not illustrate the corresponding books: No. 5, "The Poky Little Puppy" (illustrations by Tenggren) and "The Naughty Duck"; No. 7, "The Funny Little Mouse" and "The Tall Giraffe"; and No. 12, "Out of the Window" and "The Busy Elevator". The phonograph records narratively and musically recount the stories. Performers are singer Ireene Wicker, Gilbert Mack, and Mitchell Miller and Orchestra. The twelve records in this set, issued about 1948 (copyright date), are the first in the Little Golden Records series. The yellow plastic, flexible 45 rpm records are packaged in folding sleeves or albums designed to be uniform in size (about 20 x 17 cm) and in appearance with Little Golden Books. FR's drawings from *Animal Stories* appear variously on the four sides of the folding sleeves.

CR.2. *Three Bears Golden Book and Record Set* #00155. No date. The set consists of a reissue of *The Three Bears* (1948) [GB.5] and a phonograph record. The package, when open, on the left reads "READ AND HEAR A LITTLE GOLDEN BOOK AND A SPECIAL GOLDEN RECORD" and faces the second-issue book cover on the right. An ad on the package suggests that similar sets were issued for FR's Little Golden Books, *Our Puppy* (1948) [GB.8] and *The Kitten's Surprise* (1951) [GB.13], and one of Mother Goose rhymes, but we have not seen these items.

[**CR.3**]. FR's business correspondence indicates that Georges Duplaix in 1947 solicited one or more original designs for record labels for a proposed series of records based on *Animal Stories*. But we have not seen examples of these and, so, do not know if they were in fact created or used.

CR.4. *The Golden Record Bible Library*. A 24-page illustrated booklet, *Bible Songs and Stories* (distributed by Simon & Schuster, New York, 1957), is packaged in a box with ten sleeved LP record albums. The booklet features selections of FR's artwork from *The Golden Bible: From the King James Version of the Old Testament* (1946) [GB.4], with a new text by Elsa Ruth Nast. The only notable alteration to FR's original artwork is that the images of God in the center and at lower right of the first illustration are replaced (possibly by FR himself) by a sunburst and a people-less Garden-of-Eden scene. But one of FR's images of God as an old man in a white beard reappears in the same illustration on the front of the first record sleeve, No. 1. This is from FR's six-panel depiction of The Creation from the cover and repeated in opening pages of *The Golden Bible*. The other nine album sleeves have artwork by another illustrator, Steele Savage. The ten sleeved LPs and the booklet are contained in a red, drop-front, heavy cardboard box, 32.5 x 32.5 cm. The front matter of the booklet reads, in part: "10 LP Record Albums containing 16 great Stories from the Old and New Testaments and 18 Bible Ballad Songs / Starring the narrative voice of LEIF ERIKSON and the singing voice of TERRY GILKYSON . . . featuring the voices of Betty Mulliner and Norma Zimmer and full Chorus under the Choral Direction of Arthur Norman. Dramatic Records produced and directed by George Wallach, Musical Direction by Mitch Miller."

CR.5. *Scott, Foresman First Talking Storybook Box*. John Langstaff. *Over in the Meadow* [1967] [B4, AB.32]. "Special Scott, Foresman and Company Edition for *Scott, Foresman First Talking Storybook Box*. By special arrangement with Harcourt, Brace & World, Inc., New York."

The book is a reissue of the Harcourt, Brace edition of 1957 and has a 3:47 minute, 33-1/3 rpm record (in a blank white sleeve) in a pocket mounted on the rear pastedown end paper. Record produced by Shield Productions, Inc., and Jamar Records. The front matter of the book lists twenty other book-record titles in the series.

[**CR.6**]. Columbia Record sets. Two Little Golden Book narratives, *The White Bunny and His Magic Nose* (1957) [GB.20] and *The Three Bears* (revised version, 1967) [GB.36] were, according to 1967 estate correspondence, planned to be made into phonograph records. Examples not found.

CR.7. For the use of teachers in elementary school, Weston Woods Studios, Weston, CT. issued film strips, audio tapes, videocassettes, a phonograph record, and printed teacher guides for Harcourt, Brace's two books by FR and author and songster John Langstaff, *Frog Went A-Courtin'* (1955) [B4, AB.24] and *Over in the Meadow* (1957) [B4, AB.32]. No dates.

III.

Catalog of Published Graphic Art for Adults

In addition to mainly children's-book illustrations, Feodor Rojankovsky throughout his long career steadily produced for grown-ups graphic art of nearly every kind that was published in Europe and the United States: magazine covers and drawings, book covers and jackets, catalog covers and brochures, picture calendars, and magazine advertisements, travel and event display posters, scenic postcards and Christmas greeting cards.

During the First World War and before leaving Russia, Rojankovsky made many covers and drawings for the prestigious Russian art journal, *Lukomor'e,* and other pre-Revolutionary magazines. After settling in Poland in 1920, he designed many book covers and, among other kinds of graphic art work, made magazine drawings, especially the many covers and cartoons for *Szczutek*, the leading Polish magazine of humor and satire in the early 1920s.

The graphic art work in Paris in the 1920s and 1930s—including some notable work for British clients—yielded a variety of magazine advertisements, promotional brochures in the *Moderne* style, magazine and newspaper story illustrations, and several notable British travel posters. In the early 1930s, he produced covers and cartoons for *Le Rire*, the popular French magazine of satire and risqué humor. And until about 1938, he continued designing book covers for his publisher in Poznan and for several French publishers as well.

After coming to the U. S. in 1941, Rojankovsky drew advertising art and story illustrations for the *Saturday Evening Post* and other national magazines. He also designed calendars, Children's Book Week posters, Christmas cards and other work. He was now preoccupied with children's art and much of this work for American magazines and other publishers employs subjects and styles similar to his children's illustrations.

Rojankovsky never listed these hundreds of published graphics and no nearly complete collection of reproductive prints exists. From estate records and many other sources, we have identified and described a large and representative array of this non-children's artwork—more than three hundred fifty items—including the most important designs. Yet at this moment other work, mostly minor we hope, has surely eluded us.

B6

Magazine Drawings and Covers

European Magazines, 1915 - 1939 (EP.1 - EP.18)

Lukomor'e (EP.1, 1 - 55)

EP.1. *Lukomor'e* [The Cove] was a pre-Revolutionary weekly journal of literature, art, and satire featuring many prominent Russian graphic artists. While serving as an infantry officer in the Russian Imperial Army and fighting the Germans in the 1914-1917 campaign of the First World War, Rojankovsky made 87 drawings and paintings of things he saw while serving in the battle fields. These drawings, including ten cover designs, appeared in 55 issues of the magazine in 1915, 1916 and 1917 and are an important eye-witness account of the war.

The first of FR's drawings appeared in the issue of May 30, 1915 and was his first published work, at the age of 23. His last contribution to the magazine was on May 9, 1917 (by the old Julian calendar), several months before it ceased publication with the issue of October 31, 1917, as a result of the October Revolution of the Bolsheviks.

The earlier drawings of 1915 are mostly pictures of noncombat military operations in the field and of the presence of soldiers and their horses in villages. Some of the drawings in 1915 are at a Moscow military hospital sketched after the artist was wounded in the first winter of the war and evacuated. Upon return to active duty, FR drew grim scenes of the aftermath of battles and skirmishes. The last drawings in 1917 are, appropriately, street scenes of victory celebrations in Petrograd and Moscow following the liberal but short-lived February revolution. The several non-military scenes scattered throughout are idyllic views of villages and towns and romantic and peaceful scenes of people in city parks—relief for readers from many images of turmoil and war.

The full-color covers and a number of color drawings are photolithographs from watercolors or, in a few cases, from colored pencil. The many black-and-white drawings are from either pen or pencil sketches, occasionally with a wash. FR's color pictures in the magazine were frequent in 1915, but the color work dropped off and simple pen drawings became more usual as the war continued in 1916 and 1917. Most of the drawings are large, either full-page or half page.

Rojankovsky's two older artist brothers, Sergei and Pavel, also each contributed one drawing (also signed "Rojankovsky" but with the initials "S" and "P") to the same magazine, respectively, on May 2, 1915 (No. 18, p. 10) and July 9, 1916 (No. 28, frontis).

1. Issue No. 22, 30 May 1915, p. 10. Pencil. 9 x 19 cm. "Mestechko Khentsiny, Keletskoi gub." [Little Town of Khentsiny in Keletsky Province]. Distant view of village in winter. Same issue, p. 11. Pencil. 14 x 19 cm. "Parad v

Kel'tsach. Nagrazhdenie Georgievskimi krestami" [Parade in Kel'tsy. Presentation of St. George's Crosses]. Military awards ceremony. Same issue, p. 13. Watercolor. 13.5 x 19.5 cm. "V Pol'she" [In Poland]. Military arriving in a town.

2. No. 23, 6 June 1915, p. 13. Watercolor. 14 x 19 cm. "Moskovskii voennyi gospital'" [Moscow Military Hospital]. Hospital grounds.

3. No. 24, 13 June 1915, p. 13. Watercolor. 15 x 20 cm. "V Varshave" [In Warsaw]. Park scene at night.

4. No. 26, 27 June 1915, p. 13. Watercolor. 13 x 20 cm. "Razvaliny Khentsinskago zamka. Keletskoi gub." [Ruins of a Castle in Khentsiny. Keletsky Province].

5. No. 27, 4 July 1915, p. 13. Watercolor. 18 x 20 cm. "Prival" [Stopping Place]. Soldiers relaxing in field camp.

6. No. 28, 11 July 1915, p. 13. Watercolor. 14 x 19 cm. "Riazan'" [Riazan (city 200 km. SE of Moscow)]. Village scene.

7. No. 30, 25 July 1915, p. 3. Pencil. 13.5 x 19 cm. "V polevom lazarete" [In a Field Hospital]. Same issue, p. 7. Pencil. 14 x 19 cm. "Dopros plennago" [Interrogation of a Prisoner]. Soldiers questioning prisoner in front of log cabin. Same issue, p. 9. Pencil. 12.5 x 18.5 cm. "Otdykh" [Rest]. Soldiers relaxing.

8. No. 33, 15 August 1915. Cover. Watercolor. 26 x 22 cm. "U pulemeta" [At the Machine Gun]. Two soldiers manning a gun. Same issue, p. 3. Pencil. 12.5 x 19 cm. "Bezhentsy" [Refugees]. Six refugees with infants in arms. Same issue, p. 17. Watercolor. 10.5 x 12.5 cm. "Gorod v tylu" [City in the Rear]. Town square with soldiers. Same issue, p. 17. Watercolor. 8 x 12.5 cm. "Moskovskii voennyi gospital'" [Moscow Military Hospital]. Hospital grounds with recuperating patients.

9. No. 34, 22 August 1915, p. 5. Pencil. 14.5 x 19 cm. "U pereviazochnago punkta" [At a Dressing Station]. Same issue, p. 7. Pencil. 14 x 19 cm. "Rezerv" [Reserves]. Another scene of military field camp. Same issue, p. 16. Pencil. 6 x 9 cm. "Razrushennyi fol'varok" [Ruined Farm]. Small house under trees.

10. No. 35, 29 August 1915, p. 7. Pencil. 11 x 18.5 cm. "Razbivka palatok" [Pitching of Tents]. Soldiers in field camp.

11. No. 36, 5 September 1915. Cover. Watercolor. 26 x 22 cm. "Nabliudenie boia" [Observing the Battle]. Officers watching battle from a distance.

12. No. 39, 26 September 1915. Cover. Watercolor. 26 x 22 cm. "Signal" [Signal]. Burning buildings in field by night.

13. No. 41, 10 October 1915. Cover. Watercolor. 26 x 22 cm. "V pokhode pod dozhdem" [On the March in the Rain]. Soldiers marching through a town.

14. No. 42, 17 October 1915, p. 3. Pencil. 14.5 x 19 cm. "Ostavlennyi okop" [Abandoned Trench]. Aftermath of battle, with corpses.

15. No. 43, 24 October 1915, p. 4. Pencil. 15 x 19 cm. "Tiazhelaia batareia" [Heavy Battery]. Battery of artillery. Same issue, p. 5. Pencil. 18.5 x 19 cm. "Plennye" [Prisoners]. Three soldiers in field.

16. No. 44, 31 October 1915, p. 2. Pencil. 13 x 19 cm. "Nabliudenie boia" [Observing Battle]. Officers watching a battle. Same issue, p. 10. Pencil. 8 x 19 cm. "Kolonna pekhoty v pokhode" [Column of Infantry on the March].

17. No. 45, 7 November 1915, p. 7. Pencil and watercolor, in black and white. 16 x 18.5 cm. "Bezhentsy v puti" [Refugees en Route]. Village scene with cart and refugees.

18. No. 46, 14 November 1915, p. 8. Pencil. 13 x 19 cm. "Ranniaia zima v okopakh" [Early Winter in the Trenches].

19. No. 48, 28 November 1915, p. 12. Pencil. 13 x 12.5 cm. "V ofitserskoi zemlianke. Na otdykhe" [In the Officers' Dugout. At Rest]. Two officers relaxing.

20. No. 49, 5 December 1915, p. 11. Pencil. 12.5 x 18.5 cm. "Postroika saperami mosta" [Sappers Building a Bridge].

21. No. 50, 12 December 1915, p. 11. Pencil. 18 x 19 cm. "Otdykh" [Rest]. Soldiers relaxing. Same issue, p. 17. Watercolor. 11.5 x 19.5 cm. "Na Dvine" [On the (River) Dvina]. Military camp in the snow.

22. No. 51, 19 December 1915. Cover. Watercolor. 27 x 22 cm. "Razvedchiki v derevne" [Scouts in a Village]. Village scene with soldiers on horseback.

23. No. 5, 30 January 1916, p. 7. Pen. 17 x 19 cm. "Aeroplan!.." [Airplane!..]. Soldiers pointing to sky. Same issue, p. 8. Pencil. 14.5 x 19 cm. "Gizgol'dery [sic] i zmeikovyi aerostat" [Gas Tanks and Kite Balloon]. Inflating a military balloon. Same issue, p. 9. Pen. 14 x 19 cm. "V tylu" [At the Rear]. Soldiers in village with pig.

24. No. 6, 6 February 1916, p. 7. Pen. 26 x 19 cm. (full page) "Vozdukhoplavatel'nyi park" [Ballooning Park]. Two balloons aloft, with windmill. Same issue, p. 11. Pen. 16 x 19.5 cm. "U pozitsii" [At a Position]. Village scene "at a position."

25. No. 7, 13 February 1916, p. 5. Pen. 18 x 19 cm. "U provolochnykh zagrazhdenii nepriiatelia" [At an Enemy Wire Entanglement]. Dead soldier in snow. Same issue, p. 8. Pencil. 24.5 x 19 cm. (full page). "Razrushennyi snariadami kostel v Izbitsakh" [Roman Catholic Church in Izbitsy, Destroyed by Missiles].

26. No. 8, 20 February 1916, p. 2. Pen. 14 x 19 cm. Story: "Sluchai" [An Incident], by Boris Bedov. Illustrations: "Mne strashno, milyi... znaesh, mne kazhetsia, chto gde-to zdes' sovsem blizko, est' smert'" ['I am terrified, dear, you know, it seems to me that death is somewhere here very close']. Man and woman embracing. Same issue, p. 3. Pen. 25 x 18.5 cm (full page). "Kogda my prishli vo dvor, my uvideli v kontse ego gruppu liudei" [When we arrived in the courtyard, we saw a group of people at the end of the courtyard]. Illustration to story, continued, another scene. Same issue, p. 5. Pen. 25 x 12 cm. "I vot zakhvatil uzhas. Terpkii, viazhushchii, okhvatil vse telo. . ." [And here he was gripped with panic. Sharp, astringent, it seized his entire body . . .]. Illustration to story, continued, another scene. Same issue, p. 17. Pen. 19 x 26 cm (full page, horizontal). "Na pozitsii, otbitoi u nepriiatelia" [In a Position, Taken From the Enemy]. Soldiers in field.

27. No. 10, 5 March 1916, p. 3. Pen. 14.5 x 19 cm. "Les" [Forest]. Forest Scene.

28. No. 11, 12 March 1916, p. 9. Pen. 24.5 x 19 cm. "Nabliudenie" [Observation]. Soldiers climbing ladder for field observation.

29. No. 14, 2 April 1916, p. 11. Pen. 14 x 19 cm. "Ustroistvo nabliudatel'nago punkta" [Construction of an Observation Post]. Soldier mounting ladder against tree for field observation. Same issue, p. 14. Pen. 13 x 19.5 cm. "Nabliudenie za boem" [Observing the Battle]. Soldiers looking through field glasses.

30. No. 17, 23 April 1916, p. 10. Pen. 13.5 x 19 cm. "Polevaia kukhnia" [Field Kitchen]. Same issue, p. 11. Pen. 18 x 19.5 cm. "Plennye" [Prisoners]. Same issue, p. 13. Pen. 25 x 19 cm. "V blizhnem tylu" [In the Nearby Home Front]. Village scene, with soldiers embracing women.

31. No. 18, 30 April 1916, p. 7. Pen. 24 x 19 cm. "Rabota razvedchikov" [Work of Scouts]. Soldiers cutting telephone wires with sword.

32. No. 21, 21 May 1916, p. 5. Pen. 13 x 19 cm. "Na peredovykh pozitsiiakh" [In the Forward Positions]. Military field scene. Same issue, p. 20. Pen. 14 x 19 cm. "Mirnyia zaniatiia na pozitsiiakh" [Peaceful Occupations at the Positions]. Soldier holding newborn calf to cow's teat.

33. No. 23, 4 June 1916, p. 11. Pen. 22 x 18 cm. "Stoianka v lesu" [Stopping Place in the Forest]. Same issue, p. 15. Pen. 16 x 19.5 cm. "Telefonist" [Telephonist]. Soldier using a field telephone.

34. No. 24, 11 June 1916, p. 11. Pen. 19 x 25 cm (full page, horizontal). "Veselyi plennyi" [Merry Prisoner]. German prisoner dancing to accordion music.

35. No. 26, 25 June 1916. Cover. Watercolor. 26 x 21.5 cm. "Riazan'" [Riazan (city 200 km. SE of Moscow)]. Orange building with onion domes.

36. No. 28, 9 July 1916. Cover. Watercolor. 25 x 21.5 cm. "Pered poletom" [Before the Flight]. Aviators with their airplane.

37. No. 30, 23 July 1916, p. 13. Pen. 24 x 18 cm (full page). "Gospital' v fol'varke" [Hospital in a Farmyard]. Field hospital under trellises, with nurses. Same issue, p. 14. Pen. 12.5 x 19.5 cm. "Postroika mosta" [Building a Bridge].

38. No. 32, 6 August 1916, p. 15. Pen. 25 x 19 cm (full page). "Plennyi" [Prisoners]. On a march.

39. No. 33, 13 August 1916, p. 14. Pencil. 14 x 18 cm. "V Galitsii" [In Galicia]. Village scene.

40. No. 34, 20 August 1916, p. 16. Colored pencil. 15 x 19.5 cm. "Stolovaia v ambare" [Canteen in a Barn]. Officers in a field mess. Same issue, p. 17. Colored pencil. 16.5 x 19.5 cm. "Derevnia bliz pozitsii" [Village Near a Position]. A village scene.

41. No. 36, 3 September 1916. Cover. Watercolor. 29 x 19 cm. "Osen'" [Autumn]. City park, with family on a bench.

42. No. 37, 10 September 1916, p. 5. Pen. 18.5 x 23.5 cm (full page, horizontal). "Pereprava cherez most" [Crossing the Bridge]. Unit crossing, while other soldiers get water from river. Same issue, p. 8. Pen. 13.5 x 19 cm. "Deistvie nashago bronirovannago avtomobilia" [Attack of Our Armored Car]. A skirmish.

43. No. 38, 17 September 1916, p. 5. Pencil. 14.5 x 18.5 cm. "Na etape. Kukhnia." [At a Stopping Place. Kitchen]. Soldiers working in a field kitchen.

44. No. 40, 1 October 1916. Cover. Watercolor. 24 x 19 cm. "Na etape" [At a Stopping Place]. Soldiers resting in field. Same issue, p. 9. Pen. 24 x 29.5 cm (full page). "Posle raboty" [After Work]. Man repairing autos.

45. No. 44, 29 October 1916, p. 4. Pen. 16 x 13 cm. No caption. Soldier standing beside horse.

46. No. 45, 5 November 1916. Cover. Watercolor. 25 x 19 cm. "Osen'" [Autumn]. Young woman in city park, in old fashioned dress.

47. No. 50, 10 December 1916, p. 13. Pencil. 9.5 x 18.5 cm. "Gory v Galitsii" [Mountains in Galicia]. A landscape.

48. No. 1, 1 January 1917, p. 7. Pen. Half page. "Ustroistvo provolochnykh zagrazhdenii" [Construction of a Wire Entanglement]. Soldiers stringing barbed wire.

49. No. 2, 7 January 1917, p. 9. Pen. Full page. "Pitatel'nyi punkt V. M. Purichkevicha" [V. M. Purichkevich Refreshment Place]. Dining tables.

50. No. 3, 14 January 1917, p. 15. Pen. Full page. "Evakuatsionnyi punkt" [Evacuation Point]. Loading wounded between ambulances and train.

51. No. 7, 14 February 1917, p. 11. Pen. Half page. "Vziatyi okop" [Captured Trench]. Dead soldier on road near trench.

52. Nos. 9-11 (combined issue), 2 April 1917, p. 12. Pen. Half page. "Pervyia izvestia" [First News]. People reading newspapers in street and shouting. Same issue, p. 13. Pen. Three quarters page. "Sniatie venzelei" [Taking Down the Monograms]. Removing the Royal purveyor signs from shops. Same issue, p. 21. Pen. Full page. "Na Znamenskoi ploshchadi v dni revoliutsii" [On Znamensky Square in the Days of the Revolution]. Crowd scene in square. Same issue, p. 22. Pen. Half page. "Chitaiut o svobode" [They are Reading About Freedom]. People reading a news wall, small girl in foreground.

53. No. 14, 25 April 1917, p. 13. Pen. One quarter page. "Manifestatsiia o Gosud. Dumy" [Street Demonstration about the Government Duma]. Street crowd listening to speaker on platform.

54. No. 15, 1 May 1917, p. 3. Pen. Full page. "Revoliutsiia v Moskve. Manifestatsiia soldat i grazhdan u Kremlia" [Revolution in Moscow. Street Demonstration of Soldiers and Civilians at the Kremlin].

55. No. 16, 9 May 1917, p. 10. Pen. Half page. "Pitatel'nyi punkt" [Canteen]. Women nurses serving food to soldiers. Same issue, p. 15. Pen. Full page. "Parad revoliutsionnym

voiskam" [Parade in Honor of the Revolutionary Forces]. In Palace Square in Petrograd.

Ogonek (EP.2, 1 - 2)

EP.2. *Ogonek* [Twinkle] was a popular Russian weekly magazine for which FR illustrated two short stories:

1. Issue No. 29, Sunday, 17 July 1916, p. 2. Pen. Half page. People talking in a formal dining room, illustrating Vadim Belov's "Sud skoryi i pravyi" [A Swift and Just Trial].

2. No. 40. Sunday, 2 October 1916, p. 2. Pen. Quarter page. Headpiece of two men talking on telephones; p. 3, half page pen drawing of parlor scene, with man on his knees pleading with a seated woman, both illustrating Vadim Belov's "Sil'nye strasti" [Strong Passions].

Solntse Rossii (EP.3)

EP.3. *Solntse Rossii* [Sun of Russia] was a Russian art and literary magazine, for which FR painted one color cover:

Issue No. 368, 8 March 1917. Cover. Watercolor of sitting soldier (three-quarters view), wearing old-style military garb, hand resting on ceremonial sword or dagger. Patriotic theme for the liberal February Revolution. Captions: "Slava Velikoi Revoliutsii!" [Glory to the Great Revolution!] and "Geroi Revoliutsii" [Hero of the Revolution].

Szczutek (EP.4, 1 - 33)

EP.4. *Szczutek* [Fillip] was a popular Polish weekly magazine of humor and political satire, founded in Lvov in 1918. The title means "a fillip," a disrespectful flick of the index finger from the thumb.

Szczutek published four of FR's cover designs and 35 other drawings in 1920, 1921, 1922, and one, the last, in 1923. These appear in 33 separate issues of the magazine. Only the drawing titles are given here; most also have extended captions relaying the conversation among the characters depicted. A few of the drawings illustrate light verses. Most are either pencil or pen-and-ink drawings.

Most of the scenes are satirical social and political commentary on the issues of the day, some with allegorical figures. The drawings are populated with comfortable bourgeois couples at home, shapely and fashionable young women, slim female nudes in black stockings, colorful theatrical characters, people puzzling over modern art in galleries, and people sitting and conversing in cafés and green parks. One drawing of two women gossiping about a third (1921) is reproduced in Górska and Lipiński (p. 200) and in Witz and Zaruba (pl. 164).

1. Issue No. 22, 30 May 1920, p. 4. "Kultura na wsi" [Culture in the Rural Countryside]. Quarter page. Peasant woman milking a cow.

2. No. 24, 13 June 1920, p. 4. "Po obiedzie" [After Lunch]. Half page. Bourgeois couple reclining in luxury and reading the newspapers. Same issue, p. 5. No title. Half page. Elegant lady being fitted at dressmaker's.

3. No. 25, 20 June 1920, p. 8. "Czyżby Anglicy?" [How about the English?]. Full page. Soldiers loading field artillery gun.

4. No. 26, 27 June 1920, p. 8. "Piosenka wiatru" [Song of the Wind]. Full page. Slim, naked woman in meadow has shed elegant clothing to the open air; candid cameraman in distance.

5. No. 27, 4 July 1920, p. 2. No title. Heading light verse "Businessmann." Full page. Slim, naked, reclining woman floating on a pillow of clouds. Same issue, p. 5. "Najemnicy pana Wrangla" [Mr. Wrangel's Mercenaries]. Full page. Two figures in military uniforms.

6. No. 28, 11 July 1920, p. 4. "Nowobogaccy a ojczyzna" [Newly Rich versus the Homeland]. One third page. Six adults sit on circular bench around park tree.

7. No. 29, 18 July 1920, p. 5. No title. Full page. Reading mother and young girl with hoop sit and talk on park bench. Same issue, p. 8. "Obrońca" [Defender]. Full page. Well-dressed woman in large skirt with suited man to side.

8. No. 30, 25 July 1920, p. 8. "Strefa neutralina" [Neutral Zone]. Full page. Three standing figures, all smoking; two large suited men talking to a svelte younger woman.

9. No. 31, 1 August 1920, p. 5. "Z rozmów na dobie" [From a Conversation in a Café]. Half page. Chic young woman and an older man at a separate table in foreground.

10. No. 19, 4 May 1921, p. 6. No title. Half page. Two women and two men around table, as third woman plays piano. Same issue, p. 8. "Admonicja" [Admonition]. Full page. Outdoor, public café scene.

11. No. 20, 12 May 1921, p. 4. "Cafe 'Kurfürstendamm'." Half page. Three middle-class women talking at table in said café.

12. No. 21, 19 May 1921, p. 4. "Dobrzy patrjoci (Rzecz w Berlinie)" [Real Patriots (Set in Berlin)]. Quarter page. Two suited men and one woman seated at public tea room table.

13. No. 22, 26 May 1921, p. 10. "Na wystawie futurystów" [At the Futurist Exhibition]. Quarter page. Several elegant

women and men standing about and talking at an exhibition of modern art.

14. No. 23, 1 June 1921, p. 4. "Na wystawie futurystów w Poznaniu" [At the Poznan Futurist Exhibition]. Third page. Older couple discussing a modern sculpture of three nude dancers.

15. No. 29, 14 July 1921, p. 9. "W kąpielach" [At the Health Resort]. Two-thirds page. Two middle-aged women sitting and talking at round lounge table.

16. No. 33, 11 August 1921, p. 1. Cover: "Wizja" [The Vision]. Uniformed leader as giant figure with arms crossed and hovering over urban-industrial scene of rail yards.

17. No. 35, 25 August 1921, p. 12. "Głód w Rosji" [Hunger in Russia]. Full page. Gigantic war god in helmet embraces skeleton as they sit on landscape with tiny village in foreground.

18. No. 37, 8 September 1921, p. 1. Cover for theatrical issue: "Przed przedstawieniem" [Before the Performance]. Theatrical couple, one a harlequin, seated at backstage dressing table.

19. No. 42, 13 October 1921, p. 1. Cover: "Taniec marki polskiej na linie" [Dance of the Polish Mark on the Tightrope]. Rump view of ample woman circus performer with parasol teetering on high wire over watching crowd. Same issue, p. 12. "Przesilenie finansowe" [Financial Crisis]. Full page. "Goldfinger" and "Geldblum" characters discuss economics.

20. No. 43, 21 October 1921, p. 4. "Monolog Józi" [Józi's Monologue]. Half page. Man sitting on end of high-backed couch, with reclining woman whose upper body rests on his lap as she caresses his face.

21. No. 44, 27 October 1921, p. 12. "Za kulisami" [Behind the Scenes]. Full page. Two workmen discuss large sculptured head.

22. No. 46, 10 November 1921, p. 4. "Występy artystów rosyjskich we Lwowie" [Performance of Russian Musical Artists in Lvov]. Half page. Standing figure of ample, fashionably-dressed woman with hand on hip.

23. No. 49, 1 December 1921, p. 9. No title. Half page. Two men seated at café table discussing politics.

24. No. 53, 29 December 1921, p. 12. "Rodziciel daniny" [The Father of Tribute]. Full page. Two women in resigned postures seated at table.

25. No. 2, 12 January 1922, p. 9. "Pomyłka pana Michalskiego" [Michalsky's Error]. Three-quarters page. Young woman and older man seated at café table.

26. No. 3, 19 January 1922, p. 1. Cover: "Zwycięskie zapasy marki polskiej" [Victory of the Polish Mark]. Large woman in boxing costume standing over defeated opponent, with crowd in background. Same issue, p. 12. "Pocałunek" [The Kiss]. Full page. Couple kissing in front of open window with night-lighted city in background.

27. No. 6, 9 February 1922, p. 9. No title. Three-quarters page. Ample woman (back view) and thinner man (side view) standing on boulevard and talking.

28. No. 7, 16 February 1922, p. 9. "O czem się teraz mówi we Lwowie" [What They Are Talking about in Lvov Today]. Three-quarters page. Rear view of barber cutting hair of man seated in barber's chair, with assistant watching.

29. No. 10, 9 March 1922, p. 9. "Lloyd George ustępuje" [Lloyd

George Steps Down]. Full page. Two men seated, one reading, and talking at sidewalk café table.

30. No. 14, 6 June 1922, p. 9. "Na wystawie 'Zachęty'" [At the Zachety Exhibition]. Quarter page. Rear view of woman standing in art gallery, hands clasped behind her, looking at paintings.

31. No. 23, 8 June 1922, p. 12. "W garderobie" [In the Dressing Room]. Full page. Two women, one in tights, leaning with elbows on dressing table backstage at circus.

32. No. 25, 22 June 1922, p. 4. "Warszawskie Derby" [Warsaw Derby]. Quarter page. Back view of spectators at horse race.

33. No. 35, 30 August 1923, p. 9. "Wygodny malarz" [A Comfortable Painter]. Full page. Rear view of woman standing, arms raised, holding fan and mask, in stage-like setting. Rojankovsky himself is a character in the verse this illustrates.

Pani (EP.5, 1 - 2)

EP.5. *Pani* [Lady] was a stylish Polish (Warsaw) monthly magazine of literature, art, and fashion for women. FR drew one cover and four illustrations for one story:

1. Issue No. 6/7, July 1924. Cover. Black and white, titled "Tennis," 34 x 24 cm. Two young women with bobbed hair and in tennis dresses, swinging rackets on a court, with townscape in background.

2. No. 2/3, 1925, pp. 22-23. Pen. Four illustrations for a story, "Tańczyć-Tańczyć" [Dance-Dance] by J. Stycz. One half-page and three small line drawings: larger drawing of costumed merry-makers piling out of an automobile; smaller of a jazz band; dancing couples; people at a fashionable bar.

Illiustrirovannaia Rossiia (EP.6, 1 - 15)

EP.6. *Illiustrirovannaia Rossiia* [Illustrated Russia] was a Paris-based, Russian-language weekly news magazine, published from 1924-1939. In 1926, FR painted watercolors for 9 color covers (30.2 x 23.5 cm) and made pen and pencil drawings for another 6 issues of the magazine. The first contribution appeared on 6 March 1926 and the last on 16 October 1926. All are initialed in the plate. Most of the pictures depict either sentimental views of Old Russia or modernistic images of émigré life in Paris.

1. Issue No. 10, 6 March 1926, p. 3. "Russkii Monmartr" [Russian Montmartre]. Full page. Semi-cubistic image of people in the public places. Street scenes and lettered signs evoke the nightlife of the Russian district. Figures include a cabdriver, watchman, policeman, cossack dancer, and a woman sitting in a café.

2. No. 12, 20 March 1926, p. 3. Split title at top and bottom: "Mi-carême/Karnaval Parizh" [Mid-Lent/Carnival in Paris]. Full page. Sidewalk café scene at carnival time, with woman and costumed child in the foreground. Figures include people sitting at café tables, some in carnival costumes and masks, with poster-covered kiosk pillars.

3. No. 14, 3 April 1926, p. 3. "Na dispute o Zarubezhnom s'ezde" [On a Debate about the Congress in Exile]. Drawings. Seven profile portraits of prominent men. P. B. Struve is featured.

4. No. 17, 24 April 1926. Cover. Watercolor. Plump, smiling peasant girl, with arms raised above head, wearing flowered scarf and red dress with balloon sleeves. River and steamboat in background. Same issue, pp. 1-3. Four small drawings illustrate a story, "Paskhal'nyi vizit" [Easter Visit], by A. Chernyi: view of apartment courtyard; young girl reading a

book; older girl kissing a boy; girl-child teasing a bear in zoo cage.

5. No. 23, 5 June 1926. Cover in monochrome browns. Black silhouette of A. Pushkin in oval frame, this above a memorial tablet with foliage, scrolls, panpipe, and a lyre. Under the tablet, in stylized script, "8 Iiunia—Den' Russkoi Kul'tury" [8 June—Day of Russian Culture], with magazine title above in same script. Both picture and lettering bear FR's initials.

6. No. 26, 26 June 1926, p. 3. A full-page political cartoon. Titled "Emigrantskiia karty. I. Koroli" [Émigré Playing Cards. I. Kings]. Borrowing from the image on British court playing cards, caricatures of four contemporary political personalities: King of Hearts is P.N. Miliukov; King of Diamonds is P.B. Struve; King of Clubs is A. F. Kerenskii; King of Spades is A. F. Trepov.

7. No. 27, 3 July 1926. Cover. Watercolor. Titled "Zamoskvorech'e" [name of a district in Moscow]. Boy in school uniform and backpack, carrying a sling shot, and walking on a street toward the viewer. Surrounds of a birch tree and other greenery. Background of churches, houses, factories, and overhead a kite and a bright sun.

8. No. 28, 10 July 1926, p. 3. A full-page political cartoon. Titled "Emigrantskiia karty. II. Damy" [Émigré Playing Cards. II. Queens]. From British court playing cards, caricatures of four émigré female personalities: Queen of Hearts is E. D. Kuskova; Queen of Diamonds is Z. N. Gippius; Queen of Clubs is N.A. Teffi; Queens of Spades is Larissa Popova.

9. No. 29, 17 July 1926. Cover. Watercolor. Bastille Day issue. Holiday scene in modernist style of couples dancing, orchestra playing, and café tables. In the foreground, a rakish black man dances with woman in fur-trimmed jacket,

with urban background of tall buildings, tricolor banners, and lettered signs.

10. No. 31, 31 July 1926. Cover. Watercolor. Titled "Morozhenshchik" [Ice-cream Vendor]. Man in peasant costume, with a wooden ice-cream bucket on his head. Background of farm buildings, trees, and chickens. See the similar drawing in Satyricon [EP.8].

11. No. 33, 14 August 1926. Cover. Watercolor. Titled "Na Pliazhe" [On the Beach] in the plate. Crowded summer scene of bathing beach. Man in street clothing carries a towel and another sits and reads a copy of *Illiustrirovannaia Rossiia.* Several women in bathing costumes, sitting in cabana chairs, standing, or lying on towels on the sand. Background of sea, sailboats, and pier.

12. No. 35, 28 August 1926. Cover. Watercolor. Titled "Likhach" [Driver of a Smart Cab]. Huge ruddy face and upper torso of a cab driver with yellow beard, wearing blue coat and top hat. Background of cobbled street. Lettered sign on a low building shows the first three letters, TRA, probably of traktir [inn].

13. No. 37, 11 September 1926. Cover. Watercolor. Titled "Osen'" [Autumn]. Image of Russian peasant girl in orange dress with blue flowered scarf, holding a sheaf of wheat in right arm, flowers in left, and at her feet the autumn harvest of melons and fruit.

14. No. 39, 25 September 1926. Cover. Watercolor. Titled "Iarmarka v derevne" [Country Fair]. Folkish image of two peasant girls at a village fair. Gaily decorated stalls, with foods, balance scales, decorative fabrics hanging.

15. No. 42, 16 October 1926, p. 5. Four small drawings illustrate a

poem, "Motia iz Odessy" [Motya from Odessa], by Valentin Gorianskii: a running man; a man at café table; two older women seated before a standing man on a small stage; and two dolls in folk costumes.

Ukhvat (EP.7, 1 - 2)

EP.7. *Ukhvat/Oukwat* [The Grabber] was a Paris-based, Russian-language satirical magazine, of which only six issues were published in 1926 by the émigré publisher "Ptitselov." FR is known to have contributed to two of the six issues, drawing the covers, full-page cartoons and one partial-page drawing. All are signed in the plate with his initials and, with one exception, also credited as "Ris. F Rozhankovskago" [Drawing by F. Rojankovsky].

1. Issue No. 2, 1926. The front cover, captioned "Daesh' 'charme slave' (in French)"! [Give me some "Slavic charm"!], shows a fat, rich capitalist surrounded by caviar, samovar, floating musicians, holding a ballerina and exhaling a bird. "Charme slave" is the title of the story, by Teffi, that appears on p. 2. The illustration at the top of p. 2 shows a set table with chafing dish, and a window through which is seen the Eiffel Tower.

2. No. 3, 1926. The front cover, captioned "Semeinoe schast'e" [Familial Bliss] depicts a baby in a carriage reaching for a rattle; the back cover pictures a bride and dubious-looking groom, while the accompanying text has the groom thinking of what he has given up for this marriage. Full-page humorous cartoons on p. 3, captioned "Novorozhdennyi" [Newborn], showing nurse presenting baby to grandmother; on p. 5, "V Bulonskom lesu" [In the Bois de Boulogne], showing numerous people lounging, playing, reading, in the famous Parisian park; and p. 13, captioned "U sovetskago fotografa" [At a Soviet Photographer], showing a seated couple, man

in boots with Soviet army cap beside him; plus on p. 7, pair of drawings, above and below an unrelated text, showing, in upper picture, observers in hot-air balloon looking down through binoculars at, in lower picture, drinking and drunken peasants in countryside.

Satirikon (EP.8)

EP.8. *Satirikon* [Satyricon] was a Paris-based, Russian-language weekly magazine of humor and satire, which published only 28 weekly issues, from April 4 to October 15, 1931. M. Kornfeld was the editor and publisher. The magazine was an effort to revive the famous pre-Revolutionary Russian magazine of the same name. FR is listed on the masthead as an artistic contributor, but contributed only one drawing, for a series, *Goroda i gody* [Cities and Years], illustrated by various artists:

Issue No. 9, 30 May 1931, p. 10. Poetry illustration. "Vospominan'ia prezhnikh dnei. Moskva" [Recollections of Former Days. Moscow]. Pen. 25 x 20.5 cm. A nostalgic scene in an old Moscow city market. The chief figures are a young gymnasium student in a school uniform and, standing just behind, a man in a traditional smock, carrying a wooden bucket of ice cream on his head. The two have paused to look at a display of caged birds and other small animals. The drawing illustrates Sasha Chernyi's poem "Na Trube" [On the Trumpet], which appears beneath. The verse recounts a young boy who admires the caged birds, but the only coin in his pocket is too small to purchase even a sparrow.

Le Rire (EP.9, 1 - 16)

EP.9. *Le Rire* [Laughter] was a ribald French humor magazine published in Paris from 1894 through the 1950s. Between 1930 and early 1933, FR contributed watercolors for ten full-color front and back covers and made pen drawings for six full-page cartoons (in a realistic style). All are credited "Dessin de Rojan" or "Dessin de Rojankovsky" and signed in the plate. All cover and page sizes are 30 x 23 cm.

In the manner of traditional magazine cartoons, each picture portrays an anecdotal situation of everyday urban life. Most of the cartoons have titles above the picture. All have lines of dialog beneath in which the characters speak and define the humorous, often sexual situations, sometimes with double entendres.

1. Issue No. 585, 19 April 1930, p. [9]. Drawing. "Estimation." Young woman with dress dropped to waist, her breasts bared. She chats about the asset of beautiful breasts with another girl who is bending over a bowl of water washing her hair.

2. No. 587, 3 May 1930. Front cover. French family (mother, father, boy, girl) seated at table in a sidewalk café. Parents banter about the appetite of a cousin who is soon to visit.

3. No. 592, 7 June 1930, p. [9]. Drawing. "Les affaires vont mal" [Business is Going Badly]. Three prostitutes sitting at café table, talking and smoking, commenting on how bad business is and speculating about selling sex on the installment plan.

4. No. 593, 14 June 1930. Back cover. "Protectionnisme" [Protectionism]. Young man and woman lying on grass near a suburban amusement park, discussing their love relationship. She is in a foreshortened view, with her legs and feet in high heels and bright yellow anklets in bold foreground.

5. No. 598, 19 July 1930. Front cover. "Hypocrisie humaine" [Human Hypocrisy]. Viewed from the rear, a burly French sailor and a girl in knee shorts look at monkeys in a zoo cage.

The couple have their arms around each other, his right hand on her hip; they jokingly compare the sexual behavior of monkeys and humans.

6. No. 631, 7 March 1931. Front cover. Mother and daughter in city park. Mother is seated on a bench reading a book in her lap, her legs crossed and showing much thigh. Daughter, age 10 or 12, is sprawled on a chair, face down, tickling her mother's shin with a twig to get her attention, saying naively a man seated opposite is staring at the title of her mother's book.

7. No. 643, 30 May 1931, p. [5]. Drawing. "La vie d'artiste" [The Life of an Artist]. Artist at an easel in studio, with nude model leaning forward with hands on a table. The artist says he will paint her as a nymph with a satyr, while she hopes they will not have to pose together. The nude figure is similar to one that occupies a full watercolor reproduced in the FAR Gallery catalog (1973).

8. No. 650, 18 July 1931, p. [5]. Drawing. Young woman standing, her back to us, with dress hiked up above her waist. She is showing her step-ins for the consideration of her woman friend who sits on a couch. The friend comments that her panties look strong and solid; she replies that in certain sexual encounters their resistance allows time for reflection.

9. No. 655, 22 August 1931. Back cover. Bathing beach scene, with couple and child near a wicker cabana. Young mother in shorts and tank top lies face down, nibbling on a snack, making idle chatter but looking very bored. Father sits stiffly behind her, shoes off, but wearing a business suit.

10. No. 658, 12 September 1931. Front cover. Family at the zoo looking down at polar bears in a pit, one explaining that the bears change into white fur as a summer fashion.

11. No. 662, 10 October 1931. Back cover. "Une petite main qui se place" [A Small Hand that Is Placed]. Young woman alone in her Paris flat. She sits facing us, resting her head in a pillow on a table, pondering the sexual proposition her boss has made to her.

12. No. 671, 12 December 1931. Back cover. Bathing-beach scene with the same family as pictured in No. 9 above, but in slightly different poses. Here the mother lies on her stomach on beach blanket, her head turned away from her husband and biting on a cracker. The father in his business suit is lying on his back reading a magazine, while the child digs in the sand with a shovel. Three women stand closer to the water, looking out at the waves.

13. No. 676, 16 January 1932. Front cover. Two pretty women skiers lean on their poles and chat. Comically topless despite the snow and cold, they wear only shorts, ski boots, mittens, and toboggans. They comment that since they started making the ascent on foot no one else is using the ski lift either. This picture had appeared the previous year in *Fantasio*, a magazine also published by *Le Rire* [see EP.10, 2, below].

14. No. 684, 12 March 1932, p. [9]. Drawing. "Le nudisme à la montagne" [Nudism on the Mountain]. A bare-breasted female skier, as above, talks with an older and buxom woman skier who is fully clothed. The older insists she could do as well with her larger bosom, while the younger taunts that she might cause an avalanche if she tries.

15. No. 706, 13 August 1932. Back cover. "Propos rassurants" [Reassuring Words]. Two young women in bathing costumes talk at the edge of an indoor swimming pool. They make a double entendre about a banker boyfriend who has dived but not yet resurfaced.

16. No. 735, 4 March 1933, p. [9]. Drawing. "Les profiteurs du sport" [The Profiteers of the Sport]. The fight is over in a boxing ring, one boxer is being helped out, the other limp in his corner. One spectator explains to another that his only interest in the sport is as a maker of false teeth and sees business opportunity.

Fantasio (EP.10, 1 - 2)

EP.10. *Fantasio* was a humor magazine with more or less erotic stories and illustrations, published in Paris from 1906 to 1948 by *Le Rire*, which was itself a ribald humor magazine to which FR contributed [see EP.9 above]. In 1931 FR contributed two full-page, full-color drawings to *Fantasio.* The two pictures are signed in the plate as "Rojan."

1. Issue No. 588, 1 August 1931. Full-page full-color cartoon, showing a sporty young couple dancing in a bar to gramaphone music. He wears a checked jacket and striped cap, she, a striped skirt, fitted long-sleeved blouse and headband. The accompanying conversation is in somewhat coarse, idiomatic street language.

2. In an unidentified issue in 1931 appears the same full-page, full-color cartoon of two bare-breasted young women skiers, that then appeared in *Le Rire* the following year [see EP.9, 13]. Here it is given the caption "Les bains de soleil dans les Alpes" [Sunbathing in the Alps]. Apparently, the publisher, *Le Rire*, was not above occasionally lifting art from its lesser known satellite magazine for subsequent appearance in its primary magazine.

Ridendo (EP.11, 1 - 2)

EP.11. *Ridendo: Revue gaie pour le Médecin* [Laughing: A Humorous Review for the Doctor] was a Paris magazine of medical humor and sex, published twice-monthly from 1934 to 1940. When Paris was occupied in 1940, *Ridendo* disappeared for eight years, being revived in 1948. FR contributed only two cartoons, one each in the first two issues of 1934. But the magazine carried his name in the list of contributing artists until the end of 1936.

1. Vol. 1, No. 1, 5 January 1934, p. [26]. Half-page captioned cartoon: fat woman and doctor discussing her ill husband who is seated in a chair.

2. Vol. 1, No. 2, 20 January 1934, p. [23]. Full-page captioned cartoon: two attractive young women chatting at the foot of the bed of a mortally ill friend, commenting wryly on her passing.

Paris-Soir (EP.12)

EP.12. *Paris-Soir* [Paris Evening] was a large-circulation daily newspaper published in Paris from 1923 to 1944. FR illustrated a newspaper novel by O.-P. Gilbert, "Le cercle des ombres" [The Circle of Shadows], that was serialized in daily installments in *Paris Soir* from 9 May through 18 June 1937. Each installment has the same headpiece of man in shirt and pith helmet, with arm outstretched toward palm fronds. Thirty-four of the 41 installments each have one other illustration. The 34 drawings (not itemized here) are of the male characters, sometimes in adventurous situations, and of a young woman at home, all in colonial settings.

FR also illustrated many children's stories for the Sunday page *Pour les enfants* in *Paris-Soir Dimanche* [see B3, FS.6 - FS.43].

The Bystander (EP.13, 1 - 5)

EP.13. *The Bystander*, a British weekly tabloid magazine, featuring reviews, topical sketches and short stories, was published from 1903-1940. In 1934, 1935, and 1936, FR contributed three covers and two full-page illustrations. All are signed in the plate as "Rojan."

1. 23 November 1934. Front cover of the "Christmas Number, 1934," so titled. Full-color picture of two dolls, one a fashionably dressed young woman, being handed a hatbox decorated for Christmas by a toy soldier in a tall fur hat.

2. 5 June 1935. Front cover of the "Summer Number," so titled. Full-color picture of an athletic young woman tennis player, energetically running to the back of the court to complete a long swing at the ball.

3. Christmas Number, 1935, p. 1. Full-color circus drawing of a clown holding a guitar with women trapeze artists flying above. Captioned "May it go with a swing . . ."

4. 29 April 1936. Front cover of the "Flying Number," so titled. Full-color picture (from superior bird's-eye view) of top of airplane and countryside below, with two men in open cockpits, one waving up to us.

5. Christmas Number, 1936, p. 2. Full-color illustration of four circus performers standing on platform in front of signs announcing the show. Captioned "Here We Are Again."

Other European Magazines (EP.14 - EP.18)

EP.14. Article illustrations. *Tygodnik Illustrowany* [Illustrated Weekly] (Warsaw). No. 25 (1931), pp. 485-86. "Serce polskiego wybrzeza" [The Heart of the Polish Seashore] by S. Strumph Wojtkiewicz. Five watercolors of boats, harbor, and seaside scenes. In the same issue, pp. 487-88. "Na Mierzei Helskiej" [On the Helska Sandbar] by J. Janowski. Six watercolors of boats, harbor, and seaside scenes.

The 11 watercolors in these two articles were from a larger series of paintings made for a series of postcards picturing well-known places in Poland.

EP.15. Two story illustrations. *Der Querschnitt* [The Cross-Sectional] (Germany). May 1936, p. 263. "Das Zeitalter der Jungen Mädchen" [The Era of the Young Girls]. A pencil drawing of man and woman sitting on park bench in side view, with rear view of young girl standing in foreground. In the same issue, p. 292. "Wie Soll der Mann Sein?" [How Should It Be?]. A pencil drawing of young woman with bobbed hair, sitting, leaning forward and resting her head on a pillow on table top.

EP.16. Story illustration. *Séduction* (France). No. 211, 13 November 1937. An unknown number of illustrations for the story, "Perversité" [Perversity] by G. de Marithé, in this weekly sex magazine of the 1930s.

EP.17. Article illustration. *Par Avion: Organe des transports et du tourisme aériens* [By Plane: Organ of Transport and Air Tourism]. No. 5 (December-January 1938-39), pp. 21-27. Three full-page ink drawings accompany Hubert Bouchet's article "Les lignes impériales Françaises" [The Imperial French Lines]. Each 29.5 x 22.5 cm. The article promotes air travel by the French national airlines to Latin America, the Far East and French Africa, and the drawings depict romantic scenes in each region.

EP.18. Serial pre-publication of "Les inconnus dans la maison" [Strangers in the House] by Georges Simenon in 14 issues of *Match* from October 1939 to January 1940, illustrated by FR throughout. We have no indication of FR's illustrations in the first edition of the novel in book form, published by Gallimard in Paris 1940.

American Magazines, 1941-1969 (AP.1 - AP.17)

AP.1. Story illustration. *Harper's Bazaar*. December 1941, pp. 76ff. A half-page drawing of Penelope the bear surrounded by smaller animals (at the head of the story) and five small drawings of animals scattered in the text, all illustrating Munro Leaf's "Penelope." On another page, a short bio and photo of FR in "The Editor's Guest Book." As "Theodore Rojan," these are perhaps the first drawings he saw published after his arrival in the U.S. three months earlier.

AP.2. Cover design. *The New York Times Book Review*. Sunday, November 15, 1942. Children's Book Week Number. Halftone reproduction of the child and animals on the color cover (and wraparound jacket) of *The Tall Book of Mother Goose* [B4, AB.4].

AP.3. Cover design. *New York Herald Tribune Weekly Book Review*. Sunday, May 23, 1943. Reproduction of FR's poster for the 1943 Children's Spring Book Festival [B5, CP.1], here used for the paper's coverage of the annual event.

AP.4. Cover design. *The New York Times Book Review*. Sunday, November 14, 1943. Young girl in winter garb, sitting in snow, reading a children's book, and surrounded by small animals, with decorated Christmas tree. A variant of the large drawing published in *Paris-Soir Dimanche* (1938) [B3, FS.38], except here the girl holds an English-language picture book. Also used as a poster about 1943 [B5, CP.2] and for personal Christmas cards in the 1940s [B8, CA.4, 25].

AP.5. Story illlustration. *Woman's Home Companion*. January 1944. Picture/drawing of a gray Persian tomcat, for Robert L. Scott, Jr.'s story, "Sand for Tony." pp. 32ff.

AP.6. Story Illustration. *Woman's Day*. March 1947, p. 22. Color picture of boy holding young pig, for Gina Allen's "The Price of a Pig."

AP.7. Story illustration. *Saturday Evening Post.* September 6, 1947, p. 40. Picture of wart hog, plus a small head of same used as headpiece, for Will Cuppy's "The Wart Hog."

AP.8. Story illustration. *Saturday Evening Post.* August 27, 1949, pp. 34-35. In a two-page spread, a color garland of ducks in various states of flight and repose and other animals surround the opening of Don Tracy's "The Duck That Flew Backwards."

AP.9. Story illustration. *Saturday Evening Post,* April 1, 1950, pp. 32-33. In a two-page spread, seven color pictures of foxy antics surround the opening of Don Tracy's "The Fox That Didn't Like to Run." Reprinted (with truncated illustrations) in same magazine, December 1974, pp. 44ff.

AP.10. Story illustration. *Woman's Day.* December 1950, pp. 29, 93. Color garland of wild animals, oriented to the Holy Manger scene, for Ailyn Yasumura's "The Animals' Christmas Gift."

AP.11. Cover design. *AIGA Journal* (American Institute of Graphic Arts), Vol. 3, No. 3, nd [c. 1951]. Special Issue on Children's Books. Printed in three colors. FR's young daughter, Tanya, wears a paper hat and sits in a tiny chair, reading a book. The watercolor is one of three similar published images. Versions of this picture were later used in *Dog Stories* [B5, GB.16] and the poster for Children's Book Week 1959 [B5, CP.7].

AP.12. Calendar and verse illustration. *Woman's Day.* January 1951, pp. 48ff. Twelve color pictures (plus calendar cover) of children playing in seasonal activities, illustrating Seymour Barnard's verse in "The Woman's Day 1951 Calendar."

AP.13. Story illustration. *McCalls.* October 1956, pp. 46-47ff. Full-page color drawing of three cats, for Virginia Hatch's "Matchmakers."

AP.14. Story illustration. *McCall's.* July 1959, p. 142. Small color picture of a family of Irish setters, for Jane Gilbert Shellhase's "A Love Match."

AP.15. Story illustration. *Readers Digest.* February 1967, p. 73. Small color picture of Labrador Retriever sniffing and making friends with a baby seal on the front porch of a house, for Jerome B. Robinson's "Our Summer Visitor."

AP.16. Article illustration. *Readers Digest.* December 1967, p. 223. Small color picture of pigs eating from trough, for Richard C. Davids' "In Praise of Pigs."

AP.17. Article illustration. *Readers Digest.* August 1969, p. 167. Color drawing of swimming platypus, for Fred Dickenson's "Nature's Little Puzzler—The Platypus."

B7

Book Covers and General Adult Books

From 1920 to about 1938, Rojankovsky designed book covers for R. Wegner, his publisher in Lvov and later in Poznan, and for several French publishers. In later years, he designed covers for Russian-language books published in France and in the United States. The cover art listed below is credited to FR on the copyright pages, unless otherwise noted as only signed in the plate or as attributed.

Wydawnictwo Polskie (R. Wegner) (BW.1 - BW.34)

The cover designs for Wegner's literary editions sometimes vary with reissues of the same title. FR redesigned certain of his own covers for later issues, and sometimes those of other artists.

BW.1. Stanisław Adamczewski. *Serce nienasycone* [The Insatiable Heart]. Poznan, [nd]. Simple picture of an oil lamp, embossed in gold on hardcover version, printed dark-grey and white against light-grey background on softcover version. Attributed.

BW.2. Jerzy Bandrowski. Krwawa chmura: powieść [Cloud of Blood:

A Novel]. Lvov and Poznan, 1920. Asian warrior holding raised saber over the neck of a bound and kneeling prisoner. Signed "T. R." in plate.

BW.3. Jerzy Bandrowski. *Pielgrzymi: powieść* [Pilgrims: A Novel]. Lvov, 1920. Man in winter garb trudging through snow. Not credited; signed "T. R-KI" in plate. New cover for later issue (ca. 1929?) shows man in winter garb with walking stick striding across a background medley of Russian urban images. Signed "Rojan" in plate.

BW.4. Jerzy Bandrowski. *Czerwona rakieta: powieść* [The Red Skyrocket: A Novel]. Lvov, 1921. Church dome with fireworks streaking overhead. Signed "T.R." in plate. 2nd edition, 1930, new cover: multiple church domes with skyrocket streaking overhead; armored cars in foreground. Attributed.

BW.5. Jerzy Bandrowski. *Wściekłe psy* [Rabid Dogs]. Poznan, [c. 1922]. Full-color illustration depicting heads of four men in various Slavic military costumes and with weapons; the cap of the sailor is lettered [FL]OTA, 'NAVY,' in both Polish and Russian on soft cover; small illustration on back cover shows abstract battle scene in a town. Attributed.

BW.6. Jerzy Bandrowski. *Lintang: powieść* [Lintang: A Novel]. Lvov, 1922. Cover for a later issue (c. 1929?) is a modern design with saronged bare-breasted Asian woman carrying a burden on her head, with a medley of colonial city images in the background.

BW.7. Jerzy Bandrowski. *W białem miasteczku* [In the White Town]. Poznan, [1930]. Full-color illustration of several peasants in foreground with cart and snowy landscape in the background. Signed "Rojan Paris" in the plate.

BW.8. J. F. Cooper. *Pilot*. Poznan, 1929. (The cover for the 1929 issue is by T. Lipski.) FR designed cover for a later issue: map-style compass at center, surrounded by brown monochrome garland of maritime, tropical-island, and native symbols.

BW.9. Karl Gjellerup. *Pielgrzym Kamanita. Biblioteka Laureatow Nobla, Tom 14* [The Pilgrim Kamanita. Library of Nobel Laureates, Vol. 14]. Poznan, nd. Mythic novel of Buddhist history by the winner of the 1917 Nobel Prize for Literature. FR's cover is a stylized version of a Persian miniature, in color, with author, title, and series in block letters, above, below, and forming a frame.

BW.10. Knut Hamsun. *Włóczęgi: powieść* [Hoboes: A Novel]. Poznan, 1929. Girl under tree on hillside, with goat, overlooking an inlet below.

BW.11. Knut Hamsun. *A życie toczy się dalej: powieść* [The Road Leads On: A Novel]. Poznan, [1938]. Seaside scene, with people, house, boats, and juts of land; small circular maritime scene on back cover. Another, simpler cover design has an oak leaf, panpipes, tree, and house. (Primacy not known.)

BW.12. Knut Hamsun. *Głód* [Hunger]. Poznan, 1938. Suited, hatted man standing in a posture of despair.

BW.13. R. Kipling. *Kapitanowie zuchy* [Captains Courageous]. Poznan, nd [c. 1930]. Cover art credited to FR on copyright page, but example of book with cover present not examined.

BW.14. R. Kipling. *Puk z Pukowej Górki* [Puck of Pook's Hill]. Poznan, 1937. Head of man in topee and sailing ship below.

BW.15. Jerzy Kossowski. *Cyrk: powieść* [Circus: A Novel]. Poznan, 1929. Circus horse with girl riding bareback before spectators in bleachers; small picture of tent, wagon, and horses on back cover. Signed "Rożankowski 29" in plate.

BW.16. Selma Lagerlöf. *Tętniące Serce* [The Racing Heart]. Lvov, 3rd edition, 1938. First edition (1923) cover is by another artist. Third edition (1938) cover by FR has wooden house and doves in tree; small picture of rural camp on rear.

BW.17. Benito Mussolini. *Pamiętnik z czasów wojny* [A Diary from the War]. Poznan, [late 1930s]. Black, red, and green images and lettering on beige background. Front cover has a large silhouette of a saluting soldier in black and a small silhouette of a standing soldier in red; back cover shows a helmet and sword in black, red, and green.

BW.18. F. A. Ossendowski. *Lenin*. Poznan, 1930. Dust jacket and/or wrappers: black and red wraparound image of heroic Lenin, arm raised, in front of a red silhouette of Kremlin. FR possibly also decorated the front cover and spine for a cloth issue.

BW.19. F. A. Ossendowski. *Gasnące ognie: podróż po Palestynie, Syrji, Mezopotamji* [Fading Embers: Journey through Palestine, Syria, Mesopotamia]. Poznan, 1931. Silver/grey clothbound book with gold embossed picture on cover of a man in a tunic balancing an amphora on his left shoulder with his right arm, standing over the initials of the author; gold-embossed decorations on spine. Title page includes a pen drawing of two Arabs crossing the desert, one leading a camel on which the other is riding. Cover attributed; title-page probably also by FR.

BW.20. E. A. Poe. *Opowieść Artura Gordana Pyma* [Narrative of Arthur Gordon Pym]. Poznan, [1931]. Sailing ship, cliffs, and trees in green and black.

BW.21. Władysław St. Reymont. *Pęknięty dzwon* [The Cracked Bell]. Poznan, 1938. 9 stories. Front: burning city seen through hole in brick wall, with large cracked bell overlaid with white bird in flight. Back: man plowing field, explosion in back, barbed wire in fore. Attributed by a 1930's exhibition catalogue.

BW.22. R. L. Stevenson. *Wyspa Skarbów* [Treasure Island]. Lvov-Poznan, 1925. Two pirates with weapons drawn. Attributed.

BW.23. Kazimierz Waliszewski. *Katarzyna II* [Catherine II]. Poznan, [nd]. Cover design, in brown on yellow background, of one of

Catherine's monograms: ornate intertwined letters: E (for Ekaterina), I (for Imperatritsa [Empress] in the old Russian alphabet), and Roman numeral II, under the image of a crown.

BW.24. Stanisław Wasylewski. *Bardzo przyjemne miasto* [A Very Pleasant City]. Poznan, nd [1929]. 12 stories. Front: old town square, with lady in bonnet and gentleman in top hat. Back: soldier standing with hands on reposed rifle; townscape in background; barbed wire in fore.

BW.25. Stanisław Wasylewski. *Na Dworze Króla Stasia* [At the Court of King Stas]. Poznan, nd [1930s]. Front top: cupids, inscription on scroll; center, silhouette of King Stas; bottom, scrolls, quill pens, books, etc. Back: small picture. Signed "Rojan/Paris" in plate.

BW.26. Maria Disslowa. *Jak gotować* [How to Cook]. Poznan, 1934. Dust jacket design of tabletop laden with fresh food awaiting preparation. Retained on 1950s reissues (London: Tern/Rybitwa) and in English version issued as *European Cooking*.

Cuda polski (BW.27 - BW.34)

FR painted watercolors for the covers and jackets of at least eight volumes in Wegner's uniform series of guidebooks to places in Poland. Titled *Cuda polski* [Polish Wonders] (15 volumes, all 20 x 14 cm), the guides are by various authors and published by Wydawnictwo Polskie (R. Wegner), Poznan, in the 1930s. Reprinted multiple times; the entire series was reissued in hard cover from 2009 to 2011, all with FR's cover designs.

BW.27. Aleksander Janowski. *Warszawa* [Warsaw], 1930. Palatial house, statues, and pool in foreground.

BW.28. Jan Kilarski. *Gdańsk* [Danzig], 1937. Church domes and other city rooftops.

BW.29. Tadeusz Łopalewski. *Między Niemnem a Dźwiną* [Between the Niemen and the Dvina], 1938. Large rustic house in woodlands.

BW.30. Gustaw Morcinek. *Śląsk* [Silesia], 193[?]. Heavy machinery in a steel mill.

BW.31. Jerzy Remer. *Wilno* [Vilnius], 1934. Church architecture.

BW.32. Jerzy Smoleński. *Wielkopolska* [Great Poland (name for region around Poznan)], 1930. City street scene with old houses and large church.

BW.33. Jerzy Smoleński. *Morze i Pomorze* [The Sea and Pomerelia], c. 1932. Fisherman launching rowboat.

BW.34. Stanisław Wasyłewski. *Lwów* [Lvov], 1931. Rooftops of old city.

Book Covers for Other Publishers (BC.1 - BC.22)

BC.1. Bor[is] Pil'niak. *Golyi god: roman* [The Naked Year: A Novel]. Berlin and St. Petersburg: Z. I. Grzhebin, 1922. Scrolls and floral designs frame Cyrillic letter forms for the title, author, publisher and year. Signed with an unusual monogram that integrates the roman letters *T* and *R*. This book is the first edition of a significant literary event.

BC.2. N. A. Teffi (pseud. of Nadezhda Aleksandrovna Buchinskaia, née Lokhvitskaia). *Gorodok: novye rasskazy* [Little City: New Stories]. Paris: N. P. Karbasnikov, 1927. Republished by Russica, New York, 1982. Red and black on white background; red Eiffel Tower seen through window and parted lace curtains, with black samovar in foreground. Attributed (in the original) and initialed in the plate.

BC.3. Dimitrii Kobiakov. *Gorech'* [Bitterness]. *Kniga III* [Book 3]. Paris:

Ptitselov, 1927. Spray of stylized leaves and berries in black, with integrated letter forms in black and red. Attributed.

BC.4. A. M. Chernyi and V. V. Zen'kovskii, eds. *Russkaia zemlia: al'manakh dlia iunoshestva* [The Russian Land: Almanac for Young People]. Paris: YMCA Press, 1928. In circular garland of stylized flora, a birch tree in wooded setting, with radiant sun behind, all inked in black and green on soft cover.

BC.5. A. Chernyi. *Neser'eznye razskazy* [Unserious Stories]. Parizh: [s.n.], 1928. Stylized design of the winged horse, Pegasus, down on earth with a blacksmith replacing a shoe.

BC.6. Don-Aminado (pseud. of Aminad Petrovich Shpolianskii). *Nakinuv plashch: sbornik liricheskoi satiry* [The Tossed Cloak: A Collection of Lyrical Satire]. Paris: Neskuchnyi sad, 1928. Limited to 100 numbered copies; others out of series. Dark violet and black image on light violet paper; angled figure of standing man in tall hat, wrapped in a cloak, holding a guitar.

BC.7. Thérèse and Louise Bonney. *A Shopping Guide to Paris.* New York: Robert M. McBride, 1929. Same design on dust jacket and end papers of cloth edition and on wraparound covers of paperback. Humorous isometric color map of central Paris, with major buildings and sites lettered with their names; vertical red, white, and yellow bars at each end. Signed "Rojankowsky" in plate.

BC.8. Marc Chadourne. *L'U.R.S.S. sans passion* [U.S.S.R. without Passion]. Paris: Mornay, 1932. Monograph with 34 photographs. Constructivist-style design in red, black and grey on white, with art deco letters.

BC.9. Mikh[ail] Osorgin [Il'in]. *Svidetel' istorii: roman* [Witness to History: A Novel]. Paris: Moskva, 1932. Front: bold geometric layout of rectangles of red and white on largely black ground with title and author in block letters; back: black and red stripes and red circle on white background. Also privately published by author in 1932.

BC.10. T[atiana]. A. Bakunina. *Russkie Vol'nye Kamenshchiki* [Russian Freemasons]. Paris: Privately printed by the author, 1934. Design of stonemasons' drawing compass and L-square in front of classical architecture, with sun and moon.

BC.11. T[atiana]. A. Bakunina. *Znamenitye Russkie Masony* [Famous Russian Masons]. Paris: Privately printed by the author, 1935. Self-portrait drawing (in profile) by Pushkin at top of design, with FR's Masonic delta (in blue flames) and letters below.

BC.12. Boris Poplavskii. *Snezhnyi chas: stikhi, 1931-1935* [Snowy Hour: Verses, 1931-1935]. Paris: N. Tatischeff, 1936. Limited to 600 copies. Minimal design of white snowdrift against dark blue-grey background.

BC.13. Mikh[ail] Osorgin [Il'in]. *Vol'nyi Kamenshchik* [The Freemason]. Paris: Privately printed by author, 1937. Novel. Representing an initiation rite, blindfolded neophyte, with noose around neck, stands while man in Freemason's apron holds a sword point to his breast; symbol of eye (in delta) in background.

BC.14. Hector Bolitho. *George VI*. Paris: Librairie Stock, 1938. Four-color design features the British King's coat of arms with shield and rampant lion and unicorn, with framed and garlanded silhouette of King above the title line.

BC.15. Mikh[ail] Osorgin [Il'in]. *Proisshestviia zelenago mira* [Events of the Green World] . Sofia: privately printed by author, 1938. Essays. Green and black design, with oak leaf and two perching birds.

BC.16. Aleksandr Brailovskii. *Iz klassikov: perevody*. Second, English title page: *Fragments*. Introduction by G. Fedotov. New York: Asssociation of Russian Writers in New York, 1943. Literary anthology. Blazon-bearing title and, beneath, classical pedestal bearing names of classical authors.

BC.17. *Molodye poety sovetskoi Rossii: russkaia poeziia, 1940-1942.* Second, English title page: *Younger Poets of Soviet Russia: Russian Poetry, 1940-1942.* New York: Association of Russian Writers in New York, 1943. Large flag streaming from staff, over lyre, bird wing, sword, and barbed wire, on orange paper.

BC.18. Aleksei I. Chernov. *Narodnye russkie pesni i romansy.* Second, English title page: Alexis J. Chernoff. *Russian Folk Songs.* New York: A. J. Chernoff, 1949, 1953. 2 vols. Vol. 1. Red cloth with gold stamping. Front: musical motifs of harp, balalaika, sun, and running legends. Spine: musical instruments. Back: Small design of lyre. Vol. 2. Same designs, except on green cloth. FR credited on the copyright page with designing the "cover," which refers either to these stamped designs or, possibly, also to a dust jacket or to a wrappers edition, if any.

BC.19. Viktor Mamchenko. *Zvezdy v adu: Parizh 1936-1946* [Stars in Hell: Paris 1936-1946]. [New York]: Privately printed, nd [1946]. Poems. Calligraphic title in black and red letters, with design on back.

BC.20. Viktor Mamchenko. *V potoke sveta: Parizh 1946-49* [In a Stream of Light: Paris 1946-49]. Paris: Privately printed, 1949. Poems. Calligraphic title on otherwise plain covers.

BC.21. Viktor Mamchenko. *Zemlia i lira* [Earth and Lyre]. Paris: Privately printed, 1951. Poems. Calligraphic title in decorative field, with vertical, black and green floral band on left side.

BC.22. G. P. Fedotov. *Litso Rossii: Sbornik statei (1918-1931)* [Face of Russia: Collection of Articles (1918-1931)]. Paris: YMCA Press, 1967. Blue-grey front cover with letter forms in black and white; white spine with letters in black. Attributed.

General Adult Books (BB.1 - BB.6)

BB.1. Malczewski, Antoni. *Marja: powieść ukraińska* [Marja: A Ukrainian Novel]. Lvov and Poznan: Wydawnictwo Polskie, 1922. [6] + 80 pp., plus 10 leaves of plates. 13 x 11 cm.

Dark yellow, paper-covered pictorial boards, decorated front and back. Front cover design (in color) of oval emblem on a trapezoidal pedestal, decorated with various objects; small oval with flower on rear. Decorated title page. Ten full-page direct color lithographs illustrate the narrative poem.

BB.2. Mickiewicz, Adam. *Sonety krymskie* [Crimean Sonnets]. Lvov and Poznan: Wydawnictwo Polskie, 1922. 78 pp. 13 x 11 cm.

Black, paper-covered pictorial boards, decorated front and back. Cover design of man reading book, standing at open French doors, quarter moon and townscape in background. Decorated title page: a silhouette of a top-hatted man sitting on a bench under a tree. Back cover: Pegasus and date "1922."

The 18 full-page direct lithographs in pale colors for this book of poetry by the national poet were a collaborative effort of Ernst Czerper and FR, working in a similar style, each presumably doing about half of the drawings. Six are initialed by FR, three by Czerper; nine are unsigned or cryptically signed. Also 18 black-line tailpieces, all unsigned. Czerper, a German artist and close friend, also collaborated with FR in the painting of a mural in Poznan.

BB.3. *Poznań, 20 akwarel* [Poznan, 20 Watercolors]. Poznan: Ruch, 1926. [22] pp., with title page, list of illustrations, and 20 leaves of plates. 13.2 x 20 cm.

Soft, wraparound, dark paper cover, front blind-stamped *POZNAŃ*, held by cord (tied in bow at front) through two holes near spine. An oblong viewbook for the city of Poznan, with 20 color images lithographed from watercolors, of which FR painted ten, I. Rupniewski, eight, and J. Iljińczyk, two. Also published, with additions, as separate postcards [see B8, CA.1 below]. Pictures of old public squares, historic buildings, and monuments in Poznan. Sold as a tourists' souvenir of the city.

BB.4. Bobrinskoi, P. A., et al., eds. *Pamiati russkago studenchestva, kontsa XIX, nachala XX vekov: sbornik vospominanii* [In Remembrance of Russian University Days, at the End of the XIX, Beginning of the XX Centuries: A Collection of Recollections]. Paris: Svecha, 1934. 222 pp. 22.9 x 17 cm.

Grey paper wraps. Front cover has blue symbol of cross and crown in shadowed relief. One thousand copies were printed, of which 200 are numbered.

Colophon: *Vin'etki i zastavki ispolneny khudozhnikami V. F. Krivuts i F. S. Rozhankovskim. Oblozhka raboty khud. F. S. Rozhankovskago.*

Twenty-one unsigned pen drawings for head and tail pieces depict landmark architecture of Moscow and St. Petersburg, for 17 essays by various émigrés.

BB.5. Evangulov, Georgii. *Neobyknovennye prikliucheniia Pavla Pavlovicha Pupkova v S.S.S.R. i v emigratsii* [Extraordinary Adventures of Pavel Pavlovich Pupkov in the U.S.S.R. and in Emigration]. Second, French title page: Georges Evangouloff. *Les aventures extraordinaires de Pavel Pavlovitch Poupkoff en U.R.S.S. et en émigration.* Paris: privately printed by the author, 1946. 101 pp. 19.5 x 14.5 cm.

Colophon: *Illiustratsii i kontsovki g-zhi Kristi i Rozhana. Oblozhka raboty B. Grossmana.*

Thirteen line drawings and three tailpieces by Kristi and FR. The three full-page ink drawings of single figures on pp. 7, 11, and 23 are FR's work.

Humorous novel in light verse.

BB.6. Lester, Carol E. *To Make a Duck Happy*. New York: Harper & Row, 1969. x + 148 pp. 21.25 x 14.5 cm. Stated "First Edition."

Thirteen black halftones from watercolors. Green cloth covers. Pictorial end papers by FR. Dust jacket (designed by Robert Korn); photo of the author's two ducks on back panel. $4.95 on front flap.

The author's story of her two pet Pekin ducks, Patsy and Peter, whom she raised while studying their emotions in her ark-house in Sausalito on San Francisco Bay. A light adult title.

B8

Advertising and Other Commercial Art

European Advertising, 1928-1939 (EA.1 - EA.16)

EA.1. Bon Marché. Catalog cover in the series *Au Bon Marché*. "Jouets [Toys] 1928." December 1928. Two dolls (boy and girl) in close foreground, with the brightly lighted Bon Marché store and evening Christmas shoppers. Signed "T.R./Lecram."

EA.2. Bon Marché. Catalog cover in the series *Au Bon Marché*.

"Blanc" [White]. Mardi 17 Janvier [1928]. Announcing a white sale, the design is linen goods stacked to resemble an avenue of modern skyscrapers. Monogram in plate with the integrated initials "TR" in a circle and "Lecram Press." Design reprinted as full-page ad for Bon Marché in *Fémina*, January 1928, p. 9. Reproduced in Heller and Fili (1997).

FR is reported as winning a prize in the 1920s for an unidentified cover design for Bon Marché (*Publishers' Weekly*, March 17, 1956:

1402). One of the above two was presumably the winning entry.

EA.3. Grande Maison De Blanc. Promotional portfolio. *Quand la bise fut venue* [When the North Wind Came]. Paris: Lecram Press, nd [c. 1929]. 19 x 16 cm. A loose portfolio of six color images made for the luxury linen shop and department store. All signed "Rojan."

FR's best-known advertising piece is noted for its striking lithographed art deco images of seasonal social and sporting activities of fashionable Parisians. The cover and all six plates are reproduced in halftone in R.-L. Dupuy (1932). Color reproductions appear in *Commercial Art* (1931); Robinson (1976); and Robinson (1989).

EA.4. Laboratoires Rosa. Promotional gift booklet. *La Fontaine Fables*. Paris: Laboratoires Rosa, nd [c. 1930]. [12] pp. 27 x 21 cm. Album of 12 fables, each with a large three-color illustration. Though issued as promotional premium, this children's book [listed also as B3, OF.1] contains only oblique advertising matter on the inside of the back cover. Mentioned by René Thiébaut in *L'art publicitaire pharmaceutique* (1939).

EA.5. Hotel Continental (Paris). Brochure titled *Hotel Continental*, captioned "Your Residence a Palace." c. 1930. Full-color and monochrome. 18 x 14 cm. Sleek art deco images of the hotel's exterior and public spaces inside, set against iconic Paris background. Signed "Rojan" in plate.

EA.6. Société des Talons Wood-Milne. A series of magazine ads for a manufacturer of rubber shoe heels. c. 1932. Each ad has a drawing of a different animal symbolizing a sure-footed virtue of the product. Four of the ads, perhaps constituting the full series, are reproduced in R.-L. Dupuy (1932).

EA.7. British Orient Line (steamship company). Travel brochure.

Cover design for Orient Line cruise brochure, *Southward Bound*, c. 1933. Robed and veiled North African woman, balancing a large jar on her shoulder, approaches docks with cruise ship alongside. Reproduced full-color in Mercer and Gaunt (1934). Also see the Orient Line travel posters [TP.4, TP.5 and TP.6].

EA.8. British Orient Line (steamship company). Travel brochure. Cover design for Orient Line cruise brochure, *Norway*, c. 1933. Scandinavian girl in native costume reclines on a hilltop overlooking a fjord with a steamship. Included in McGill University's 2009 exhibit. Also see the Orient Line travel posters [TP.4, TP.5 and TP.6].

EA.9. Whipsnade Zoo. (a) Informational leaflet, *Whipsnade Zoo*, 4 pp. 20.5 x 13 cm. [1937]. Color drawings (2) of exotic zoo animals and savannah decorate three borders of front and back of the folded sheet. Text promotes visits to the zoo, giving bus directions and fares from London. (b) The same two drawings (but in black halftones) decorate the title page and Acknowledgements page (at rear) of Julian S. Huxley's *Official Guide to Whipsnade Zoological Park* (London: Zoological Society of London), 1937. 18.5 x 12.5 cm. 82 pp.

EA.10. British paper manufacturer (unidentified). (a) Brochure with 20 Mother Goose drawings, given away as a premium by a paper company. About 1936. Drawings also used to decorate (b) the outer wrappings of the company's brand of toilet tissue. All reported to be uncredited. Examples not located.

EA.11. *Albums du Père Castor*. Paris: Flammarion, 1938. [8] pp. 20.5 x 18 cm. Advertising catalog for Père Castor books. Cover drawing of a beaver standing on a box lettered "Flammarion 1938" and holding a stack of books; left margins of two opening pages have six other drawings of beavers doing various human activities. The beaver on the cover was Flammarion's logo for the series and is used to this day. This catalog seen is only one of numerous such catalogs, which were issued probably every year. In addition, FR did new illustrations for many ads for the Père Castor books, mostly drawings of animals.

EA.12. British Post Office, special telegram form for St. Valentine's Day, 1938. The full-color design at top of the message form is a theatrical stage with parted curtains, with humorous images of postmen delivering Valentines to ladies waiting in open windows, and with a large figure of a woman recipient standing center-stage. A close copy of FR's design appeared in the London *Daily Express*, February 14, 1938, credited only as "after this year's Post Office Valentine Design."

EA.13. Perrier. Full-page (39 x 28 cm) magazine advertisement for the bottled water, with a black-ink drawing of a Roman legionnaire (in full profile) holding high his helmet, as if a bowl, in supplication to the heavens. *L'Illustration* (Paris), 8 July 1939, Annonces III. Signed "Rojan."

EA.14. Perrier. Another full-page ad (39 x 28 cm), a black-ink drawing of the front half of a camel with a fully robed bedouin astride. Captioned "La soif" [The Thirst]. *L'Illustration* (Paris), 12 August 1939, Annonces-I. Signed "Rojan."

EA.15. Perrier. Another full-page ad (39 x 28 cm), a black-ink drawing, with trees, fountain and a young woman with a water jug facing landscape with chariots approaching an arch. Captioned "Déja les Romains précurseurs . . . ." [Already, the Roman precursors . . . .]. *L'Illustration* (Paris), 1941, Annonces-I (photo of print offered for sale does not show precise date). Signed "Rojan."

EA.16. Perrier. Another full-page ad (39 x 28 cm), a black-ink drawing of the seven Pléiades in Renaissance costume gathered in a ruin, one singing, accompanied by a young man with a lute. Captioned "Un de la pléiade a chanté. . . ." [One of the Pléiades sang . . . .]. *L'Illustration* (Paris), 1941, Annonces-I (photo of print offered for sale does not show precise date). Signed "Rojan."

American Advertising, 1942-1951 (AA.1 - AA.18)

AA.1. De Beers Consolidated Mines. Full-page color ad for diamond engagement rings. Young woman in a romantic garden wistfully watches a swan in the water. *Saturday Evening Post*, June 6, 1942, p. 47.

AA.2. Carter's Ink. Three different color pictures, each with a white mother cat and her nine kittens in anecdotal situations and with fitting captions. Each kitten's color symbolizes Carter's nine tinted fountain pen inks. *Saturday Evening Post*, April 3, 1943, p. 93; October 16, 1943, p. 112; April 1, 1944, p. 79; and full-page in *Life*, Sept. 6, 1943, p. 119; and April 17, 1944, p. 114.

AA.3. Frank H. Lee Co., Danbury, CT. Color ad for Lee Water Bloc Hats. Copyright 1945. Rabbits, carrots, and Lee hats. Examined tear sheet; c. 1945 magazine publication not identified.

AA.4. Casite auto oil additive. Color ad of many animals on roadside staring after a swiftly passing auto, including Casite's symbol of a cartoon bull. Credited. *Saturday Evening Post*, April 20, 1946, p. 70.

AA.5. National Electrical Manufacturers Association. Ad for water heaters and ranges. Drawing of a long-legged giraffe leaning down to eat grass. Initialed FR. Appears in *Architectural Forum*, September 1947, *Practical Builder*, September 1947, and *American Builder*, October 1947.

AA.6. National Electrical Manufacturers Association. Another ad for water heaters and ranges. Drawing of sad dog: "Will the house you build today be a 'dog' tomorrow?" Opposite page has smaller ad with cocker spaniel, slipper in his mouth: "It's not puppy love—Women really want electric water heaters." Initialed FR. *Architectural Forum*, November 1947, pp. 44-45. Also in *Practical Builder* (November 1947) and *American Builder* (December 1947).

AA.7. Sharp & Dohme. Color ad with animal pairs boarding Noah's

Ark. Reproduced in *Twenty Second Annual of Advertising Art* (1943), p. 103, from the Exhibition of the Art Directors Club of New York at the New York Public Library, Spring 1943. Place of 1942 magazine publication not identified.

AA.8. The Travelers. Borderless panel drawing, a three-stage vertical strip of a falling cat who, unlike humans, always lands on its feet. *Saturday Evening Post*, May 15, 1948, p. 101. Reproduced in *Twenty Eighth Annual of Advertising and Editorial Art* (1949), design No. 28, from the exhibition held by the Art Directors Club of New York at the Museum of Modern Art, March 15 to April 17, 1949.

AA.9. Ford Motor Co. Two ads. First, nine animals surrounding a Ford sedan, each animal making an appropriate utterance of approval. Captioned "Ford's out front with everybody!" *Saturday Evening Post*, September 28, 1946, p. 37. Reproduced in the *Twenty Sixth Annual of Advertising Art* (1947), design No. 7, from the national exhibition of advertising and editorial art shown at the Metropolitan Museum of Art, Spring 1947. Second, a similar ad captioned "Ford's out front down on the farm!" pictures seven farm and domestic animals, each symbolizing a favorable quality of the sedan. *Saturday Evening Post*, March 13, 1948, p. 53.

AA.10. Manhattan Shirt Co. Full-page color ad for Manhattan Shirt Company, captioned "Easter Tint Ties by Manhattan," with big-eyed Easter Rabbit wearing necktie and holding basket of eggs. *Esquire*, April 1947, p. 159.

AA.11. Phillips Petroleum Co. Full-page color ad with Mother Goose in high-top shoes, shawl, and bonnet, with a swirl of cellophane tape about her. Captioned "Long Live Mother Goose," the text explains that a petroleum extract is used to make the stickum on Scotch tape—a time-honored means of repairing battered children's books, such as Mother Goose stories. *Saturday Evening Post*, January 10, 1948, p. 9.

AA.12. Coast Fishing Co., Wilmington, CA. A series of 10 mostly vertical half-page color ads for the "Puss 'n Boots" brand of cat food. *Saturday Evening Post*, 10 issues, 1947-48. Each ad shows a different animal, whose name corresponds to selected letters of the alphabet; decorative letter forms also by FR. Nine of the 10 ads (excepting "B for bear") were compiled into a children's partial ABC book distributed for product promotion (*The Puss 'n Boots Book*, 1949) [B4, AB.18]. The booklet was promoted by the company in *Life* in 1949-50 in ads, not drawn by FR, that offered the following: "Send three Puss 'n Boots labels and 10¢ in coin for 24 pages of delightful animal pictures by Feodor Rojankovsky. Coast Fishing Company, Dept. E, Wilmington, California."

AA.13. Stephen F. Whitman & Son, Philadelphia, PA. Whitman's Sampler (boxed candy). Two color ads. First, large drawing of rabbit with ribbons in its mouth, suspending a box of candy. *Saturday Evening Post*, March 13, 1948, p. 14. Second, similar design, except the rabbit is now in motion, "hopping your way." *Saturday Evening Post*, April 16, 1949, p. 18.

AA.14. John Morrell & Co. 1948 advertising calendar, titled "Fairy Tales," and children's prints of twelve traditional fairy tale scenes. Copyright 1947. [Also listed as B5, CP.4].

FR painted 12 watercolors illustrating famous fairy tales, one for each month, which were made into a 12-leaf, full-color advertising calendar for the meat-packing firm. Issued in two calendar sizes: the large version is 70 x 35 cm overall; the small version is 46.5 x 21 cm overall.

The 12 images were also issued as loose, frameable children's prints and in two sizes. The larger (on heavier paper, sheet size 50.5 x 37.5 cm) were sold for 50 cents each. The somewhat smaller prints, on lighter paper, are 42.5 x 34.5 cm. All prints marked "Painted for John Morrell & Co. by F. Rojankovsky, 1947" and Morrell's copyright line.

The calendar prints include "Snow White," for which FR was awarded the Art Directors Club Medal in 1948 for color work in advertising (Carrick, 1949). "Snow White," sitting in a glade and surrounded by animal companions, is reproduced in the *Twenty Seventh Annual of Advertising Art* (1948). Reproductions from the Annual National Exhibition of Advertising and Editorial Art shown at the Grand Central Galleries, June 1-19, 1948. Also reproduced in Pitz (*American Artist*, 1948).

In addition, the pictures appear as 12 double-page spreads in *Favorite Fairy Tales* [B5, GB.10]. Four of the most popular paintings are also reproduced in *F. Rojankovsky's Wonderful Picture Book* [B5, GB.38].

AA.15. John Morrell & Co. Calendar for the year 1950. Copyright 1949. Titled "The Greatest Calendar Show on Earth." Features 12 full-color circus scenes by FR, plus a pictorial advertising cover sheet decorated by another artist. Overall size: 49.5 (full calendar length) x 21 cm. Any variant calendar sizes or loose prints, as for the 1948 Morrell calendar above, not found [also listed as B5, CP.5].

In December 2000 the Ottumwa Regional Health Center, in the Morrell company's home city, donated five of the 12 original circus scenes, which they owned, to the Children's Care Hospital in Sioux Falls, SD, which already owned the other seven. All twelve original paintings are now on display for the children at the hospital.

AA.16. Kaiser-Frazer Sales Corp., Willow Run, MI. Two-page color ad captioned "The Henry J—America's most important new car." Color picture of dog ("smart"), bull ("tough"), squirrel ("thrifty"), and kitten ("nimble") with the new automobile. *Saturday Evening Post*, November 11, 1950, pp. 76-77.

AA.17. Baker and Taylor Co., Hillside, NJ. Advertising leaflet, *Books for Christmas,* with sample color cover by FR, about 1951. Issued by a printing firm to promote catalogs for Christmas gift books. Offers choice of FR's cover or one by another artist (this shown on back). Design of bundled little girl walking in snow, wearing red hat and carrying an umbrella and a bag of picture books, while reading book held in mittened hands.

AA.18. "1951 Engagement Calendar" (cover); "1951 Calendar of Animals" (title page). Spiral bound, 17 x 14 cm. Six full-color lithographs of animals. Other "Decorations by Hertha List." A Pixie Publication, No. XC 359. Issued in, probably, six variants (we have seen three), each using on the cover a different one of the six pictures inside, but otherwise identical and with the same catalog number.

European and American Posters (TP.1 - TP.11)

TP.1. Poznan Trade Fair, 1922. Titled "II Targ Poznański, 19-27 Marca 1922" (Also titled in French and English). Other lettering below indicates location and visitor information services. Color lithography, 67.5 x 48.5 cm. Initialed "T.R." Modern design with detailed scene of rail terminal and its busy platforms. Preserved in National Museum, Poznan. Reproduced in Mulczyński (1996).

TP.2. Poznan Trade Fair, 1924. Three promotional designs: (a) Titled at top "1924 4TP" and captioned below "IV Targ Poznański 27.4-4.5. Poznań." Color lithography, 90 x 61 cm. Initialed "T.R." Modern design emphasizing letter forms, with symbol of winged helmet. (b) The same design and lettering (but with less detail in feathers and a less rotund helmet) appear on a leaflet for the fair. 31.5 x 19.5 cm. (c) A similar design (but with more shading in the feathers) is used on a second poster for the 1924 Fair, titled "1924 4TP" and captioned "IV Polnische Exportmesse 27. 4.-4. 5. Poznań." Color lithography, 91 x 70 cm. Examples of all three preserved in the National Museum, Poznan, Poland.

TP.3. Titled "Blanc," 132 x 91.5 cm. Shown and offered for sale at $4.00 as part of a larger collection of posters by prominent French artists in the exhibit "Street Murals: The Modern French Poster" at the Bookshop for Boys and Girls, Boston, MA, 1932. Probably the same design as the cover of *Au Bon Marché*, January 1928, and an ad in *Fémina*, 1928 [EA.2].

TP.4. British Orient Line. Captioned "Norway" at the top and "Orient Line Cruises" at the bottom. Scandinavian boy in native costume on hillside (with reindeer), with sea, islands, and village below. Similar to the poster below with Scandinavian girl [TP.5]. Color lithograph. Also see the Orient Line's brochures, *Southward Bound* and *Norway*, about 1933 [EA.7 and EA.8].

TP.5. British Orient Line. Captioned "Norway" at the top and "Orient Line Cruises" at the bottom. Scandinavian girl in native costume on hillside (with reindeer), with sea, islands, and village below. Similar to the poster above with Scandinavian boy [TP.4]. Color lithograph. Also see the Orient Line's brochures, *Southward Bound* and *Norway*, about 1933 [EA.7 and EA.8].

TP.6. British Orient Line. Captioned "Norway Cruises" at the top and "Orient Line" at the bottom. Indigenous Sami reindeer herder in native costume, with a gun in his right hand and holding the reins of the reindeer behind him, with a house and fjord in the background. Color lithograph. Also see the Orient Line's brochures, *Southward Bound* and *Norway*, about 1933 [EA.7 and EA.8].

TP.7. London Transport. Titled "For the Zoo," Color lithograph, 102 x 63.5 cm, 1935. A zebra, fox, leopard, and giraffe with her baby decorate the poster. Directs passengers to London Zoo, giving hours and admission fees. Made in two versions, lettered: (a) "A Choice of Stations—Regents Park, Camden Town, St. Johns Wood" and (b) "By Tram to Camden Town." Both preserved in the London Transport Museum.

TP.8. Southern Railway Co. (British). Titled "Riviera—For Sunshine the Whole Year Round," 102 x 63 cm, 1935. Color lithograph. Southern vista in bright colors; large cacti and subtropical foliage in foreground; house with striped beach umbrellas on roof in mid view; hazy hills and blue sea in background. Preserved in the Victoria & Albert Museum, London.

TP.9. Southern Railway Co. (British). Titled "Kew Gardens," with quotation from John Milton: "Towers and battlements it sees, Bosom'd high in tufted trees." Color lithograph, by Bayard Press, 101 x 63 cm, 1937. Skyward view up the gnarled trunk of ancient tree surrounded by foliage, with woodpecker at the trunk and, still in flight, a descending bird. Preserved in the Victoria & Albert Museum, London; National Railway Museum, York.

TP.10. Children's Spring Book Festival. Sponsored by the *New York Herald Tribune*, May 1943 [listed also as B5, CP.1]. Painting of little girl, viewed from the back, seated at a wooden picnic table and reading a picture book spread on the table before her; she sits on two other books for elevation. Reproduced on cover of *New York Herald Tribune Weekly Book Review*, Sunday, May 23, 1943. Derived from a sketch made in Paris, 1930s, of a young friend of the artist. An early variant is in *Calendrier des enfants* (1936) [B3, PC.12a].

TP.11. Russian Relief Drive, Palm Beach, Florida, March 1946. FR designed two posters (examples not located) to advertise a local Russian relief drive to send packages to persons in the postwar Soviet Union. Probably a local project of the American Society for Russian Relief, Inc, New York, which was especially active at this time.

Postcards, Music, and Greeting Cards (CA.1 - CA.4)

CA.1. Postcards. A series of at least 31, probably more, scenic postcards with views of public squares, old buildings, and monuments in Poznan and other cities in Poland, c. 1925. Color lithographs from watercolors. Each separately titled and all marked: "Nakład Polskiego Tow. Ksiegarni, Kolejowych 'Ruch' S.A." All credited on the margins to "T. Rożankowski" as the painter. FR signed at least one of these paintings as "Rożan." Ten of the scenes of Poznan are in the viewbook *Poznań—20 Akwarel* (1926) [B7, BB.3]; three are reproduced in Warkoczewska (1995), an exhibition catalog, and seven were included in the corresponding exhibit in Poznan.

While FR painted most of these postcard scenes while living in Poland, shortly after he migrated to Paris in late 1925, he painted at least one additional Polish urban scene for postcards, and probably more. We have seen only one, a contemporary tea room scene, credited to "T.Rojan, Paris."

CA.2. Postcards. Series of 11 scenic postcards of Polish seaside and maritime sites. Undated. All reproduced in *Tygodnik Illustrowany* [Illustrated Weekly] (1931). Similar to above series.

CA.3. Cover of musical score of *Balalaïka: Pièce musicale en 3 actes, 12 tableaux de Maschwitz* [Balalaika: Musical Revue in 3 Acts, 12 Scenes by Maschwitz]. Music by G. Posford, B. Grün, and R. Stolz. Paris: Editions Max Eschig/Editions Royalty [1936]. Produced by Maurice Lehmann at Théâtre Mogador.

Stylized color illustration of Russian peasant with balalaika, standing beside tree with a bird. The operetta was an American film in 1939 starring Nelson Eddy. Sheet music for individual songs was also issued with FR's same drawing on the cover, but in monochrome (red on beige background).

CA.4. Christmas cards. FR painted at least 25 watercolors that were commercially published as traditional Christmas cards.

The first 12 cards (Dash series Nos. 15F1-15F12) were contracted in October 1949 and issued by the Irene Dash Greeting Card

Company, New York, most likely for the 1950 season. Another twelve cards (Dash series Nos. 15F13-15F24) in the same style and format were also issued. Both series were probably each issued as varietal boxed sets of twelve cards. All the cards are full-color lithographs filling the face (with narrow margins) of folding cards, 16.5 x 12.5 cm. Each has a printed seasonal greeting inside. Many have been reissued, down to the present, first by Irene Dash and later by the American Artists Group, the successor firm. Most of the pictures are of playful small animals in snowy, woodsy settings and feature various symbols of Christmas.

1. Winter scene, with steepled church, pond and skater, sleighers, and trumpeting angels, surrounding a white ground with "Merry Christmas." Dash No. 15F1.

2. Cat and dog watch fireplace, with stocking hanging from mantel. Dash No. 15F2.

3. Wreath with fourteen animals sitting on holly and pine branches, surrounding a white ground with "Greetings of the Season." Dash No. 15F3.

4. Man and woman, from porch rail, watch bird feeder and deer. Dash No. 15F4.

5. Manger scene, Holy family, with animals watching. Dash No. 15F5.

6. Rooster, hen on nest, chicks, and Christmas wreath. Dash No. 15F6.

7. Snowy scene of children caroling at door of cabin. Dash No. 15F7.

8. Bear dressed as Santa, attended by small animals. Dash No. 15F8.

9. Eskimo child holding wreath, on back of reindeer. Dash No. 15F9.

10. Six animals dancing around Christmas tree. Dash No. 15F10. Reproduced in Gruber (1950).

11. Animal orchestra with bear, fox, raccoon, rabbit, squirrel, bird, chipmunk, and mouse, directed by a little-girl angel. Dash No. 15F11.

12. Red Squirrel nibbling at pine cone. Dash No. 15F12.

13. Seventeen small animals dancing around evergreen and wreath in snow-laden forest. Dash No. 15F13.

14. Santa Claus in sleigh pulled by four reindeer in a snowy forest. Dash No. 15F14.

15. Snowy village scene through window, with Christmas tree inside. Dash No. 15F15.

16. Dog and cat looking at Christmas tree, with tropical foliage outside large window. Dash No. 15F16.

17. Seven animals in front of forest cabin looking at Christmas tree through its brightly lit window. Dash No. 15F17.

18. Mother deer licking her fawn in a snowy forest. Dash No. 15F18.

19. Snowy winter scene, looking across a stone railing at a horse-drawn sleigh, village, valley and mountains beyond, encircled by snow-covered branches. Dash No. 15F19.

20. Baby bear and small animals picnic in snow in front of cabin with wreath over door. Dash No. 15F20.

21. Snow-covered stump, on top of which five mice encircle a tiny Christmas tree, with two other mice and a chipmunk playing instruments, while an owl and a mole watch. Dash No. 15F21.

22. Twelve animals dancing across the page, in four rows of three, variously carrying branches of holly and evergreens, a Christmas tree, and a basket. Dash No. 15F22.

23. Baby bear pulls sleigh with rabbit, kitten, and Christmas tree. Dash No. 15F23.

24. Strolling vixen dressed as Russian peasant, carrying rooster and Christmas tree, and two kits carrying packages. Dash No. 15F24.

Other Dash/American-Artists-Group Cards

American Artists subsequently issued one other Christmas card with a new drawing by FR, a kitten with a neck bow emerging from a Christmas gift box, and seven other "junior" cards, with designs that were excerpted from some of the original 24 cards.

Privately Printed Christmas Cards

Rojankovsky also designed and privately printed multiples of at least five Christmas cards, many of which were individually hand-colored by the artist. For special friends, he occasionally painted original Christmas cards.

25. Black-and-white print, some hand-colored, of a much-reproduced picture of young girl in woods, sitting at base of decorated Christmas tree, attended by small animals. 1940s. 14.5 x 16 cm. Versions of this drawing published several times. [B3, FS.38; B5, CP.2; B.6, AP.4].

26. Black-and-white print, many hand-colored, of little girl in winter garb and holding bag of gifts, with one hand on small Christmas tree. About 1952. 16 x 12 cm.

27. Color print of village scene seen through a window—snow, rustic buildings, yard, with figure carrying Christmas tree. 1956. 16.5 x 20.5 cm. Many block printed in multicolors by one operation: colors applied to each area of the block and the print was then pulled .

28. Black-and-white (with green accents) print of hobby horse covered with letter forms, titled "An Alphabet of Christmas." Full 26-letter ABC of Christmas inside. 1966. 15.5 x 12 cm. Printed by Martin Connell for family use. The design is from the proposed end papers of a book planned but never published as such, called "The Tall Book of ABC." The image later appeared on the published cover of *F. Rojankovsky's ABC* (Golden Press, 1970) [B5, GB.37].

29. Black-and-white print, many hand-colored, of snowy woods scene with rustic cabin, man on sleigh, and birch tree. 1967. 17.5 x 12.5 cm.

B9

Erotic Book Illustrations—Paris in the 1930s

Between 1932 and about 1937 in France, Feodor Rojankovsky illustrated with explicit pictures six erotic literary books and, as an artist's book, a portfolio without words. The six books are new editions of French erotic literary standards and today are well-known, valued, and much collected in Europe and America. A few have taken their place as classics of the genre. This small but significant body of work is most usefully viewed in the cultural context of Paris of the 1930s and as continuous with the artist's career in the graphic arts. A review of this work rounds out the picture of a man in and of his time and place.

The largest and nearest complete public collection of Rojankovsky's published erotic illustration is held at the Kinsey Institute for Research in Sex, Gender, and Reproduction at Indiana University, Bloomington. The Kinsey holds and, with scholarly reserve, attributes to Rojankovsky, the six most important of the seven published works, including the portfolio and both authentic editions of Radiguet's *Vers libres*.

Reflection on the open cultural climate in Europe between the two wars and on the situation of émigré artists in France makes us less surprised that Rojankovsky drew erotic pictures—and more surprised if he had not. By the early 1930s Rojankovsky had earned a reputation in Paris as a children's illustrator, but also as a journeyman draftsman of skill and roguish imagination. It is hardly surprising that a talented graphic artist chose to make some extra money by illustrating one of Everyman's favorite topics. He lavished his best draftsmanship and color work on some of these projects and they are properly among his best work.

Illustrated literary and anecdotal erotica may be construed as fairy tales and picture books for grown-ups, catering to mostly unattainable fantasies and sometimes dark and ugly dreams. Both fairy tales and erotica are but dreams set in a romantic past or never-never present where such improbable doings may be imagined without the complications of reality and personality. The ancient fairy tales were didactic for adults, speaking to a number of visceral human problems, releasing anxieties, and were often bawdy.

A large company of often distinguished graphic artists in France illustrated erotic books early in the XXth century. More than a few children's-book illustrators also made erotic expressions in certain of their art. And illustrators of standard literary works, many with erotic themes, also occasionally illustrated children's books. The list includes women artists, it bears noting, and several devoted themselves to erotic books.

The best known women illustrators were an international cast: Suzanne Ballivet, Mariette Lydis, May den Engelsen, Léonor Fini, Gerda Wegener, Gertrude Hermes, and Clara Tice. Working across genres, the American Tice also illustrated a children's alphabet book, *ABC Dogs* (New York: Funk, 1940). Wegener illustrated fairy tales, such as Eric Allatini's *Contes de mon père le jars* (1919). And the list of diversions from conventional gender and genre preoccupations surely continues.

A literary parallel caps the one seeming paradox. Felix Salten, author of beloved *Bambi*, early in his career authored *Die Kleine Veronika* (1903), an erotic story of a naive country girl who learns city ways and, anonymously, *Josefine Mutzenbacher, oder Die Geschichte einer Wienerischen*

Dirne, von ihr selbst erzahlt (1906) about the career of a Viennese prostitute.

The communities of Russian émigré artists in Europe between the two wars were microcosms of the larger artistic society and culture. Several prominent Russian artists and illustrators created erotica like their French and German counterparts. Around 1920, Konstantin Somov and Boris Grigoriev made books and portfolios with explicit erotic images. Grigoriev favored French and German brothel scenes, Somov eighteenth-century court fantasies. Other eminent Russian émigrés such as Leon Bakst, George Annenkov, Natalia Goncharova, W. N. Masiutin, and Dmitri Mitrokhin created less explicit (so far as we know) but nonetheless erotic pictures. More to the point, Grigoriev, Annenkov, Goncharova, and Mitrokhin also illustrated noted children's books.

In Rojankovsky's immediate circle of graphic artists, his friend from the Lecram Press, Gaston de Sainte-Croix, also drew explicit pictures for erotic texts, and continued this work into the 1950s. Sainte-Croix, too, illustrated a few children's books, including the re-illustration in 1959 of Père Castor's edition of Marie Colmont's *Histoire du nègre Zo'hio*, originally illustrated by Rojankovsky just before he left France. Another friend, the Russian woodcut artist Valentin Le Campion, also illustrated erotic texts and made many explicit erotic book plates for private collectors. Rojankovsky obtained many of his commissions through Robert Chatté, a famous figure in clandestine erotic book production in Paris in the 1930s.

Rojankovsky was well versed in contemporary French erotic art. His humorous naturalism resembles certain of the deft and prolific French illustrators of the 1920s and 1930s and is sometimes confused with the unsigned work of André Dignimont and Marcel Vertès. Rojan's erotic illustrations began to appear in 1932, at the time he had begun to draw risqué covers and captioned cartoons for *Le Rire*, the ribald and racy French humor magazine. In style and spirit, many of the book illustrations were continuous with the pictures in *Le Rire*, but the sexual innuendo and double entendres were now made explicit.

The texts of the six literary titles illustrated by Rojankovsky had all been published in earlier editions and some long before illustrated by other artists, such as Félicien Rops. Several were favorites of the genre and illustrated time and again by various artists, especially in the heyday of erotic publication in the 1920s and 1930s. Béranger's *Chansons galantes*, Protat's *Examen de Flora*, and *Le théâtre érotique de la rue de la Santé* were all originally published in the mid-nineteenth century. Radiguet's *Vers libres*, Louÿs' *Poésies érotiques*, and Spaddy's *Dévergondages* were first published in the 1920s, all before Rojankovsky's versions.

Rojankovsky's pictures have held interest through the years, and his best work compares more than just favorably with the similar work of his contemporaries. Collectors today pay handsomely for one of the 510 copies of the portfolio *Idylle printanière* with hand-colored lithographs or for one of the original edition of 125 copies of Radiguet's *Vers libres* printed by pochoir, and the later enlarged edition is similarly pricey. Reflecting this interest, color images from these two works have been reproduced in several anthologies and magazines.

Hand-drawn and painted erotic images from the imagination have a long history through the centuries. Well before the 1930s, the tradition of artists' erotica was breaking up in favor of the greater realism of still photography and grainy, silent stag films. But photography of this subject usually falls into inescapable literalism, leaving little to the imagination or to art. The older traditions of graphic art and illustration continue to hold a secure and special place in cultural nostalgia, and have an appeal that clinical videos and slick magazine photography can never equal. In today's pop-cultural atmosphere, hand-drawn images have been revived in the new erotic comix.

Rojankovsky's almost genteel images of the 1930s were what turned grandfather on, and today they seem quaint and dated. Indeed, their chief interest is for the modern cultural history of erotic imagery, and that says a great deal about their appeal down to the present. Today, the field of historical and contemporary erotica is established as an area of academic cultural studies, is taught in many American universities, and is a topic of dispassionate scholarly, even of sympathetic feminist, contemplation. It is no longer a scandal in the cultural closet.

Paris was Europe's traditional center for erotic literary publishing and artistic expressions of human lust and sexual abandon. The commercial trade in elegantly printed and illustrated books flourished between the wars, and the editions were of a quality little seen since. The British and Germans went to Paris for the books, pictures, and photographs that could not be published in their own countries. American tourists liked the challenge of smuggling contraband books past U.S. Customs. But most of this production was not for export. The French *amateurs* of erotica were themselves heavy consumers of explicit tales and pictures and many of the private masculine libraries of the bourgeoisie contained "curiosa" in luxury bindings.

Whatever their tastes, French bibliophiles of means often belonged to small, private book clubs or societies that commissioned artists to illustrate books for limited editions of several hundred copies that were sold *hors commerce* to the small membership. Some editions also had a small number of special copies printed on luxury papers, some few of these with an original drawing laid in or with a separate suite of prints. The private presses that specialized in erotic productions often emulated this elite publishing style, and most of Rojankovsky's erotic books were published in this manner.

In addition to the published books and portfolios, Rojankovsky also produced for private collectors a number of independent erotic drawings and watercolors, ranging from explicit sexual images to conventionally posed female nudes of the pin-up variety. He also made up unique portfolios of paintings and embellished and extra-illustrated unique, single copies of published books already illustrated by other artists, but too tamely for the collectors. The French film actor Michel Simon (1895-1975), an avid collector of erotica, bought a quantity of Rojankovsky's original independent work and surely all the published work. The Simon collection was later sold from his estate and is now scattered.

How many unique books and portfolios were made by Rojankovsky in the 1930s is open to conjecture. They are difficult to locate in private collections and even more difficult to examine. Most are known through secondary sources. Weiermair (1995) reports one notable example in an anonymous private collection: Apulée [Apuleius]. *L'âne d'or. Suit*[e] *de douze dessins originaux pour L'âne d'or d'Apulée.* [c. 1935]. According to Weiermair, the portfolio contains a sequence of 12 "original aquarelles" and had an edition of only three copies, each original: one with a red-haired woman, one with a blonde, and one with a brunette. Weiermair reproduces in color two of the 12 pictures of the brunette version. These two paintings were probably conceived as scenes from Book 10, where Lucius, still in his transformation as an ass, is seduced by an eager and capacious woman. The hand-lettered portfolio cover of one copy, presumably designed by FR, is also reproduced.

Illustrators of erotic books generally followed the styles of mainstream book illustration, and book illustration generally followed the leading decorative and graphic styles of the period. Until about 1900 many erotic illustrators drew dark, obsessive images of nineteenth-century bourgeois sexual transgressions—the Freudian stuff of repressed dreams. Another popular erotic mood was created by the Austrian Franz von Bayros, who followed the filigreed 1890s style of Aubrey Beardsley and its excesses of Rococo decoration. In the first decades of the 20th century, romantic eighteenth-century court fantasies of powder and crinoline were as popular in erotica as in fancy gift editions of fairy tales for children. In the 1920s and 1930s, the costume fantasies and *tableaux* of George Barbier emphasized decorative design over raw erotic feeling. Edouard Chimot and Louis Icart favored stylish, elongated women in gauzy boudoir settings.

The modern, 1930s look of Rojan's drawings and watercolors gave them special interest in their day. The gaily-colored romantic naturalism made the vicarious erotic experience seem continuous with real, everyday life and not set apart in a fantasy world. The drawings had the look of 1930s magazine illustration and advertising art, though some of the settings were historical and the characters in (and out of) period costumes.

His sexual actors are young, and all are pretty and lithe. A superb draftsman of the human figure and a master of the quick but sure sketch, he imagined these human entanglements with mischievous male humor and drew the complete erotic catalog of his day. The genre of male heterosexual erotica has its own conventions, idioms of expression, and favored themes—its own language—and Rojankovsky understood and expressed it fluently in his own accents.

Rojan's most fetching little book is Raymond Radiguet's *Vers libres* (circa 1935). Only 125 copies were printed, and its popularity called for a second edition of 250 copies, augmented with additional verses and four additional drawings by "R", as the new preface alluded to the artist, no longer so anonymous.

The pictures are in harmony with the naughty lyrics by the young novelist. Radiguet (who died of typhoid at age 20) entered Paris literary circles at age fifteen as the companion of Jean Cocteau and is mostly remembered for his supposedly autobiographical novel *Le diable au corps* (1923), published in the year of his death. Today, the illustrated *Vers libres* is highly valued and collected both for Rojankovsky's pictures and for its status as the first illustrated edition of Radiguet's verse. In 1998 the Kinsey Institute at Indiana University chose the second edition of *Vers libres*, as an example of an attractive, art-worthy book from their collection for an exhibit in their public reception area.

The aquarelles reproduced by pochoir in *Vers libres* celebrate spontaneous and unashamed youthful sexuality in the great out-of-doors—in wooded glades and among the sand dunes at seaside. The light palette, favoring yellows and reds, drenches the preoccupied figures in sunlight. A striking image familiar to many from reproductions is an in-text drawing of a standing, stylishly dressed woman, one leg raised over and around the opening lines of Radiguet's verse "Saison," her flapperish finery hoisted up in front, as she prepares herself to mount her lover who lies ready on the page opposite.

The most popular and reproduced of Rojankovsky's published erotica is *Idylle printanière*, a portfolio of 30 drawings without a written text. The album is an early modern period piece in every respect—its hand-colored lithographs, the early 1930s costumes of its two actors, the style of their sexual encounter, and finally the wordless, film-strip presentation of the sexual script and its 30 scenes—a quarter of them without nudity.

On a fine spring afternoon, a tall and well-dressed man meets an equally fashionable young woman on the Paris Métro. They leave together and, after a persuasive *tête-à-tête*, agree to pursue their sudden passion in a *cinq à sept*. On the way to the hotel in the backseat of a boxy Paris taxi—and in broad daylight—they impatiently indulge in comical, topsy-turvy sexual antics. Emerging from the taxi, the young woman stares directly at us, rumpled and wide-eyed from the preliminaries. In the hotel, the couple follow an erotic script as in stop-motion frames of a film, inviting the voyeur to inspect the details of their joy.

Our heroine is a thoroughly modern Little Red Riding Hood, going about her business in the city but waylaid in the Métro, and this time caught and gobbled up by the suave wolf.

* * *

Béranger's *Chansons galantes* (1937), with mildly erotic lithographs from aquarelles, is the only such work formally credited to "Rojan" on the title page. The other books and portfolios with more explicit illustrations do not bear his name and are unsigned, at least in the ordinary copies we have seen. By other reports, certain of the deluxe issues are signed and laid-in original drawings are signed, and certain other copies were signed as presentations. In any case, abundant evidence supports the attributions and they have remained unchallenged.

Unsigned book illustrations may be attributed to an artist on the basis of traditional knowledge in publishing history, in the rare book trade, or in librarianship—by the agency of supposedly authoritative scholars, anthologists, editors, auction catalogers, or specialist librarians. All the published editions listed here have at least two such attributions.

The illustrations also may be reasonably attributed to Rojan solely on the basis of artistic style and certain tics in the drawings. Many original erotic drawings and watercolors are in private collections, some with strong provenances, and several have been reproduced in anthologies. These and other drawings may be compared with the images in the published books and all the more support the attributions.

The title pages of erotic books of this period often omit places of publication or give false cities, and state fictitious publishers or misleading dates, as well as giving pseudonymous authors. These evasions were intended to confuse the authorities who occasionally attempted to censor the editions, or perhaps just to create a clandestine aura to entice collectors.

All circumstantial evidence suggests that all of Rojankovsky's published erotic works were drawn in France between 1932 and 1937. Yet Spaddy's novel *Dévergondages*, statedly published in Brussels, bears the date of 1948, and has the color lithographs gathered at the end. Spaddy's novel was first published in 1937. Rojankovsky probably made these drawings in 1937 or shortly later for an unrealized edition of the novel, and someone held them over and published the new edition after the war. We have no evidence that the artist did this kind of work after about 1937; he left Europe in 1941 and started his American career. The bibliography includes seven published titles, their later and variant editions.

Bibliography (ER.1 - ER.7)

ER.1. Protat, Louis. *Examen de Flora, à l'effet d'obtenir son diplôme de putain* [The Examination of Flora, for the Purpose of Obtaining Her Prostitute's Diploma]. [No publisher indicated]: Paris, nd [c. 1932]. 45 + [3] pp. 19 x 12.5 cm. Paper covers. Fourteen pochoir illustrations from watercolors. Unsigned. Limited to 315 copies.

Colophon: "*CET OUVRAGE A ÉTÉ TIRÉ À QUINZE EXEMPLAIRES SUR JAPON ET À TROIS CENTS EXEMPLAIRES SUR VÉLIN, TOUS NUMÉROTÉS.*"

The 15 copies on Japon include loose enclosures of an original watercolor.

A previously published book of poetry attributed to Louis Protat. An early edition, according to *L'Enfer de la Bibliothèque Nationale* (Apollinaire, 1913), had been condemned to destruction by judgement of the Tribunal Correctionnel de la Seine in 1852. Félicien Rops illustrated the frontis of an edition in 1864.

ER.2. Albert Glatigny and others. *Le théâtre érotique de la rue de la Santé* [The Erotic Theatre of the Rue de la Santé]. Paris: [No publisher indicated], 1932. 135 + [3] pp. 20.4 x 15.7 cm. Twenty pochoir illustrations from watercolors, of which five are out-of-text. Cream paper covers, with only the title on the front. Unsigned. Limited to 270 copies.

Colophon: "*Cet ouvrage a été tiré à 20 exemplaires sur Japon et 250 exemplaires sur vélin. No. [000].*" (Numbered with mechanical stamp).

Originally published in 1864 with a frontis by Félicien Rops, the text of this book by four minor, nineteenth century French authors has a history of censorship. FR's pictures for this new edition illustrate each of the five bawdy playlets.

ER.3a. *Idylle printanière* [Spring Idyll]. no pl. [Paris?]: no publisher indicated, nd [c. 1933]. A portfolio of 30 loose lithographs, without a text.

Publisher's portfolio of light blue paper-covered boards and cloth spine, about 33.5 x 26 cm, with white silk ties. Paper label with *Justification du Tirage* and decorative devices pasted to inside of front cover. Design on title page, plus 30 black lithographic drawings, each hand-colored with pencil, and each inserted in a folded, cutout mount. The image sizes (slightly variable) are about 17 x 11 cm and printed on cream-colored laid paper, sheet size 27.5 x 19 cm. Unsigned. Limited to 516 copies.

Colophon: "*JUSTIFICATION DU TIRAGE. Le présent album, non mis dans le commerce, comprenant 30 planches originales et un frontispice, tiré à la presse à bras sur vergé teinté d'Arches, a été édité à 516 exemplaires dont 500 numérotés de 1 à 500, exclusivement destinés aux Bibliophiles souscripteurs et 16 marqués de A à P réservés aux Collaborateurs et Amis de l'Artiste, l'exemplaire marqué A comprenant les dessins originaux, les épreuves et une suite en noir étant destiné à l'Auteur.*"

Except perhaps for the 16 reserve copies, FR probably did not personally hand-color the 516 copies of 30 leaves each, though he likely provided a model. The variations of color shading and detailing (ranging from delicate and subtle to heavier and brighter) within and among the several copies we have examined suggest the coloring was done by hired hands.

The first eight scenes are reproduced in color in the *Journal of Erotica* (1994); four are reproduced in Weiermair (1995); one in Tilly (1986).

ER.3b. *Idylle printanière.* No publisher indicated, nd [mid-1930s]. Unstated second edition.

Same as the first edition of 516 copies above, except the label with the new *Justification du Tirage* has different decorative devices. Otherwise, the binding size, color, and materials; paper size, color and type; image sizes; and the mountings are the same. Unsigned. Limited to 310 copies.

Colophon: "*JUSTIFICATION DU TIRAGE. Le Présent Album, non mis dans le commerce, comprend 31 [30 plus cover drawing] Planches originales sur Vergé teinté, entièrement coloriées à la main, aux crayons de couleurs. Le tirage a été strictement limité à 310 exemplaires, tous numérotés à la main dont 10 marqués de A à J, réservés aux collaborateurs et à des hommages.*" (Numbered by hand in blue ink).

A side-by-side comparison with the drawings in the first edition reveals small differences in the sketches, especially in the hatching of the backgrounds and drapery and a few small re-emphases in the figures. In preparing plates for lithographs, FR routinely retouched the printing surfaces, sometimes even redrew certain pictures. Such revisions may be seen, for example, between early printings of the Père Castor books of this same period.

Other early, full or partial editions of *Idylle printanière* may exist. An example, purportedly from such an edition, was in 2000 offered for sale on the Web and, with four sample pictures shown, described only as "an early post-war edition, c. 1945 with 20 [cf. 30 in the original edition] colored lithographs in their original folio cover with slip-case. Size 7.75" x 11"." The ten pictures omitted from the narrative of 30 pictures are perhaps the ten opening scenes without nudity. The dealer did not respond to requests for further and clarifying information.

ER.3c. *Paris Spring 1933.* London: Erotic Print Society, 1983. A retitled, facsimile edition of *Idylle printanière.*

Except for the new title on the front cover of the portfolio, this is a photographic facsimile of one copy of the original edition of 516. The portfolio case (about the original size) is of grey boards, darker grey cloth spine, with grey ribbons. Reproductions of all 30 hand-colored lithographs are printed on the left side of a folio sheet of laid paper, which is folded once to expose the print through a cutout—to resemble the original mounted presentation. Image sizes (slightly variable) are the same as the originals, about 17 x 11 cm, and show the darker, original cream paper on the margins. Limited to 500 copies.

The date of 1933 featured in the new title is probably close to the date of actual publication, which remains uncertain. The 1994 catalog of the Erotic Print Society states that the portfolio was "originally entitled *De Montparnasse à Pigalle*," though we have no record of such a title.

The same decorative label but carrying the new colophon text, now reads: "*The Erotic Print Society/ London/ mcmlxxxiii/ CERTIFICATE OF LIMITATION/ PARIS SPRING 1933. This is to certify that this numbered copy is a faithful reproduction of the privately published 1933 edition of* Idylle Printanière *attributed to Fedor Rojankowski. This, the DeLuxe edition, available only by subscription, is printed on 125gsm Archive paper and is limited to Five Hundred copies only of which this is No [000].*"

ER.4a. Radiguet, Raymond. *Vers libres* [Free Verses]. Champigny: Au Panier Fleuri, nd [c. 1935]. [38] pp. 26 x 18 cm. Pochoir prints from watercolors on Arches paper. Twenty-seven illustrations and other drawings, including three double-page and several out-of-text. Paper covers. Unsigned. Limited to 125 copies.

Colophon: "*JUSTIFICATION / Il a été tiré de cet ouvrage 125 exemplaires numérotés de 1 à 125. Exemplaire No. [000].*"

First illustrated edition: the first edition of the literary text was: Champigny: Au Panier Fleuri [c. 1925], also in a limited edition of 125 copies, but it was not illustrated. The introduction to the "second thus" illustrated edition below (Nogent: Au Panier Fleuri) describes this illustrated edition of 1935 as the second edition of the literary text.

The full-page illustration opposite "Ébauches," is reproduced in color in *Journal of Erotica* (1994, vol. 7). The main design for "Saison" is reproduced in Kearney (1982).

ER.4b. Radiguet, Raymond. *Vers libres.* Second illustrated edition. Nogent: Au Panier Fleuri, nd [c. 1936-38]. [34] pp. 28.2 x 19.2 cm (uncut). Pochoir prints from watercolors. Twenty-five illustrations and other drawings, including one double-page and several out-of-text. Paper covers. Unsigned. Limited to 250 copies.

Colophon: "*De cet ouvrage, non mis dans le commerce, édité pour les seuls souscripteurs, il a été tiré trois exemplaires sur Japon ancien à la forme contenant chacun un dessin original, quatre exemplaires sur Japon nacré, numérotés de I à VII. / Deux cent quarante-trois exemplaires sur Vélin de Vidalon, nmérotés [sic] de 8 à 250. / Exemplaire No. [000].*"

The three copies on Japon ancien and the four on Japon nacré each include an original ink and watercolor drawing.

The Introduction states this as the third edition of the literary text and mentions the success of the first illustrated edition (above) with its "illustrations de R...," a coded reference to "Rojan."

This second illustrated edition drops verses and illustrations for "Le petit journal" and "Ébauches" and adds three verses and new illustrations for "Bains publics," "L'autre bouche" and "Jeux innocents."

ER.4c. Radiguet, Raymond. *Vers libres.* A counterfeit edition by another hand. La Varenne: A La Corne d'Abondance, nd [1938?]. Quarto. Paper covers. Limited to 300 numbered examples printed on Arches.

Reportedly, a faithful imitation of Rojankovsky's illustrations of the first edition, though the pictures are larger. Some copies are augmented with a suite of plates in black and white. We have not inspected this edition and take the description from a dealer's catalogue (Privat l'art de voir, No. 1-86).

ER.5. Louÿs, Pierre. *Poésies érotiques* [Erotic Poems]. Rome: no publisher indicated, 1937. viii + 71 pp. 21.3 x 15 cm. Seventy-three in-text line drawings in orange ink, illustrating 61 verses attributed to Louÿs. Plain white stiff wrappers. Unsigned. Limited to 311 copies.

Colophon: "*Il a été tiré de la présente édition, entièrement souscrite, imprimée par un amateur au dépens de quelques autres: UN exemplaire sur vieux Japon, accompagné d'une suite en noir sur Ingres à la forme et de 35 dessins originaux, portant le numéro UN. CINQ exemplaires sur Arches teinté à la forme, accompagnés d'une suite en noir sur Ingres à la forme et de 4 dessins originaux coloriés par l'artiste, numérotés de 1 à 5. QUINZE exemplaires sur Arches teinté à la forme, accompagnés d'une suite en noir sur Ingres à la forme et d'un dessin original colorié par l'artiste, numérotés de 6 à 20. CINQUANTE exemplaires sur Arches teinté à la forme, accompagnés d'une suite en noir sur Ingres à la forme, numérotés de 21 à 70. DEUX CENT TRENTE exemplaires sur vélin B.F.K. de Rives à la forme, numérotés de 71 à 300. Il a été tiré en outre DIX exemplaires réservés aux collaborateurs, numérotés de I à X.*" (Numbered by mechanical stamp.)

Marcel Vertès earlier illustrated this title in 1932.

ER.6. Béranger, Pierre-Jean de. *Chansons galantes* [Gallant Songs]. Paris: Éditions de la Belle Étoile, 1937. 157 + [2] pp., including a half title. 23.5 x 19 cm. Sixteen full-page lithographs from watercolors, with black-line end pieces and small devices throughout.

Buff-colored paper wraps. Front cover lettered: BÉRANGER/ CHANSONS GALANTES, with small design of a standing naked woman (rear view) wearing a bonnet. Spine lettered: BÉRANGER/CHANSONS GALANTES/PARIS. "Par Rojan" on title page. Limited to 1516 copies.

Colophon: "*Cette édition a été tirée à 16 exemplaires sur Hollande Van Gelder et 1.500 exemplaires sur vélin Navarre.*" (Numbered by mechanical stamp.) *Achevé d'imprimer* appears in the end matter: "*Ce volume, édité par Paul Cotinaud, a été achevé d'imprimer le quinze juin mil neuf cent trente-sept, sur les presses de l'union typographique, Henri Leduc, Directeur. Les Aquarelles ont été reproduites par le procédé Duval-Beaufumé.*"

Les Gaietés de Béranger were published in 1864 with a frontispiece by Félicien Rops. FR's new illustrations are mildly erotic scenes with discreet female nudity—in keeping with the traditions of galantiana.

ER.7. Spaddy [pseudonym]. *Dévergondages* [Wantonness]. Bruxelles: Aux Dépens d'un Amateur, 1948 [art work c. 1937]. 152 pp. 21.5 x 16 cm. Sixteen out-of-text color lithographs, gathered at the end of the text block. Unsigned. Limited to 250 copies.

Colophon: "*Cette édition, comprenant 16 lithographies en couleurs, entièrement souscrite et non mise dans le commerce, a été tirée à 250 exemplaires composés et numérotés comme suit: 16 exemplaires sur Japon de Barjon comportant chacun une aquarelle originale et une suite en noir des illustrations, numérotés de I à XVI. 234 exemplaires sur Vélin de Rives numérotés de 17 à 250. EXEMPLAIRE No. [000].*" (Numbered by mechanical stamp).

The drawings date from about 1937 or shortly later. The text was originally published in Paris (Duflou, 1937) and reprinted in 1970 (Paris: Jérôme Martineau). A brief textual excerpt (in English) is in Phyllis Kronhausen's Erotic Fantasies (New York: Grove Press, 1970), pp. 341-346. According to Kearney (1982), "Spaddy" is the pseudonym of either Jean Gros or Renée Dunan. Discussed in Pia (1978) as an object of official censorship.

Appendix A1. The Artist At Work by Feodor Rojankovsky

In 1964, Ruth Hill Viguers, then editor of *The Horn Book*, invited the 1956 Caldecott Medal winner, Feodor Rojankovsky, to write an article for "The Artist at Work," a column Viguers had launched in December 1963. Despite recurrent health problems, Rojankovsky accepted. After eye surgery in 1964 and again in 1965, he prepared a handwritten draft in his native Russian. But the essay was not submitted, and Rojankovsky soon fell into his last illness; he died in 1970. Thirty-five years after the essay was invited, we found a rough version, translated into English, in the *Lucille Ogle Papers* at the University of Oregon. We adapted it with the approval of the artist's daughter, Tatiana Rojankovsky Koly, and submitted it finally for publication. *The Horn Book* published it posthumously in September 1999. It is reprinted here with their permission.

This is Rojankovsky's only authored essay, other than the transcription of his Caldecott acceptance speech.

> My earliest thoughts of drawing pictures came in the 1890s when as a young child I pored over the illustrated books in my father's library. My father was the headmaster of a secondary school in my home city of Reval [then in Imperial Russia, now the capital of Estonia and named Tallinn] and owned many beautiful books. Here I felt my first love of the exact reproduction of the simplest objects, an eye for detail, and an appreciation of graphic art. I remember puzzling over the delicate tint of the wine in a goblet pictured in a huge book on French decorative arts brought home from the 1889 International Exhibition in Paris. Years later I learned that it was called *rosé* and was accurately colored! Another book that fired my imagination was F. Gershteker's *The Universe: Stories for*

Children (Petersburg, 1885). Many years later I found a copy in a Paris bookstall and have kept it to this day.

My younger sister and I played a game with my father's collection of oval photographs of his former students that helped me to learn characterization in story illustration. We studied the students' physiognomies, deduced their character traits or "types," and fitted them to characters in stories. I learned the rudiments of art technique from my two older brothers, both artists and my first teachers. And in school, with the encouragement of an excellent teacher of natural history, I illustrated my notebooks and taught myself the first steps towards a layout and the graphic embellishment of texts. Looking back, an inexorable logic brought me to become a children's illustrator, and I think such an emergence is spiritually necessary for any master of the art.

In a long career, beginning in Russia [from 1915], Poland [after 1920], France [after 1925] and later in America [after 1941], I have used nearly every reproductive method available to me. Most of my early illustrations were reproduced as simple line cuts or, occasionally, as color halftones. I was not often free to experiment and choose the best reproductive method but was constrained by those used by my publishers, and the results were often disappointing.

But over time and as I moved from country to country, technologies improved and the possibilities for reproducing my drawings and watercolors became more rich and varied. At Mourlot Frères in Paris, I drew on stones to make the five-color direct lithographs for *Daniel Boone* (1931) and other Domino Press books. Working with Paul Faucher on the Père Castor series for Flammarion [about 1933], I learned offset printing from zinc plates. I personally created the separation of colors on six or seven plates and the impressions were close to my preconceived originals. This method achieved a clearness and brightness of my main colors and, with skill, kept the subtle nuances in subordinate colors. In the United States, my artwork for the Artists and Writers Guild and the Golden Books was reproduced by photolithography. In the 1950s I made color separations on acetate for *Frog went A-Courtin'* and other books. This method returned to the artist some control over the color work and results resembled the old hand methods.

The work of the children's-book illustrator is a wonderful and noble calling. Many artists dedicate their whole creative life to it. The illustrator appears to the eyes of children before they can speak and opens an enchanting world. Taking them firmly by the hand, the illustrator of picture books leads children into a wider world. At first, books interpret the child's familiar world close at hand—home, pets, garden, and school—and later lead the child to faraway and unknown worlds. . . .

This dialogue between the illustrator and his child readers continues and, eventually, develops into a rewarding friendship. Many children have written me letters asking questions about my books—and I tried to answer most. By guiding the child's way of seeing, the illustrator becomes a teacher, a partner with parents in rearing children. The illustrator helps form the personalities of developing children, leading them from level to level in the growth of their reading skills and visual experience.

The illustrated book, little by little, leads young people to a sense of citizenship in the world and should present more and more complex pictures of people and things. The illustrated book is also the child's first picture gallery, expanding at each level of development new wonder and love for the variety of nature. Books must pass just ahead of children and young people, leading them forward into the world.

Today, we are living in an astonishing age, a parade of new technologies and scientific discoveries. We illustrators now have the task of introducing children to the modern era. In my own lifetime, I have seen aeronautics progress from balloons to airplanes with jet engines. In my hometown of Reval I saw the horse replaced by the automobile, and steam locomotives by electricity. From America I saw Sputnik, and finally saw man leaving his cradle on earth and going into space. Themes for illustrated books are numerous and rich, and we must keep up with the world to do our best.

Appendix A2. Chronology: Feodor Rojankovsky, 1891 - 1970

1891. Born December 24 to parents Lydia Kiprianovna (Kordasevich) and Stepan Fedorovich Rojankovsky in Mitau/Mitava, a town then in Imperial Russia, but today in independent Latvia and named Jelgava. Feodor was the second youngest of six (five surviving) children. His father was headmaster and teacher of Latin and Greek at a secondary school for boys.

1893. The family moved to Reval, the capital of Estonia (today named Tallinn), where his father had been reassigned as the headmaster of Revel'skaia Aleksandrovskaia Gimnaziia, another secondary school for boys.

1897. Father, Stepan, died in the summer. Mother, Lydia, moved to St. Petersburg to be near her older daughter, Aleksandra; the two youngest children soon followed.

1901. After four years in St. Petersburg, Lydia and her two children returned to Reval, where Feodor completed his last year in a dual-language (Russian-German) primary school.

1902. In Reval, began secondary school (gimnaziia) in same school where his father had been headmaster.

1909. Went to Yalta to join brother, Pavel, an electrical engineer who headed a technical school. Continued studies and painted murals and decorations for public spaces.

1911. Went to family friends in Moscow. Decided on career in art and began studies at the studio of Fedor Rerberg.

1912. Entered the Moscow School of Painting, Sculpture and Architecture in 1912 and studied for two academic years.

1914. Drafted in August 1914, began three years of service in the First World War as an infantry reserve officer in the Russian Imperial Army, commanding a motorized unit.

1918. In the wake of the Bolshevik Revolution of October 1917, went to Poltava in the newly independent Ukraine, near the family estate of sister Aleksandra's husband. Illustrated books for the new Republic's Poltava Zemstvo.

1919. Mobilized by the White Army in the Russian civil war of 1918-1920 and served as an officer in the camouflage corps. The Red Army drove his unit of Whites into Poland, where his military service ended in Polish detention camps formed for the containment and demobilization of Whites.

1920. Remaining in Poland, he went to nearby Lvov and soon thereafter to Poznan, beginning the long association with the publishing firm of Rudolf Wegner, illustrating books and covers. Made the first of many drawings (1920-1923) for the satirical magazine *Szczutek*. Began work as a stage decorator at the Teatr Wielki, the Poznan theater and opera. During the next five years in Poland, also made extended excursions to Warsaw in search of other art and design work.

1922. Traveled briefly to Danzig (Gdańsk) and, for longer, to Berlin, seeking to expand his career. But the 1923 German hyperinflation ruined the economy and many Russians left.

1923. Returning to Poland, resumed work as a scene painter at the Poznan opera house. Also worked for a Polish fashion magazine, illustrated more books and covers, and did other free-lance work. Left Poland in 1925.

1925. Settled in Paris in late 1925, living in greatly reduced circumstances for a year or so.

1926. Began illustrating for the Russian-language weekly news magazine, *Illiustrirovannaia Rossiia,* and for publishers of émigré children's books.

1927. Got regular job as an art director with the Lecram Press, a large Paris studio for "la publicité," and remained three years, until about 1930. Resided at No. 11 rue Madame, in the artists' quarter of the 6th Arrondissement, near Saint-Germain-des-Prés, through 1932.

1930. Began working with Esther Averill and Lila Stanley to design stationery and greeting cards for an American firm.

1931. Publication with Averill of Domino Press's *Daniel Boone* in

October. Met Yvette (surname not known), a French woman, who became his companion until he left France in 1941.

1933. Publication of FR's first children's book in Paul Faucher's Père Castor series for Flammarion publishers. In January moved from central Paris to Plessis-Robinson in the suburbs, at No. 3 avenue Payret-Dortail. Inducted into the French Freemasons, the Grande Loge de France, November 1933.

1934. Signed an exclusive five-year contract with Faucher to illustrate more Père Castor books. Averill and Stanley returned to the U. S. But FR stayed in contact with Averill and was to illustrate two more books for the Domino Press, now relocated in New York.

1935. Began vacationing, summer and winter, at Argentière, in the Savoie region of the French Alps. In subsequent years, began building a little house in the area, named "Villa Rambles."

1937. Moved from Plessis-Robinson to a duplex house in Meudon, another Paris suburb, at No. 10ter rue Hérault. Began illustrating for *Paris-Soir.*

1940. Nazis occupy Paris in June. Vacated Paris region and took refuge in Forgeneuve, in the family home of his editor Paul Faucher. Spent several months there painting landscapes of the local region and helping in Faucher's relocated progressive school. The house in Argentière, which was in the Non-occupied Zone of France, was completed sometime in 1940. Went there in late 1940 and continued to produce Père Castor books. Avoided the Occupied Zone.

1941. Signed exclusive contract with agent Josef Riwkin and editor Georges Duplaix to work for Artists and Writers Guild, facilitating his immigration to the U.S. Traveled alone to New York, arriving on September 12. Brief stay as a guest in agent Riwkin's townhouse at 48 Charles Street, before occupying an apartment at 45 West 11th Street.

1942. *The Tall Book of Mother Goose* (1942) was published—his first major book in the U.S. Spent summer of 1942 with friends in Westport, Connecticut. In the fall, took another apartment at 50 West 8th Street (between Fifth and Sixth avenues).

1943. Guild sponsored a trip to Los Angeles and Hollywood, where he worked a few weeks as a visiting artist at the Disney Studios. Also visited friends in Sante Fe, New Mexico, for the month of September 1943.

1944. Moved to yet another apartment nearby at 20 West 9th Street, a converted brownstone, and lived here until 1949. FR and fiancée Nina Fedotova made autumn-winter trip to Los Angeles and Carmel and spent the first of three consecutive summers in Bar Harbor, Maine.

1946. Married Nina Georgievna Fedotova, April 12. Nina (1916-1992) was the daughter of Georgii Petrovich Fedotov (1886-1951), the prominent Russian and émigré historian, political essayist, and religious thinker. Built a seaside house in Palm Beach, Florida, 615 North County Road, and wintered there until 1950-51, when the house was sold.

1948. Birth of daughter Tatiana, called Tanya, in New York. Family summered at home of friends in the Russian Village (now a Historical District) of Southbury, Connecticut, and infant daughter baptized in St. Sergius Chapel.

1949. FR and family moved to a rented house, 223 Alexander Road, Lakewood, New Jersey, in the semi-rural Russian enclave.

1951. First trip back to France since coming to the U.S. in 1941. The last exclusive contract with the Artists and Writers Guild expired and released him for free-lance projects.

1952. FR and family returned to France in summer of 1952 and remained 15 months, residing in the Paris suburb of Plessis-Robinson. Bought land for a summer home in La Favière on the French Riviera, completing it in 1953.

1953. Returned to U.S. in November 1953 and in early 1954 bought a family house at 17 McIntyre Street, Bronxville, NY, a suburb north of New York City in Westchester County, living there until 1960.

1956. Won the Caldecott Award for best illustrated book of 1955, for the illustration of John Langstaff's *Frog Went A-Courtin'*.

1957. Made second extended trip to France, staying 14 months—two summers (1957 and 1958) in La Favière and the winter of 1957-58 in Paris at No. 7 rue d'Olivet in the 7th district.

1959. First trip back to Russia, with the family. Reunion with younger sister, Tatiana, after a separation of 41 years. Thereafter, he visited Russia about every two years.

1960. Sold the Bronxville house in mid-1960 and moved to France, the family settling at No. 103 avenue de Versailles, Paris 16. Until mid-1965 the family lived between the Paris apartment and their summer home in La Favière, and FR made two trips back to the U.S. to attend to business.

1965. After five years in France, family returned to the U.S. in June, again to Bronxville, buying a house at 91 Cassilis Avenue, where they lived until FR's death—and years afterwards. In the late 1960s, FR had increasingly serious health problems, but kept working on book projects.

1968. Became a naturalized U.S. citizen and made his last biennial trip to Russia.

1970. Died on October 12, of cancer, at home in Bronxville, age 78, after a two-year illness. Funeral at St. Vladimir's Seminary in Crestwood, New York. Buried at Woodlawn Cemetery, Bronx, NY.

Appendix A3. The Artist's Names and Signatures

The artist's name in Russian is Федор Рожанковский, pronounced, roughly, as F'YO-dor Ro-zhan-KOFF-skee. The early art work published in Russia and some in Paris is signed in Cyrillic, often with the two initials, occasionally with a monogram formed with the Cyrillic letters Ф and P.

Feodor Rojankovsky is today the standard bibliographic form for this illustrator and appears on most of his later books. In some bibliographic records, his surname appears as *Rozhankovskii*, *Roshankovskii*, *Rojankovski*, or *Rojankowski*. Transliterations of Russian names vary by country and change over the years.

When living in Poland, 1920-25, the artist transliterated his surname to Polish as *Różankowski*. Credits on his published work in Poland render his given name as *Teodor* or, rarely, *Tadeusz Różankowski* (Polish *Teodor*/*Tadeusz* are equivalant to Russian *Fedor*). He sometimes signed in plates as T. R.

The Russian surname *Rozhankovskii*/*Rojankovsky* is a habitational name of remote Polish origin. In Polish, *różanka* means "rose grove or plantation." The surname, with the Russian suffix *-ovsky* (Polish *-owski*), was bestowed upon one's male ancestor who owned a grove of roses, or lived near one. Or, more proximately, bestowed on one who hailed from a village or town whose name meant "rose grove." The Rojankovskys were originally from the village of Rozhanka in Lvov province in Galicia, where they were small landowning gentry.

In France after 1925 he spelled his surname *Rojankovsky* because the French *j* is similar to the Russian/Polish *zh*/*ż* sounds, and he signed once in 1929 with the variant *Rojankowsky*. He briefly retained *Teodor* and signed French work in the late 1920s with the initials *T.R.*, occasionally making a monogram of the two initials. But *Fedor Rojankovsky* was the usual form after 1930.

By 1927 he also adopted the mononym *Rojan*, promoted this identity in his commercial studio work, and signed certain of his other work with the mononym, sometimes as *F. Rojan.* The Paris editions of the Domino Press books are signed *F. Rojankovsky* and *Fedor Rojankovsky* and the many Père Castor books as *Rojankovsky, F. Rojankovsky*, *Rojan*, or *F. Rojan.*

In the United States, he used *Theodore Rojan* on his first American magazine publication in December 1941. Throughout the 1940s his Manhattan telephone listings were as *Theodor Rojankovsky.* At first, he transliterated his given name as *Fedor* but soon as *Feodor*, pronounced the same, and he sometimes signed as *F. Rojankovsky* in the first years. But the American picture books mostly bear the now familiar form *Feodor Rojankovsky.*

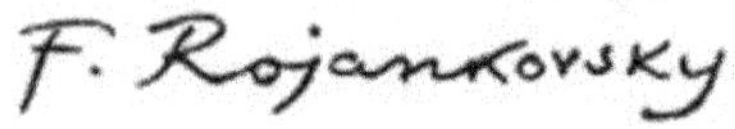

Appendix A4. Checklist of Illustrated Books

I. Children's Books

POLISH BOOKS & RUSSIAN ÉMIGRÉ BOOKS

PO.1. Zbierzchowski. *Oczyma dziecka.* 1921.
PO.2. Burnett. *Mały Lord.* 1925.
PO.3. Mark Twain. *Przygody Tomka Sawyera.* 1925.
PO.4. Szelburg. *Renine wierszyki.* nd [c. 1925].
PO.5. Ossendowski. *Słoń Birara.* 1938.

RU.1. Chernyi. *Zhivaia azbuka.* 1926.
RU.2. Chernyi. *Dnevnik foksa Mikki.* 1927.
RU.3. Chernyi. *Molodaia Rossiia.* 1927.
RU.4. Chernyi. *Koshach'ia sanatoriia.* 1928.
RU.5. Kodrianskaia. *Globusnyi chelovechek.* 1954.
RU.6. Smirnova. *Zaichata.* 1955.

DOMINO PRESS BOOKS

DP.1. Averill and Stanley. *Daniel Boone.* 1931.
DP.2. Averill and Stanley. *Powder/Poudre.* 1933.
DP.3. Averill. *Flash/Éclair.* 1934.
DP.4. Averill. *The Voyages of Jacques Cartier.* 1937.
DP.5. Mariotti. *Tales of Poindi/Les Contes de Poindi.* 1938, 1939.

APPENDIX A4

PÈRE CASTOR BOOKS

PC.1. Celli. *Les petits et les grands.* 1933.
PC.2. Reynier. *En famille.* 1934.

Le roman des bêtes
PC.3. Lida. *Panache l'écureuil.* 1934.
PC.4. Lida. *Froux le lièvre.* 1935.
PC.5. Lida. *Plouf canard sauvage.* 1935.
PC.6. Lida. *Bourru l'ours brun.* 1936.
PC.7. Lida. *Scaf le phoque.* 1936.
PC.8. Lida. *Quipic le hérisson.* 1937.
PC.9. Lida. *Martin-pêcheur.* 1938.
PC.10. Lida. *Coucou.* 1939.

PC.11. Rojankovsky. *ABC du Père Castor.* 1936.
PC.12. Lacôte. *Calendrier des enfants.* 1936.
PC.13. Andersen. *Ce que fait le vieux est bien fait.* 1939.
PC.14. Colmont. *Quand Cigalou s'en va dans la montagne.* 1939.
PC.15. Colmont. *Michka.* 1941.
PC.16. Colmont. *Pic et Pic et Colégram.* 1941.

Les "Petits Père Castor"
PC.17. François. *Mes amis.* 1941.
PC.18. Lida. *Les animaux du zoo.* 1941.
PC.19. Nelly-Roussel. *Les oiseaux du zoo.* 1941.
PC.20. François. *Drôles de bêtes.* 1941.
PC.21. François. *Une histoire de souris.* 1942.
PC.22. François. *La maison des oiseaux.* 1942.
PC.23. Perrault. *Cendrillon.* 1942.
PC.24. Grimm. *Les musiciens de la ville de Brême.* 1942.
PC.25. Nodier. *Histoire du chien de Brisquet.* 1942.
PC.26. Colmont. *Histoire du nègre Zo'hio.* 1942.
PC.27. Anonymous. *Le Royaume de la mer.* 1948.

OTHER FRENCH CHILDREN'S BOOKS AND BOOK COVERS

OF.1. La Fontaine. *La Fontaine Fables.* nd [c. 1930].
OF.2. Mariotti. *Les Contes de Poindi.* 1941.
OF.3. Dumas. *Tom, Jacques & Cie.* 1942.
OF.4. *Collection Maïa.* c. 1927-1942. (covers only).

BRITISH AND AMERICAN CHILDREN'S BOOKS

AB.1. Moncrieff. *The White Drake and Other Tales.* 1936.
AB.2. Dunne. *An Experiment with St. George.* 1939.
AB.3. Cothren. *The Adventures of Dudley & Gilderoy.* 1941.
AB.4. *The Tall Book of Mother Goose.* 1942.
AB.5. *The Tall Book of Nursery Tales.* 1944.

Just So Stories
AB.6. Kipling. *The Elephant's Child.* 1942.
AB.7. Kipling. *How the Camel Got His Hump.* 1942.
AB.8. Kipling. *How the Leopard Got His Spots.* 1942.
AB.9. Kipling. *How the Rhinoceros Got His Skin.* 1942.
AB.10. Kipling. *Four Famous Just So Stories.* 1942 (Pop-up box).
AB.11. Kipling. *The Butterfly That Stamped.* 1947.
AB.12. Kipling. *The Cat That Walked by Himself.* 1947.

AB.13. [Rojankovsky]. *Grandfather's Farm Panorama.* 1943.
AB.14. [Rojankovsky]. *Choo-Choo Panorama.* 1945.
AB.15. Andersen. *The Ugly Duckling.* 1945.
AB.16. Averill. *Daniel Boone.* 1945.
AB.17. Newcomb. *Cortez the Conqueror.* 1947.
AB.18. Abbott. *The Puss 'n Boots Book.* 1949.
AB.19. Prishvin. *The Treasure Trove of the Sun.* 1952.
AB.20. Bishop. *All Alone.* 1953.
AB.21. Kalashnikoff. *My Friend Yakub.* 1953.
AB.22. Tchaika. *Trouble at Beaver Dam.* 1953.
AB.23. Koch. *I Play at the Beach.* 1955.
AB.24. Langstaff. *Frog Went A-Courtin'.* 1955.

AB.25. Averill. *Cartier Sails the St. Lawrence.* 1956.
AB.26. Reisenberg. *Balboa.* 1956.

Music for Living Series
AB.27. Mursell. *I Like the Country.* 1956.
AB.28. Mursell. *I Like the City.* 1956.
AB.29. Mursell. *In Our Town.* 1956.
AB.30. Mursell. *Now and Long Ago.* 1956.
AB.31. Mursell. *Near and Far.* 1956.

AB.32. Langstaff. *Over in the Meadow.* 1957.
AB.33. Thayer. *The Outside Cat.* 1957.
AB.34. Fritz. *The Cabin Faced West.* 1958.
AB.35. Rand. *The Little River.* 1959.
AB.36. Varley. *The Whirly Bird.* 1961.
AB.37. Kalashnikoff. *The Defender.* 1962.
AB.38. Rand. *So Small.* 1962.
AB.39. Rojankovsky. *Animals in the Zoo.* 1962.
AB.40. Fisher. *Cricket in a Thicket.* 1963.
AB.41. Rojankovsky. *Animals on the Farm.* 1967.
AB.42. Graham. *A Crowd of Cows.* 1968.
AB.43. Daniels. *The Falcon Under the Hat.* 1969.
AB.44. Wahl. *The Mulberry Tree.* 1970.
AB.45. Hall. *A Year in the Forest.* 1973.

THE GOLDEN BOOKS

Simon & Schuster

GB.1. Lockwood. *Golden Book of Birds.* 1943.
GB.2. Duplaix. *Animal Stories.* 1944.
GB.3. *Pictures from Mother Goose.* 1945 (Large, loose portfolio).
GB.4. Werner. *The Golden Bible.* 1946.
GB.5. *The Three Bears.* 1948. Cf. 1967 edition.
GB.6. Jackson. *Big Farmer Big* (insert *Little Farmer Little*). 1948.
GB.7. McGinley. *A Name for Kitty.* 1948.

GB.8. Nast. *Our Puppy*. 1948.
GB.9. Duplaix. *Gaston & Josephine*. 1948.
GB.10. *Favorite Fairy Tales*. 1949.
GB.11. Jackson. *The Big Elephant*. 1949.
GB.12. Rojankovsky. *The Great Big Animal Book*. 1950.
GB.13. Nina [Rojankovsky]. *The Kitten's Surprise*. 1951.
GB.14. Rojankovsky. *The Great Big Wild Animal Book*. 1951.
GB.15. Coatsworth. *Cat Stories*. 1953.
GB.16. Coatsworth. *Dog Stories*. 1953.
GB.17. Coatsworth. *Horse Stories*. 1954.
GB.18. Coatsworth. *Dogs, Cats, and Horses*. 1957 (new cover).
GB.19. Watson. *The True Story of Smokey the Bear*. 1955.
GB.20. Duplaix. *The White Bunny and His Magic Nose*. 1957.
GB.21. *Little Golden Mother Goose: 75 Favorite Rhymes*. 1957.
GB.22. *More Mother Goose Rhymes: 57 Favorite Rhymes*. 1958.
GB.23. *Mother Goose Rhymes: 154 Childhood Favorites*. 1958.
GB.24. Werner. *A Catholic Child's Bible: Old Testament*. 1958.
GB.25. Purcell. *Baby Wild Animals*. A Golden Stamp Book. 1958.
GB.26. Daly. *Wild Animal Babies*. 1958.

Golden Press

GB.27. Buell. *Treasury of Little Golden Books*. 1960.
GB.28. Defoe. *Robinson Crusoe*. 1960.
GB.29. Watson. *Animal Dictionary*. 1960.
GB.30. Rojankovsky. *Wild Animals*. 1960.
GB.31. Memling. *10 Little Animals*. 1961.
GB.32. Memling. *I Can Count*. 1963.
GB.33. Krinsley. *The Cow Went Over the Mountain*. 1963.
GB.34. Scarry. *Hop, Little Kangaroo*. 1965.
GB.35. Risom. *I Am a Fox*. 1967.
GB.36. Daly. *The Three Bears*. 1967. (New edition).
GB.37. Rojankovsky. *F. Rojankovsky's ABC*. 1970.
GB.38. Rojankovsky, Nina, ed. *Rojankovsky's Wonderful Picture Book*. 1972.

II. Books for Adult Audiences

GENERAL ADULT BOOKS

BB.1. Malczewski. *Marja.* 1922.
BB.2. Mickiewicz. *Sonety krymskie.* 1922.
BB.3. *Poznań, 20 akwarel.* 1926.
BB.4. Bobrinskoi. *Pamiati russkago studenchestva.* 1934.
BB.5. Evangulov. *Prikliucheniia Pavla Pavlovicha Pupkova.* 1946.
BB.6. Lester. *To Make a Duck Happy.* 1969.

EROTIC BOOKS

ER.1. Protat. *Examen de Flora.* nd [c. 1932].
ER.2. Glatigny. *Le théâtre érotique de la rue de la Santé.* 1932.
ER.3. [Rojankovsky]. *Idylle printanière.* nd [c. 1933].
ER.4. Radiguet. *Vers libres.* nd [c. 1935].
ER.5. Louÿs. *Poésies érotiques.* 1937.
ER.6. Béranger. *Chansons galantes.* 1937.
ER.7. Spaddy. *Dévergondages.* 1948. [art work c. 1937].

Appendix A5. Selected Exhibitions and Awards

Solo Exhibitions

Salon Garliński, Warsaw, May 15-30, 1924. Thirty-two paintings, theatrical and costume designs, and woodcuts filled one room.

New York Public Library, old Central Children's Room, opened March 3, 1943. Complete retrospective of the French Domino Press and Flammarion books. Among the new American books were the four Kipling books of *Just So Stories* (1942) and *The Tall Book of Mother Goose* (1942). Original art included drawings for *Cartier* and *Cortez* and for the yet unpublished *The Tall Book of Nursery Tales* (1944) and *The Cat That Walked By Himself* (1947), and several watercolors of French landscapes.

FAR Gallery, New York, February 6-17, 1973. Posthumous solo exhibit of paintings and watercolors. Fritz Eichenberg authored the catalog essay.

Exposition d'Aquarelles et de Dessins de Feodor Rojankovsky. Alliance Française de Puerto Rico, San Juan, PR, February 16 to March 2, 1973. Posthumous solo exhibit. Catalog.

La maison des trois ours: hommage à Rojankovsky. La maison de l'image et du son de Villeurbanne (near Lyon), October 14, 1998. Exhibit on theme of FR's illustration of *The Three Bears*, with many books and examples of original art. The exhibit traveled to other librairies in France at least into January 2000. Catalog.

Group Exhibitions in Europe

Exhibits of the Students of Moskovskoe Uchilishche Zhivopisi Vaianiia i Zodchestva (Moscow School of Painting, Sculpture and

Architecture). Published catalogs of the 31st-38th exhibits include FR among the students whose work was exhibited. His work would have appeared in the 35th exhibit, 1913-14, and/or the 36th exhibit, 1914-15.

German Book Museum, Leipzig, 1924. Entries in Polish Books and Woodcuts. Widely reviewed in the Polish press, and said to be the first exhibit of Polish art on German soil.

International Exhibition of Book Arts. Leipzig, 1927. *Sonety Krymskie* included in the Polish entry.

Russian House, Meudon, France, November 7, 1927. FR was head of the art section for the opening event. Designed the art exhibit and included some of his recent work.

Slavic Ex Libris. Muzeum Przemyslowym (Industrial Museum), Krakow, 1930. Included FR's bookplates for Polish patrons.

International Children's Books. Annual exhibits in the galleries of Librairie Fischbacher, Paris, 1933 and 1934. Included FR's *Albums du Père Castor* and Domino Press titles.

Christmas Bazaar. Galerie La Renaissance, Paris, December 30, 1934. FR was among the 17 prominent Russian artists and sculptors who exhibited.

Albums du Père Castor. Flammarion et Cie. gallery, Paris, 1972. Exhibit on the occasion of the publication of the 350th album.

Albums du Père Castor. International Library for Young People, Munich, Germany, 1973. Exhibit.

Albums du Père Castor. Bibliothèque de l'Heure Joyeuse, 1982. Opening of a traveling show. Exhibit for the occasion of the 50th anniversary of the Père Castor books, 1931-1981.

Livre, Mon Ami. Lectures enfantines, 1914-1954. Bibliothèque Forney, Paris, September 10 to October 19, 1991. Included original art and early Père Castor and Domino Press books. Catalog.

An Acquaintance with Poznań: Views of Places on Postcards in the Years 1889-1939. National Museum, Poznan, June-September, 1995. Included FR's postcards made from 1924 watercolors of Poznan scenes. Catalog.

Illustrateurs de livres d'enfants russes. Bibliothèque Forney, Paris, October

5 to December 27, 1997. Included several picture books and an original drawing. Catalog.

Les Russes de La Favière. Musée d'Arts et Histoire, Bormes-les-Mimosas, France, September 5 to November 14, 2004. Included several originals of FR's art for the Père Castor books, plus a number of drawings and paintings unrelated to his book illustrations. Catalog.

L'Enfer de la Bibliothèque: Eros au secret. Bibliothèque Nationale de France, December 4, 2007 to March 2, 2008. Exhibit from the celebrated erotic collection of the BNF includes examples of FR's erotic books. Catalog.

Group Exhibitions in the United States and Canada

A Few Contemporary European Illustrated Books. American Institute of Graphic Arts (AIGA), New York, February 1931. Included *Sonety Krymskie* and *Marja* as items 23 and 24.

Street Murals: The Modern French Poster. The Bookshop for Boys and Girls, Women's Educational and Industrial Union, Boston, February 1932. Included FR's poster titled "Blanc." Catalog essay by Esther Averill, dateline Paris, 1931.

AIGA, New York, December 15-19, 1942. "Exhibition of three outstanding graphic artists (Russian, Brazilian and Czech) [FR, H.A. Rey and Hugo Steiner-Prag] who have recently begun to work in the U.S."

Art Directors Club of New York, 1943, 1947, 1948, 1949. Advertising art included in four annual spring exhibits at various prominent New York museums and gallery spaces. Catalogs for each.

Philadelphia Art Alliance, Rittenhouse Square, Philadelphia, PA, December 1944. Exhibit of original illustration art.

Junior League Club of New York City, May 12, 1945. Original drawings for *Animal Stories* and *The Tall Book of Nursery Tales*, along with the printed books. Exhibit also circulated to other cities by the American Federation of Arts.

24th Annual Exhibition of American Bookmaking. AIGA, New York, 1945. *Animal Stories* (1944) selected as one of "50 Books of the Year 1944," from entries of all kinds of illustrated books. Catalog.

31st Annual Exhibition of American Bookmaking. AIGA, New York, 1953. *Treasure Trove of the Sun* (1952) selected as one of "50 Books of the Year 1952," from entries of all kinds of illustrated books. Catalog.

AIGA Children's Book Show. New York, 1958. Exhibition of 79 books chosen as the "best made" in the three years 1955-1957, from 300 publishers' submissions.

Society of Illustrators, Annual Exhibition. New York, January 19, 1960.

Art and the Alphabet. The Museum of Fine Arts, Houston, Texas, May 26 to July 30, 1978. Exhibit included eight original drawings and dummy for *Animals in the Zoo* in section on "Modern Alphabet Books." Catalog.

Myth, Magic, and Mystery: One Hundred Years of American Children's Book Illustration. The Chrysler Museum of Art, Norfolk, VA, June 2 to September 8, 1996. Show traveled to Memphis, TN and Wilmington, DE. Included original art from Daniel Boone. Catalog.

A Carnival of Animals: Beasts, Birds and Bugs in Original Illustrations from Children's Books. From the Mazza Collection, Findlay University, Findlay, OH. Meridian International Center, Washington, DC. April-May 2000, and the Ohio Arts Council's Riffe Gallery, Columbus, OH, January-April, 2004. Included an original b&w illustration, done in graphite, pen and ink, and watercolor, for *The Ugly Duckling* (1945).

Golden Legacy: Original Art from 65 Years of Golden Books. National Center for Children's Illustrated Literature, Abilene, Texas. Exhibit opened in New York from July 4, through August 28, 2008, at the Children's Museum of Manhattan, in conjunction with the publication of Leonard Marcus's *Golden Legacy* (2007). The exhibit subsequently appeared at the Center in Abilene from November 1, 2007 to January 4, 2008, and continues on tour under their auspices to libraries and museums around the country through the end of 2013. Includes five paintings by FR, one each from *Animal Stories* and *A Name for Kitty*, and three from *The Three Bears* (1948).

Art Deco and the Decorative Arts in the 1920s and 1930s. McGill Library/ Bibliothèque, McGill University, Montreal, Quebec, Canada. Exhibit paid homage to Art Deco on the occasion of the 10th

World Congress being held in Montreal in May, 2009. Included FR's Orient Line cruise brochure, *Norway* [See EA.8].

Group Exhibitions in Japan

Picture Books in the 20th Century: Gifts to Children. Exhibit traveling to several Japanese cities, March 1999-February 2000. Sponsored by Asahi Newspaper Company. Included FR's Children's Book Week poster, with its original watercolor. Catalog.

Picture Book Gallery (online). International Library of Children's Literature. National Diet Library. Tokyo, Japan. A permanent, public website displaying many classic picture books, including a number of FR's. <www.kodomo.go.jp/**gallery**/index_e>

Awards and Citations

Best Children's Books of 1942. National award, 1943. For the first four Kipling books of *Just So Stories.*

Citations. December 31, 1945, and March 12, 1946. From United States Treasury Department. "Distinguished Services in Behalf of the War Finance Program," for designing posters for the School Savings Program during WWII.

Gold Medal of the Art Directors Club. New York, June 1, 1948. For color work in advertising shown at the 27th Annual Exhibition of Advertising and Editorial Art. (For the 1948 Morrell "Fairy Tales" calendar.)

Silver Medal of the Silver Jubilee of the Limited Editions Club. New York, Waldorf-Astoria, May 11, 1954. Named one of eight living artists who had done "influential and significant work in book illustration" in the quarter century, 1929 to 1954.

Spring Book Festival Award. May 12, 1955. Sponsored by the *New York Herald Tribune.* Award for best book in the picture-book age group: *Frog Went A-Courtin'* (1955).

Caldecott Award. June 19, 1956. The nation's highest award to children's-book illustrators, for his color work in *Frog Went A-Courtin'* (1955). Sponsored by the Children's Library Association.

Certificate of Excellence, American Institute of Graphic Arts, Children's Book Show. New York, 1958. Show exhibited 79 books as the "best made" in the three years 1955-1957, chosen from 300 publishers' submissions.

National Children's Book Week Poster. 1959. Invited poster design on theme, "Go Exploring in Books," sponsored by the Children's Book Council.

Citation for Merit, Society of Illustrators, Annual Exhibition. New York, January 19, 1960.

Public Collections with Original Art by Rojankovsky

Bakhmeteff Archive, Columbia University, New York, NY. FR's illustrated letters to Mstislav Dobuzhinsky, in the M. Dobuzhinsky collection.

Bowling Green State University, Bowling Green, Ohio. Originals of two unpublished illustrations in the collection of Jan Wahl's papers.

Children's Care Hospital, Sioux Falls, SD. Twelve Morrell circus paintings.

Children's Literature Center, Library of Congress, Washington, DC.

De Grummond Collection, University of Southern Mississippi, Hattiesburg, MS.

Kerlan Collection, University of Minnesota, Minneapolis, MN.

Knight Library, University of Oregon, Eugene, OR.

La Mediathèque du Père Castor, Forgeneuve, Meuzac, France. Originals of illustrations for the Père Castor books and illustrated letters in the correspondence between FR and Paul Faucher.

Lilly Library, Indiana University, Bloomington, IN.

Los Angeles Public Library, Children's Literature Department, Los Angeles, CA.

Mazza Collection, University of Findlay, Findlay, OH.

Mead Art Museum, Amherst College, Amherst, MA. Three paintings/drawings and one print by FR.

Moulin de Senlis, 1, rue du Moulin-de-Senlis, Montgeron 91230, France. Cycloramic mural by FR in former orphanage.

Muzeum Narodowe [National Museum], Poznan, Poland.

National Museum of American History, Div. of Cultural History, Smithsonian Institution, Washington, DC.
University Library, University of California, Los Angeles, CA.
Zetlin Museum of Russian Art, Ramat-Gan, Israel.

Public Collections with Printed Poster and Display Art by Rojankovsky

Bibliothèque Forney, Paris
London Transport Museum, London
Museum für Gestaltung, Zürich
Muzeum Narodowe, Poznan, Poland
National Railway Museum, York, U.K
Nelson-Atkins Museum of Art, Kansas City, MO
Victoria & Albert Museum, London

References and Sources

Adamovich, Marina. "Portret sem'i na fone epokhi." *Novyi zhurnal.* no. 264 (2011): 279-291. Interview by the editor-in-chief of the New York Russian-émigré quarterly with FR's daughter, Tanya Rojankovsky Koly, who recalls aspects of the lives of her maternal grandfather, Fedotov, and of her father.

Ade [mononym only]. "Polski koniak." *Świat* (Warzaw). 17, no. 11 (March 18, 1922): 36-40. Article on the Polish distiller Jósef Grabowski and his factory in Poznan describes his private office decorated with three panoramic murals (also pictured) by FR and Ernst Czerper.

Alderson, Brian. "Just-So Pictures: Illustrated Versions of Just So Stories for Little Children." *Children's Literature.* New Haven: Yale University Press, 1992. 147-174. Critical appraisal, with photo of the rare pop-up box FR designed for an early promotion of the books.

Alekseeva, Liudmila. "Fedor Rozhankovskii." *Sputnik studenta.* no. 2 (1962). Minneapolis: University of Minnesota. Article (in Russian) for the Russian Club.

Alexander, Irene. "Rojankovsky Adds Scenes to Sketchbook: Noted Russian Artist Finds Inspiration in Brief Visit." *Monterey Peninsula Herald.* Monterey, CA. (November 14, 1944): 10. Account of visit to Carmel, with unusual biographical facts.

American Institute of Graphic Arts. *50 Books of the Year 1944.* New York: AIGA, 1945. Exhibition catalog describes and illustrates winning entry of *Animal Stories.*

———. *50 Books of the Year 1952.* New York: AIGA, 1953. Catalog describes and illustrates winning entry of *The Treasure Trove of the Sun.*

Apollinare, Guillaume. *L'Enfer de la Bibliothèque Nationale.* Paris: Mercure de France, 1913. Celebrated descriptive bibliography of the many erotic works in the collection of the Bibliothèque Nationale in Paris. Currently in print, reproduced by several publishers.

Arbuthnot, May Hill, and Zena Sutherland. *Children and Books.* Fourth Edition. Glenview, IL: Scott, Foresman and Company, 1972. 62-63, 118. A brief entry, "Feodor Rojankovsky, 1891-1970," plus a comment deploring "two objectionable pictures" in *The Tall Book of Mother Goose* (1942).

Archives of American Art. Smithsonian Institution, Reference Department. Washington, D.C. Rockwell Kent papers: Feodor Rojankovski, 1944-45, item nos. 436-441. FR's letters to and from Kent about proposed visits and signing books.

Association Les Trois Ourses. *La maison des trois ours: hommage à Rojankovsky.* Paris: Édition les trois ourses, 1998. Commemorative album with essays about FR and his work, to accompany a traveling exhibit. Remembrances and essays by Tatiana R. Koly, Tatiana Mailliard-Parain, François Faucher, Michel Duplaix, Christian Lacroix, and others.

Averill, Esther. "Avant-Gardes and Traditions in France," in Bertha E. Mahoney and Elinor Whitney, compilers. *Contemporary Illustrators of Children's Books.* Boston: Bookshop for Boys and Girls, 1930. 89-96. The artistic status of the picture book in France in the year before *Daniel Boone.*

———. "Fedor Rojankovsky and 'Les Peaux-Rouges'." *The Horn Book.* Vol. 8, no. 1 (February, 1932): 26-32. Introduces FR to American readers and recounts publishing event of *Daniel Boone.*

———. [attributed]. Untitled, anonymous two-part article about *Daniel Boone. The Horn Book.* Vol. 8, no. 1 (February 1932): 132-133. How the "Domino Cat" (the feline mascot who lived in the Paris offices of the Domino Press) was FR's life model for the squirrel, the beaver, the fox, and even Boone's coonskin hat.

———. "A Publishers Odyssey." *The Horn Book*, Part I, Vol. 14, no. 5 (September 1938): 275-281; Part II, Vol. 14, no. 6 (December 1938): 391-396; Part III, Vol. 15, no. 1 (January 1939): 21-23. The publishing saga of *Daniel Boone* and other titles by the Domino

Press. Reprinted in Norma R. Fryatt, ed., *A Horn Book Sampler on Children's Books and Reading.* Boston: Horn Book, 1959. 70-85.

———. "Feodor Rojankovsky, Illustrator." *The Horn Book.* Vol. 19 (May 1943): 151-157. More biography, with comments on FR's recent American books. Reproduces an independent watercolor and two sketches of children.

———. "Unfinished Portrait of an Artist, Feodor Rojankovsky." *The Horn Book.* Vol. 32, no. 4 (August 1956): 246-253. Averill's address upon the occasion of the Caldecott Award. With a photograph of the artist and his young daughter, and some of his drawings. Text reprinted in B.H. Miller and E. W. Field, eds., *Caldecott Medal Books: 1938-1957.* The Horn Book Papers, Vol. II. Boston: The Horn Book, 1957, and in L. Kingman, ed., *Newbery and Caldecott Medal Books: 1956-1965.* Boston: The Horn Book, 1965.

———. "Rojankovsky-Averill Correspondence." *Phaedrus.* Vol. 11 (1985): v-xv: "Feodor Rojankovsky and the Domino Press: A Few Letters Translated and Edited with Notes by Esther Averill." Retitled "Rojankovsky-Averill Letters" and issued as a pamphlet in a limited and numbered edition of 50 copies, signed by Averill and Nina Rojankovsky. Averill's translation, with her notes, of letters FR wrote her between 1932 and 1939. Much biographical material, and illustrated with drawings that adorned the letters.

———. "A Publisher's Perspective: French Publishing." *The Horn Book.* (January-February 1990): 104-108. Highlights of modern French children's publishing in the 1920s and 1930s, the milieu in which FR worked.

Bader, Barbara. *American Picturebooks, from Noah's Ark to the Beast Within.* New York: Macmillan, 1976. 118-127, 295-301; notes: 574, 586. An excellent critical treatment of FR's work and a history of Golden Books.

Benois, Alexandre. "Detskii zhurnal *Ogon'ki.*" *Poslednie novosti.* Paris (June 13, 1933): 4. Discussion of the new children's magazine, praising FR's drawings.

———. "Novaia detskaia knizhka." *Poslednie novosti.* Paris (November 18, 1933). Also in I. S. Zil'bershtein and B. N. Savinov, eds. *Aleksandr*

Benua razmyshliaet . . . . Moscow: Sovetskii khudozhnik, 1968. 261-263. Benois praises *Daniel Boone.*

———. "Khudozhestvennyia pis'ma: Detskiia knizhki." *Poslednie novosti.* Paris (9 December 1933): 3. Review of the 1933 Christmas exhibit at Fischbacher, singling out *Les petits et les grands* and *Poudre* for praise.

———. "Khudozhestvennyia pis'ma: Rozhdestvo v Parizhe." *Poslednie novosti.* Paris (January 5, 1935): 3. Reviews 1934 Christmas show at Fischbacher and discusses *Éclair* and *Panache.*

Bernard, Kate. "Art Market" (column). *Harpers and Queen.* (September 1993): 28. Reproduces a small erotic picture credited to "Fedor Rojan Kowsky" [sic]. From a full-page pochoir in *Vers libres*—opposite the verse "Ébauches."

Beston, Henry. "The Voyages of Jacques Cartier." *The Horn Book.* Vol. 14, no. 1 (January-February 1938): 19-21. Article praising Averill's new book, as illustrated by FR.

Biblioteka Raczyńskich. *Ekslibrisy wielkopolski: Katalog wystawy.* Poznan: Muzeum narodowe, 1958. Rare documentation of FR's bookplates.

Bibliothèque Forney. *Tolmer: 60 ans de création graphique dans l'Île St Louis.* Paris: Bibliothèque Forney. Catalog of exhibit, Paris, May 22-July 5, 1986. FR was among the artists who designed for Alfred Tolmer, about1929-30.

———. *Livre mon ami: Lectures enfantines, 1914-1954.* Paris: Bibliothèque Forney, 1991. Catalog for a 1991-92 exhibit (including FR's original art and early books) with a color page from *Daniel Boone.* FR discussed in context of 1930s "Renaissance" in French children's books.

Bland, David. *A History of Book Illustration: The Illuminated Manuscript and the Printed Book.* Cleveland, OH: The World Publishing Company, 1958. 356, 398-9, 426. Attests to the innovation and influence of FR's books in the Père Castor series, praises his first books in America, and credits him for "effecting a minor revolution in the West." With illustration from 1945 edition of *Daniel Boone.* Revised edition (Berkeley: University of California Press, 1969) retains the same passages.

Bocci, Richard. "Preface," *Spring Romance/Pariser frühlingsromanze/Idylle printanière*. Paris: Bibliothèque de l'Image, 2000. 5-8. Essay correctly attributes *Idylle printanière* to FR, but promotes several biographical and bibliographical errors.

Bretonnelle, Jean. "Rojan: l'éveilleur de rêves." *Bulletin de l'Association Mémoire d'Image*. no. 24 (Printemps 2011). Discussion of FR's work as a children's-book illustrator, primarily for Père Castor, but also other work for children and adults.

Bruller, Jean. "L'œil du bibliophile." *Arts et métiers graphiques*. Vol. 28 (March 10, 1932): 46-51. Bound-in insert (opposite page 48) on heavy buff paper reproduces the cover of *Daniel Boone* by full-color lithography.

Bychkov, Sergei. "Fedor Rozhankovskii snova v Rossii." *Sobranie*. no. 1 (March, 2013): 116-123. An interview with FR's daughter, Tanya Rojankovsky Koly, about her father's life and work in both Europe and America.

Carlisle, Olga Andreyev. *Voices in the Snow: Encounters with Russian Writers*. New York: Random House, 1962. The author's childhood (early 1930s) recollection of FR in his suburban Paris studio, his entertainment of children there, and a comment on his Slavic faces in pictures of children (p. 22).

Carrick, Martin W. "Art Directors Club Medal." *Twenty Seventh Annual of Advertising Art*. New York: Art Directors Club of New York and Pitman Publishing Corporation, 1948. 75. Praise for FR's work upon the occasion of the award, with background on the winning artwork for Morrell's 1948 calendar.

Chernyi, Sasha. *Sasha Chernyi: Izbrannaia proza*. Moscow: Kniga, 1991. Commentary by A. Ivanov. Reproduces the complete text of *Dnevnik foksa Mikki*, with FR's cover and drawings; three additional covers by FR for Chernyi's books; FR's drawing of Chernyi (1927); photo of FR (circa 1955); and a biographical sketch (with errors) of FR.

Children's Book Council. *75 Years of Children's Book Week Posters: Celebrating Great Illustrators of American Children's books*. New York: A. A. Knopf, 1994. Pictures FR's 1959 poster.

Commercial Art. Vol. 10 (January 1931): 13. Color reproductions of four leaves from the portfolio, *Quand la bise fut venue.*

Commire, Anne, ed. "Rojankovsky, Feodor (Stepanovich), 1891-1970 (Rojan)." *Something About the Author.* Vol 21. Detroit: Gale Research Company, 1980. 127-131. A terse bibliography and some biographical material.

Cuevas, Clara. "Mi padre vive a traves de su arte." *Puerto Rico illustrado.* (March 1973): 8-9. An interview with FR's daughter, Tatiana, recalling his life and career.

Deitz, Paula. "Rockefeller Center Gets a Topiary Zoo." *New York Times* (August 16, 1984): Section C, 12. Description of the topiaries, with photo, derived from *Wild Animals* (1960).

Der Kalte Blick. Postcard. Reproduction of an erotic watercolor by FR of an amorous country couple, here titled "Ländliche Liebe." nd [c. 1930]. Collection Engel, Galleria Erotica, Köln. Edition *Der Kalte Blick*, no. 1011. nd [c. 1995]. The other image (no. 1012) attributed to FR in this postcard series is by another artist.

de Saint-Rat, A. L. "Children's Books by Russian Émigré Artists: 1921-1940." *The Journal of Decorative and Propaganda Arts.* Vol. 11 (Winter 1989): 92-105. The best critical overview of the émigré children's illustrators, especially of the Paris group, and of FR's place among them. Illustrated in color.

Desse, Jacques. "Les lettres illustrées de ROJAN." Ricochet-Jeunes.org. www.ricochet-jeunes.org/oeil-du-libraire/article/64-les-lettres-illustrees-de-rojan (accessed April 18, 2013). Excerpts from FR's charming illustrated letters to his illustrator friend, Gaston de Saint-Croix, dating from 1932 - 1951.

Döpp, Hans-Jürgen. *The Erotic Museum in Berlin.* London: Parkstone Press, 2000. Reproduces eight watercolors that are erroneous or dubious attributions to FR by the Museum (viz, pp. 96, 97, 100, 105, 106, 107, and 122). But the carnal version of "Little Red Riding Hood and the Wolf" in six panels of watercolors (pp. 146-147) is possibly by FR. Also reproduces four scenes from FR's *Idylle printanière.*

Doyle, Brian, compiler. *The Who's Who of Children's Literature.* New York: Schocken Books, 1968. 346-47. Brief career summary.

Dupuy, R. -L. "Fedor Rojankovsky, Paris." *Gebrauchsgraphik*. Vol. IX, no. 12 (1932): 40-47. Halftones of the title and six pages from *Daniel Boone* and some of the French advertising art.

Eichenberg, Fritz. "New Picture Books." *The Horn Book*. Vol. 20 (January 1944): 15-24. Singles out FR's first books in U.S. for special praise (p. 18).

———. "The Cover Artist." *AIGA Journal*. Vol. 3, no. 3 [c. 1951]: 36. A short article praising FR's success in his first ten years in America and discussing his cover picture for this special issue on Children's Books.

———. "Feodor Rojankovsky, Friend of Children." *American Artist*. Vol. 21 (January 1957): 28-35. Independent drawings and paintings are reproduced. Also translated into Russian for *Amerika* (no. 14, nd [1957]: 44-47), a publication of the U. S. Department of State; also in the English-language edition, *America Illustrated*, 1957. A similar essay by Eichenberg appears in the catalog of the FAR Gallery.

Erotic Print Society. *The Catalogue*. London: The Erotic Print Society, 1994. 5-10. Describes a new edition of *Idylle printanière*, retitled *Paris Spring 1933*, and reproduces in color four illustrations (one a detail) from the portfolio.

FAR Gallery. *Feodor Rojankovsky: A Retrospective Exhibition of Watercolors and Drawings, 1923-1969*. New York: The FAR Gallery, 1973, [16] pp. Catalog for a posthumous exhibit, February 6-17, 1973. Contains an essay by Fritz Eichenberg, "Feodor Rojankovsky, 1891-1970: A Tribute to a Friend." The catalog has an illustrated cover (four gouaches of animals by FR). Reproduces nine other works in the exhibit—five landscapes, three female nudes, and a portrait of a seated woman. Those not signed by Rojankovsky when he drew them were initialed "N. R." by Nina Rojankovsky. A two-paragraph notice of the show appeared in *Publisher's Weekly* (January 1973). Notices appeared in *The Art Gallery Magazine* (February 1973): 66, with reproductions of catalog illustrations, and in *The Art Gallery Guide* (February 1973).

Fascination: le musée secret de l'érotisme. Paris. no. 15 [1982]. Cover design features an image from *Idylle printanière*.

Faucher, Paul. "La mission éducative des Albums du Père Castor."

L'École nouvelle française, no. 87 (nd). Conférence de Zurich prononcée en 1957.

———. "Comment adapter la littérature enfantine aux besoins des enfants." *Vers l'éducation nouvelle.* no. 179 (January-February 1964): 11-22. A 1958 conference paper on his theories of children's books, using FR's Père Castor books as one example.

Faulsitck, Edith M. "Feodor Rojankovsky of Bronxville: Winner of the Caldecott Medal." *Westchester Life.* (August 1956): 9, 15. An interview, with a photo of FR in his Bronxville studio.

Feaver, William. *When We Were Young: Two Centuries of Children's Book Illustration.* New York: Holt, Rinehart & Winston, 1977. Reproduces design from *Daniel Boone* (pl. 73) and *Calendrier des enfants* (pl. 84), plus short bio (p. 94).

Fernandez, Jesse. "Rojankovsky." *Sunday San Juan Star Magazine.* (March 4, 1973): 16. Account of career and review of exhibit in San Juan, PR, with reproduction of cover for *Illiustrirovannaia Rossiia* (Paris).

Flammarion et Cie, editors. *À l'enseigne du Père Castor.* Paris: Flammarion, 1982. A bibliography of the series.

Frenzel, H.K. "Kinderbücher—Children's Books." *Gebrauchsgraphik.* Vol. 12, no. 2 (February 1935): 10-33. Pages 18-19, 22-23, 28-29 have halftone reproductions from *Poudre, Panache*, and *Éclair.*

Gankina, Ella Zinov'evna. "Russkaia detskaia kniga v Parizhe." In *Ierusalimskii bibliofil: al'manakh.* Jerusalem: Filobiblon, 1999, 229-247. Discusses FR's work in Paris with Domino Press and Père Castor.

Goldthwaite, John. *The Natural History of Make-Believe: A Guide to the Principal Works of Britain, Europe, and America.* New York: Oxford University Press, 1996. In a chapter on the nursery rhyme, credits *The Tall Book of Mother Goose* (1942) with "waking up the literature."

Gollerbach, S. "Na zapadnoi storone v russkom N'iu Iorke." *Novyi zhurnal.* no. 147 (1989). A recollection of FR and other friends during the 1950s and 1960s.

Górska, Hanna, and Eryk Lipiński. *Z dziejów karykatury polskiej.* Warsaw: Wiedza powszechna, 1977. Includes FR in discussion of Polish caricature and satire in the 1920s and reproduces a published drawing (p. 200).

Greason, Rebecca. *Tomart's Price Guide to Golden Book Collectibles.* Radnor, PA: Wallace-Homestead Book Co., 1991. Entries for FR are incomplete and have errors of fact, but useful for the 14 photographs of his covers.

Grimley, Gordon. *Erotic Illustrations.* New York: Bell Books, 1974. Reproduces (pl. 144-156) in halftone 13 unpublished watercolors and drawings, obliquely attributed with this caption: "These thirteen small watercolors and drawings, c. 1950 (?), were produced for a volume which seemingly never appeared. The work is clearly that of an artist of stature who is said to have produced them, on commission, during youthful poverty, and who is now renowned for his 'normal' children's-book illustrations." Most are probably by FR; others seem uncharacteristic and are less likely by FR. The most likely ones are surely earlier than suggested, probably the early 1930s, and seem to be studies for Radiguet's *Vers libres* or a similar project. In any case, none of FR's work in this genre was done after the 1930s.

Grońska, Maria. *Grafika w ksiażce, tece i albumie: Polskie wydawnictwa artystyczne i bibliofilskie z lat 1899-1945.* Wrocław: Zakład norodwy im. Ossolińskich, 1994. Lists and describes illustrations in *Sonety krymskie* and *Marja* (1922) as notable pre-war Polish book illustration.

Gruber, L. Fritz. "Christmas and New Year's Cards." *Graphis.* Vol. 6, no. 32 (1950). Page 346 has a halftone reproduction of a card published by Irene Dash Greeting Card Co.

Harling, Robert. "Somebody Discovers the Case." *Typography.* no. 1 (November 1936): 19-23. Article on publishers' bindings singles out Domino Press's trade editions of *Flash* and *Poudre* as examples of good bindings on children's books. Pictured, p. 22.

Harper's Bazaar, eds. "The Make-Believers." *Harper's Bazaar.* (July 1944): 40-41. Short article and photo of FR and a child reading, with similar articles about Roy Rogers, Joe Shuster, Serge Prokofieff, and others.

Hearn, Michael Patrick, Trinkett Clark and H. Nichols B. Clark. *Myth, Magic, and Mystery: One Hundred Years of American Children's Book Illustration.* Norfolk, VA: Roberts Rinehart Publishers and The

Chrysler Museum of Art, 1996. Reviews career and reproduces original painting from *Daniel Boone.*

Heller, Steven, and Louise Fili. *French Modern: Art Deco Graphic Design.* San Francisco: Chronicle Books, 1997. 34. Reproduces a 1928 catalog cover of *Au Bon Marché* signed and credited to "TR," which is FR initialing "Theodor."

Henderson, the Rev. Jane Geffken. "Lent is Not Tidy," Library of Sermons from the Pulpit. Exeter Congregational Church, users.rcn.com/exetercongchurch/sermon_archive/serm_3-12-00 (accessed November 9 2012). Pastor uses illustration from FR's *The Golden Bible* for a sermon text.

H. J. B. W. [initials only]. "Feodor Rojankovsky." *The Junior Bookshelf.* (London). Vol. 9 (November 1945): 85-89. A discussion of the Domino Press books and the Père Castor series, many of which were also published in England.

Hogarth, Grace. "A Publisher's Perspective." *Horn Book.* Vol. LXV, no. 4 (July-August 1989): 526-528. Passage about the transition to offset color printing in U.S. and FR's picture books.

Hopkins, Lee Bennett. *Books Are by People.* New York: Citation Press, 1969. 234-237. An interview with FR. An attenuated version is in Hopkins. *Pauses: Autobiographical Reflections of 101 Creators of Children's Books.* New York: HarperCollins, 1995.

Horiuchi, Seiichi. *110 Illustrators' Work in the Children's Book World.* Vol. 2. Tokyo: Fukuinkan Shoten, Publishers, 1984. 11-16. Reproductions from *Daniel Boone* and the Père Castor series, with an essay (in Japanese) about the artist.

Horn Book, eds. "The Hunt Breakfast." *The Horn Book.* Vol. 32 (August 1956): 226, 228, 303. A checklist of 32 books by FR then available in the U.S.

Hürlimann, Bettina. *Three Centuries of Children's Books in Europe.* Cleveland: World Publishing Co., 1968 [1959]. 136-139. Critical discussion of FR's role in the Père Castor series.

———. "Three Remarkable Editors of Children's Books." *The Horn Book.* (February 1974): 17-23. A discussion of Père Castor (Paul Faucher), Tadashi Matsui, and Shankar Pillai, noting Faucher's editorial role at Flammarion, the importance of émigré Russian artists in the Père Castor series, and of FR as its "chief artist."

Husarski, Wacław. "Plastyka: Salon Garlińskiego." *Wiadomości literackie.* no. 22 (1924): 5. A review of FR's 1924 show at the Salon Garliński in Warsaw, reproducing two original works.

———. "Kronika artystyczna." *Tygodnik illustrowany.* no. 23 (1924): 381. Review of FR's 1924 show at the Salon Garliński, citing Russian influences and his unusual technique of making multicolor wood block prints.

Ito, Motoo, Masako Yokoyama and Makiko Tsuda, eds. *The Century of Picture Books.* Tokyo: Asahi Shimbun Co., 1999. 32-33. Exhibition catalog in Japanese. Reproduced original paintings for FR's *Daniel Boone, Animals on the Farm,* and the 1959 Book Week poster.

Jan, Isabelle. "French Children's Classics." *Wilson Library Bulletin.* Vol. 47, no. 2 (October 1972): 62-71. About Paul Faucher and the *Père Castor* books, with mentions of FR.

Japanese Board on Books for Young People (JBBY). *The Artists and the Picture Book: The Twenties and the Thirties.* Tokyo: JBBY, 1991. Edited by Honda Keiko and Fukumoto Yumiko. (English-language edition, 1992, without illustrations.) Catalog in Japanese for the exhibition (same title) at the Tokyo Metropolitan Teien Museum, 5 April-26 May 1991. Pages 200-201 have color reproductions from five books included in the exhibit, *Daniel Boone, Froux, The Children's Year, The Tall Book of Mother Goose,* and *ABC du Père Castor,* plus a discussion of FR's contributions (by Shima Tayo) in both editions.

J.B.M. [initials only]. "André Hellé is [now FR's] only worthy rival." *Creative Art.* Vol. 11 (September 1932): 76, 78. A review of *Daniel Boone.* Reproduces two illustrations.

Jennett, Seán. "The 4th International Exhibit of Book Design." *Printing Review* (U.K.). Vol. 18, no. 64 (Winter 1953-54): 22-25. Praises the graphic work in *The Treasure Trove of the Sun,* reproducing a two-page spread and a full-page insert.

Johnston, Robert H. *"New Mecca, New Babylon": Paris and the Russian Exiles, 1920-1945.* Kingston and Montreal: McGill-Queen's

University Press, 1988. Background on the Russian émigré communities between the wars—FR's milieu.

Jones, Delores B. *Bibliography of Little Golden Books.* New York & Westport, CT: Greenwood Press, 1987. Introduction is an excellent history of the Golden Books, and the check list includes FR's 17 titles in this subseries.

———. *Best in Children's Books Index.* Hattiesburg, MS: de Grummond Children's Literature Collection, University of Southern Mississippi, 1997. 60 pp. Mimeo. Locates FR's many works in the series of books.

Journal of Erotica. London: Midsummer Books. Vol. 5 (1994): 28-31. Reproduces in color the first eight plates from the 30-plate portfolio *Idylle printanière.* Vol. 7 (1994): 25. Reproduces full-page and in color a single pochoir print from Radiguet's *Vers libres*, the image opposite the verse "Ébauches."

Kearney, Patrick J. *A History of Erotic Literature.* London: Macmillan, 1982. 161. Large halftone of an illustration from *Vers libres*, heading the poem "Saison."

Kerorguen, Yan de. *La colline russe.* Paris: B. Grasset, 1979. About Russian Hill at La Favière and FR as a notable resident.

Keyes, Emilie. "Russia-Born Children's Artist Finds Congenial Resort Home." *Palm Beach Post.* (January 9, 1946): 2. FR's visit to Palm Beach as guest of Georges Duplaix, with an interview and biographical facts.

Kingman, Lee, J. Foster, and R. G. Lontoft. *Illustrators of Children's Books: 1957-1966.* Boston: The Horn Book, 1968. 166 *et passim.* Short biography.

Klemensiewicz, Zygmunt. *Bibliografia ekslibrisu polskiego.* Wrocław: Wydawnictwo zakładu narodowego im. Osslińskich, 1952. Documents some of FR's bookplates, which had been exhibited.

Klemin, Diana. *The Art of Art for Children's Books: A Contemporary Survey.* New York: Charles N. Potter, 1966. 45-55. Reproduces two-page spread from *The Whirly Bird.*

Kleppner, Amy. "Doors to the Past." *Vermont Magazine.* (May-June 2008): 49-51. Describes kitchen doors of her house painted by FR in the early 1940s.

Kodrianskaia, Natalia. "Vystavka F. Rozhankovskogo." *Novoye russkoye slovo.* New York. (March 28, 1943): 8. A praise-filled review of FR's March 1943 show at the New York Public Library.

Korff, Alice Graeme. "Children's Books, 1944-1945." *The Magazine of Art.* Vol. 38 (May 1945): 191-93. Commentary on *Animal Stories* and *The Tall Book of Nursery Tales,* from the jury's endorsements for their first annual Children's Book List.

Kovalevskii, P. E. *Zarubezhnaia Rossiia.* Paris: Librairie des cinq continents, 1971. 270. Mentions FR among prominent Russian émigré artists; otherwise good background.

Kovarskaia, Vera. "Khudozhnik detskikh grez." *Novoye russkoye slovo.* New York. (December 16, 1970): 2. Obituary with artistic praise.

———. *Novoye russkoye slovo.* New York (February or March 1973). Review of posthumous exhibit at FAR Gallery, 1973.

Kunitz, Stanley J., and Howard Haycraft, eds. "Autobiographical Sketch." In *The Junior Book of Authors.* 2nd edition, rev. New York: H. W. Wilson Co., 1951. 260.

Lacroix, Christian. *Lacroix: Pieces of a Pattern.* New York: Thames and Hudson, 1997. With pictures from FR's bear stories, the French fashion designer cites the books' influences on his childhood and later personal taste in interior design.

Landron Bou, Iris M. "El maravilloso mundo de Rojankovsky." *El nuevo dia.* (February 22. 1973): 27-29. Article about FR, including six reproductions from the exhibit in San Juan, PR.

La Revue des livres pour enfants. no. 186 (April 1999): 46ff. Special issue, "Autour du Père Castor," has several brief articles pertaining to FR, with many of his illustrations.

Lasunskii, Oleg. "Iz tvorcheskogo nasledia Semena Abramovicha Lutskogo." In Mikhail Parkhomovsky, ed. *Evrei v kul'ture russkogo zarubezh'ia: Stat'i, publikatskii, memuary i esse.* Tom V. Bet-Shemesh, Israel: Pub. by editor, 1996. 77-79. Lasunskii describes how the original drawing for the cover of M. Osorgin's *Vol'nyi kamenshchik* (Paris, 1937) was prized by the author and passed to Lutskii after Osorgin's death.

Leikind, O. L. "Rozhankovskii Fedor Stepanovich," *Iskusstvo i arkhitektura russkovo zarubezh'ia.* http://artrz.ru/menu/1804645939/1804786154.html (accessed June 15, 2013). A career synopsis.

———, K. V. Makhrov, and D. Ia. Severiukhin. "Rozhankovskii, Fedor Stepanovich." In *Khudozhniki russkogo zarubezh'ia, 1917-1941: Biograficheskii slovar'*. St. Petersburg: Izdatel'stvo Notabene, 1999. 496-497. A career synopsis.

Lemmens, Albert, and Serge-Aljosja Stommels. *Russian Artists and the Children's Book, 1890-1992*. Nijmegen: L.S., 2009. Discusses FR's work in France and in New York.

Le Monde. "Féodor Rojankovsky." 4 November 1970: 26. Obituary.

Le Monde. (article initialed Fl. N.). "La marque Rojan: L'illustrateur russe influence encore décorateurs, créateurs de mode et graphistes." Section VI (29 January 1999). Review of exhibition catalog and commemorative volume, *La maison des trois ours: hommage à Rojankovsky* (1998).

Le tour du monde (bookseller). *Catalogue 40. Livres érotiques, coquins, galants, curieux*. Paris, 1996. Item 330 offers Radiguet's *Vers libres*, second illustrated edition, with a color reproduction of one pochoir.

Leventhal, Albert R. "The Children's Book in the Mass Market." *Publishers' Weekly*. Vol. 164, no. 21 (November 21, 1953): 2106-2108. An account of the economics of publishing Golden Books.

Lévèque, Françoise, and Serge Plantureux. "Rojan (Rozhankovskii)." In *Livres d'enfants russes et soviétiques, 1917-1945*. Dans les collections de l'Heure joyeuse et dans les Bibliothèques françaises. Catalogue en forme de dictionnaire des illustrateurs. Paris: Agence culturelle de Paris, 1997. 236-239.

Lewis, John. *The Twentieth Century Book*. London: Studio Vista, Ltd., 1967. 199. Brief review of Père Castor books and reproduces the cover of *Scaf* and two pages from *Panache*.

Linders-Nouwens, Joke. *Ik hou zo van . . . de Gouden Boekjes: het verhaal van de Gouden Boekjes in Nederland*. Amsterdam: Rubinstein, 2010. Discussion of Golden Books, including FR's, published in the Netherlands.

Locher, Frances Carol, ed. *Contemporary Authors*. Vols. 77-80. Detroit: Gale Research Company, 1979. 459-460. The same biographical material is more expansive in Commire (1980).

Londeix, Georges. *Exposition d'aquarelles et de dessins de Feodor Rojankovsky*.

Santurce, P.R.: Alliance française de Puerto Rico, 1973. Mimeo, 11 pp. Illustrated exhibition catalog with texts by Londeix and F. Eichenberg.

McElderry, Margaret K. "Rojankovsky Wins Caldecott." *Library Journal*. Vol. 81, no. 6 (March 15, 1956): 740-742. By FR's editor at Harcourt Brace when he won the 1956 Caldecott Medal. Several facts about FR's career not in other sources.

Mahoney, Bertha E., L.P. Latimer, and B. Folmsbee, compilers. *Illustrators of Children's Books, 1744-1945*. Boston: The Horn Book, 1947. 353-354, 435, *et passim*. A short biography.

Marcus, Leonard. *Golden Legacy: How Golden Books Won Children's Hearts, Changed Publishing Forever, and Became an American Icon Along the Way*. New York: Golden Books, an imprint of Random House Children's Books, 2007. A history of Golden Books, with extensive discussion of FR's life and work, with Golden Books and elsewhere, including an interview with his daughter, Tanya, photos, and reproductions of illustrations and book covers.

Médiathèque Intercommunale du Père Castor. Archives du Père Castor. http://www1.arkhenum.fr/bm_pere_castor. (accessed October 26, 2013). Examples of original art by FR in the Père Castor archives.

Mercer, F. A., and W. Gaunt, eds. *Modern Publicity 1933-34*. London: Studio Publications, 1934. Section 3 contains color reproduction of cover for the Orient Line cruise brochure *Southward Bound*.

Miaeots, Ol'ga. "Fedor Rozhankovskii - khudozhnik, kotoryi liubil detei i zverei." Otdel detskoi literatury VGBIL im. M. I. Rudomino. deti-inostranki.livejournal.com/52204.html (accessed May 26, 2013). Summarizes FR's work in France and America, with the expressed wish that his books may be translated into Russian.

———. "Russkii stil' - eto chest' i dostoinstvo." o-funambulo. o-funambulo.livejournal.com/34036.html. (accessed May 26, 2013). Tells how the author first discovered FR through a French librarian who gave her a copy of *Daniel Boone*.

Mikotajuk, Andrea. *Arts Magazine*. Vol. 47, no. 4 (February 1973): 85-86. Review of a gallery show. Reproduces a watercolor, "Porch, Nantucket," shown at the FAR Gallery, Feb. 6-17, 1973.

Mnukhin, L. A., ed. *Russkoe zarubezh'e: khronika nauchnoi, kul'turnoi i obshchestvennoi zhizni, 1920-1940, Frantsiia.* 4 vols. Paris: YMCA Press and Moscow: Eksmo, 1995-1997. Discussion of scientific and cultural life of Russian emigrés in France.

Moore, Anne Carroll. "The Three Owl's Notebook." *The Horn Book.* Vol. 32, no. 3 (June 1956): 178-180. Obliquely expresses concern over the Caldecott award to *Frog Went A-Courtin'.*

Moynihan, William T., and Mary E. Shaner, eds. *Masterworks of Children's Literature.* Vol. 8, *The Twentieth Century.* New York: Stonehill Publishing and Chelsea House, 1986. 208. Russian folk influences on FR's style.

Mulczyński, Jarosław. *Słownik grafikon Poznania i Wielkopolski XX wieku urodzonych do 1939 roku.* Poznan: Krzysztof Matusiak, 1996. 357-359. Full article on FR's Polish work, 1920-1925, with bibliography.

Murray, John J., and Bruce Fox. *Fisher-Price, 1931-1963.* Revised. Florence, AL: Books Americana, 1996. Credits and pictures in color FR's "Woofy Wagger" pull toy of 1947.

Musée d'Arts et Histoire. *Les Russes de La Favière.* Bormes-les-Mimosas, France: 2004. Catalog for the 2004 exhibit of the same name and part of the series, *Le regard de la mémoire.* Includes reproductions of FR's illustrations for several Père Castor books and of other non-illustration paintings and drawings.

N. A. [initials only]. "Khudozhnik-illiustrator F. S. Rozhankovskii." *Novoye russkoye slovo.* New York. (October 6, 1941): 3. Reporting FR's recent arrival on S.S. Navemar, with a brief review of his life and career.

National Archives. *Ship Passenger Arrival Records.* Microfilm Publication T-715. Roll 6577, Page 13, Line 30. Washington, DC: National Archives and Records Administration. Information stated to immigration officials upon arrival in 1941.

Néret, Gilles. *Erotica Universalis.* Vol. II. Köln: Taschen Verlag, 2000. Reproduces in color 28 (of 30) color plates from FR's *Idylle printanière*, one of FR's unpublished drawings for Bataille's *Histoire de l'œil*, and 16 selections from a knock-off of FR's illustrations for Radiguet's *Vers libres.*

———. *Erotica: 20th Century.* Vol. I. Köln: Taschen, 2001. Reproduces five of the knock-off illustrations for *Vers libres* (see Néret 2000); a detail of one drawing is used for this anthology's cover design, which is also falsely attributed to Rojan. Also reproduces 20 plates from FR's *Idylle printanière.*

New York Post. (September 12, 1941): Section 1, 1ff. Article about arrival of S. S. Navemar with group photo of passengers and another of FR waving from the deck rail, standing with his co-passenger Irene Lebedeva.

New York Times (obituary). "Feodor Rojankovsky, 78, Dies; Illustrator of Children's Books." (October 13, 1970): 48. With a career summary and photo.

Obolensky, Alexis. "Extraits d'un entretien avec l'artiste." In *Alexis Obolensky: peinture, terre-cuite, bois.* Palace Edition: Saint-Petersbourg, 1995. Catalog in French and in Russian. Obolensky cites childhood encounters with FR and their influences on his own art.

——— [Obolenskii, Aleksei]. "Bezdna na vostoke (Beseda s Vladimirom Bondarenko)." Zavtra. zavtra.ru/denlit/047/81.html (accessed May 11, 2000). Interview by Bondarenko with Obolensky. Both men mention FR's influence on them. Obolensky recalls FR as his childhood art teacher and friend of the family in La Favière, and Bondarenko mentions his correspondence as a young man from Leningrad with FR.

Ogle, Lucille. *Lucille Ogle Papers, 1934-1973.* Collection 201. Special Collections, Knight Library, University of Oregon, Eugene, OR. Contains over 100 items of correspondence between FR (and Nina Rojankovsky) and Ogle, mostly personal greetings, letters about book projects and business matters. Also book-related original art, proofs, and some independent work.

Opalov, Leonid. "V studii khudozhnika-illiustratora Rozhankovskogo." Article from an unidentified Russian-language newspaper (West European?), c. 1939-40.

———. "Magneticheskaia lichnost' russkogo khudozhnika-illiustratora Fedora "Rozhankovskogo." From an unidentified Russian-language newspaper (North American?), with byline dated July 1944, p. 3. Interview, including an account of FR's visit to Hollywood.

Parmegiani, Claude-Anne. *Les petits français illustrés, 1860-1940.* Paris: Éditions du Cercle de la librairie, 1989. 262-273. Overview of FR's French books, with interpretation of *The Three Bears* (1967).

———.“Le roman de la vie.” *La revue des livres pour enfants.* no. 175-176 (June 1997): 95-102. FR's artistic relationship with Faucher and his Père Castor books.

Pia, Pascal. *Les livres de l'enfer: bibliographie critique des ouvrages érotiques dans leurs différentes éditions du XVIe siècle à nos jours.* Paris: Librairie Arthème Fayard, 1998. Second edition, expanding the two-volume edition published by C. Coulet et A. Faure, 1978, with additions from the Michel Simon collection and elsewhere. A standard reference and descriptive bibliography of older French erotica. Lists FR's two editions of Radiguet's *Vers libres* and Spaddy's *Dévergondages*, and exposes the imitative edition of *Vers libres.*

Pitz, Henry Clarence. *A Treasury of American Book Illustration.* New York and London: American Studio Books and Watson-Guptill Publications, 1947. Several reproductions from various books.

———. “Book Jackets of Today.” *American Artist.* Vol. 12 (April 1948): 49-53. Singles out for praise the jacket design of *Animal Stories.*

———. “27th Annual Exhibition: Art Directors Club of New York.” *American Artist.* Vol. 12 (September 1948): 42-47. Reproduces (p. 44) the calendar painting of “Snow White.”

———. *Illustrating Children's Books: History, Technique, Production.* New York: Watson-Guptill Publications, 1963. Large color reproductions from several books.

Privat l'art de voir. Backfile of quarterly catalogs of this Paris bookseller, from 1984 to the present, list several offerings of FR's published erotica.

Publishers' Weekly, eds. “New Ten-Cent Store Line.” *Publishers' Weekly.* Vol. 129 (February 22, 1936): 899. Background on the Artists and Writers Guild.

———. “Rojankovsky and His Books for Children.” *Publishers' Weekly.* Vol. 146, no. 18 (October 28, 1944): 1741-1744. Summary of the European career, with details not found elsewhere.

———. “Jean Lee Latham & Feodor Rojankovsky Win Newbery and

Caldecott Awards." *Publishers' Weekly*. Vol. 169, no. 11 (March 17, 1956): 1400-1402. Brief career summary.

———. "Obituary Notes" [Feodor Rojankovsky]. Vol. 198, no. 19 (November 9, 1970): 35. With career summary.

Quignard, Marie-Françoise, and Raymond-Josué Seckel. *L'Enfer de la Bibliothèque: Eros au secret.* Paris: Bibliothèque Nationale de France, 2007. Catalog of the 2007-8 exhibit of the same name. Includes examples of FR's erotic books.

Raeff, Marc. *Russia Abroad: A Cultural History of the Russian Emigration, 1919-1939.* New York: Oxford University Press, 1990. Background on the Russian émigré communities between the wars.

Robinson, Julian. *The Golden Age of Style.* New York: Harcourt Brace Jovanovich, 1976. 92 ,105. Reproduces two color images from *Quand la bise fut venue.*

———. *The Brilliance of Art Deco.* New York: Bartley & Jensen Publishers, nd [c. 1989]. 166-167. Reproduces two other color images from *Quand la bise fut venue.*

Roginski, Jim, ed. Compiled by Muriel W. Brown and Rita Schoch Foudray. *Newbery and Caldecott Medalists and Honor Book Winners: Bibliographies and Resource Material Through 1991.* Second edition. New York: Neal-Schuman Publishers, 1992. Repeats the extensive but incomplete list of books, originally supplied by Nina Rojankovsky for the 1982 edition.

Rojankovsky, Feodor. Autobiography. A rough Russian ms., illustrated, in FR's personal papers recalls his early life. Portions of this document, translated by FR's wife, Nina, and his daughter, Tanya, were a key source for our account.

———. "Caldecott Award Acceptance." *The Horn Book.* Vol. 32, no. 5 (August 1956): 241-245. Also reprinted in same places as Averill (1956). A candid autobiographical speech upon receiving the Caldecott Medal.

———. "The Artist at Work." *The Horn Book.* Vol. 75, no. 5 (September/October 1999): 636-639. Posthumous publication of an article intended for the journal in 1964. (See Appendix A1 above.)

Selz, Jean. "La renaissance des livres d'enfants en France." *Arts et métiers graphiques*. no. 56 (1 January 1937): 31-41. FR's books with Faucher in context of other design developments. Two actual pages, one each from *ABC du Père Castor* and *Roman des bêtes*, are tipped in between pages 32 and 33, and the selection varies with each copy of the journal in this issue.

Seslavinskii, Mikhail. *Randevu: russkie khudozhniki vo frantsuzskom knigoizdanii pervoi poloviny XX veka*. Moskva: Astrel', 2009. 334-349. Discusses lives and work of 33 Russian artists in emigration in the first half of the 20th c. Substantial entry on FR, including many reproductions. Some biographical and bibliographical inaccuracies.

———. *Frantsuzskie bibliofil'skie izdaniia v oformlenii russkikh khudozhnikov-emigrantov (1920 - 1940-e gody)*. Moskva: ID Universitetskaia kniga, 2012. Discusses illustrations by Russian émigrés in non-children's books, with several references to FR and a reproduction from *Chansons galantes*.

———. "Tamizdat. 100 izbrannykh knig." *Pro knigi: zhurnal bibliofila*. no. 32 (2012): 63-73. List of 100 major Russian émigré books. no. 93 is FR's *Dnevnik Foksa Mikki* [B1, RU.2a].

———. "Khudozhnik knigi Fedor Rozhankovskii: Interv'iu s T. F. Rozhankovskoi i A. A. Papchinskim." *Pro knigi: zhurnal bibliofila*. no. 3 (2013): 6 - 23.

Shultz, Lev [signing "L. Sh."]. "Fedor Rozhankovskii." *Russkaia mysl'*. Paris. (November 12, 1970): 11. Obituary by FR's friend, the émigré Russian sculptor.

Silvey, Anita, ed. *Children's Books and Their Creators*. Boston: Houghton Mifflin, 1995. 562-563. A short career sketch, by Sheryl Lee Saunders.

Sosinskii, Vladimir. "Vstrechi s Rozhankovskim." *Detskaia literatura*. Vol. 7, no. 77 (May 1972): 77-81. Sosinskii, a friend in Paris in the 1930s and later in NY (before returning to the USSR in 1960), writes on FR's life and career—but from a Soviet slant, suggesting that FR was exploited by capitalist publishers. Contains biographic and bibliographic errors. An abridged version of this article was published under the same title in *Golos rodiny* [Moscow] (September 1972): 6. *Golos rodiny* was a Soviet newspaper for Russians abroad.

Stockum, Hilda van. "Through the Illustrator's Eyes." *The Horn Book.* Vol. 20 (May 1944): 176-184. Praise for *The Tall Book of Mother Goose* (1942), citing the naturalism of the drawings of children, with reproduction of "Little Miss Muffet."

Struve, Nikita. *Soixante-dix ans d'émigration russe (1919-1989).* Paris: Fayard, 1996. FR is among the biograpical entries for prominent personalities of the emigration.

Sutton, Katherine. "Armour Villa in Pen and Pencil." *The Villa Voice.* (November/December 2013): 1-3. Article on the studio that FR built at his first home in Bronxville, with photographs, then and now, and samples of FR's illustrations showing neighborhood houses.

Taysman, Phillippe. "Les polissonneries de Béranger." *Fascination: le musée secret de l'érotisme.* no. 29. Paris; [1986]: 32-38. Article discusses various illustrated editions of Béranger's *Chansons galantes*, with sample illustrations from each. Reproduces four images from FR's 1937 version.

Thiébaut, René. *L'art publicitaire pharmaceutique: essai biblio-iconographique, 1894-1939.* Nanterre: Published by author, 1939. Entry 169 is FR's *Fables de La Fontaine* for Laboratoires Rosa.

Thomé, J.-R. "Feodor Rojankovsky." *Le courrier graphique.* no. 98 (February-April 1958): 3-10. Career review, with a dozen drawings reproduced, including an illustration for a never-realized edition of *Treasure Island.*

Tilly, Andrew. *Erotic Drawings.* New York: Rizzoli, 1986. Reproduces a color plate from *Idylle printanière.*

Vaucaire, Michel. "Le livre d'enfants." *Art et décoration.* Vol. 58 (December 1930): 161-76. The status of French picture books in 1930, the stage onto which FR stepped.

Viguers, Ruth Hill, M. Dalphin, and B. M. Miller, compilers. *Illustrators of Children's Books, 1946-1956.* Boston: The Horn Book, 1958. 52, 171-172. Short bio sketch.

Visson, Assia R. "A Golden Portfolio Containing the Pictures from Mother Goose." *Gazette des beaux-arts.* 6th series. Vol. 28 (1945): 64. Review of the 1945 portfolio, with comments on the value of popularizing art.

Vollmer, Hans, ed. *Allgemeines Lexikon der Bildenden Künstler des XX. Jahrhunderts.* Vol. 6. Leipzig: Veb E. A. Seemann Verlag, 1962. 381-382. A brief entry, but with unusual details.

Wahl, Jan. "Jan Wahl, 1933." [an autobiography by Wahl]. In *Something about the Author: Autobiography Series.* Vol. 3. Adele Sarkissian, ed. Detroit: Gale Research Company, 1987. 293-331. Recalls a first meeting with FR in the 1960s.

Wallis, Mieczysław. "Sztuki plastyczne: Wystawy w salonie sztuki Czesława Garlińskiego." *Robotnik.* Vol. 30, no. 142 (May 25, 1924): 2. Review of FR's 1924 show at the Salon Garliński, characterizing him as a modernist of great promise.

Wankie, Władysław. "Ze sztuki: Wystawy w Salonie Garlińskiego." *Kurier Warszawski.* Vol. 104, no. 160/161 (1924): 14. Review of 1924 show at the Salon Garliński, singling out for praise a woodcut, a watercolor "Portrait," and 20 illustrative studies.

Ward, Martha Eads, and Dorothy A. Marquardt. "Rojankovsky, Feodor." In *Illustrators of Books for Young People.* 2nd ed. Metuchen, NJ: Scarecrow Press, 1975. 140. Repeats entry in their *Authors of Books for Young People* (Scarecrow, 1971).

Warkoczewska, Magdalena. *Pocztówki z widokami dawnego Poznania: 1898-1939: ze zbiorów Muzeum historii miasta Poznania.* Poznan: Muzeum narodowe w Poznaniu, 1995. Catalog for postcard exhibition includes FR's painted scenes of seven historical sites in Poznan; three are reproduced in halftone.

Weiermair, Peter, ed. *Erotic Art, from the 17th to the 20th Century.* Frankfurt am Main: Edition Stemmle, 1995. Catalog for the exhibit *Der Kalte Blick—Erotische Kunst 17. bis 20. Jahrhundert*, Frankfurter Kunstverein, Frankfurt am Main. Reproduces four color plates from *Idylle printanière* and two images from *L'âne d'or.*

Wessel, Miriam A. "Newbery and Caldecott Awards—1955." *American Library Association Bulletin.* Vol. 50, no. 4 (April 1956): 227. Brief biography on FR as winner of the Caldecott.

West Virginia Pulp & Paper Company. *West Virginia Inspirations for Printers: 1948, 1949.* no. 169, *The Animal Kingdom.* No place: W. Va. Pulp & Paper Co., 1948. 370. Color reproduction, fable of fox and grapes, made for Puss 'n Boots cat food ad.

Who's Who in American Art. Vol. 5. New York: R. R. Bowker, 1953. 357. Short entry.

Who Was Who in America with World Notables. Vol. 5, 1969-1973. Chicago: Marquis Who's Who, 1973. 617. Information not in other sketches.

Williams, Robert C. *Culture in Exile: Russian Emigrés in Germany, 1881-1941.* Ithaca, NY: Cornell University Press, 1972. Background on the Russian émigré communities between the wars.

Witz, Ignacy, and Jerzy Zaruba. *50 lat karykatury polskiej, 1900-1950.* Warsaw: Arkady, 1961. This anthology includes FR among Poland's prominent caricaturists (p. 10), gives a brief bio of the artist (p. 43), and reproduces a drawing from the satirical journal *Szczutek* (pl. 164).

Young Wings editors. "Elephants Without Trunks and Other Funny Animals" [and] "Biographical Sketch" *Young Wings: Magazine of the Junior Literary Guild.* (August 1942): 5, 9. Promotes the Guild's edition of the *Just So Stories*, with a bio of FR.

Zetlin Museum of Russian Art, The Maria and Mikhail. Ramat-Gan, Israel: Art and Culture Authority, City of Ramat-Gan, nd [*c.* 1996]. Reproduces a color gouache of "Woman Playing a Guitar" (1929), from the Zetlin's establishing donation in 1976. FR's painting was chosen to represent the Zetlin collection on the color cover of the supplement *Dosug* of *Novosti nedeli*, a Russian-language newspaper in Israel, 5 July 1996, which ran an article (pp. 2-3) about the collection.

www.ingramcontent.com/pod-product-compliance
Lightning Source LLC
Chambersburg PA
CBHW030422100426
42812CB00028B/3060/J
* 9 7 8 0 5 7 8 1 3 5 5 8 8 *